46268
GOP
kw

JAPANESE
for
Young English Speakers

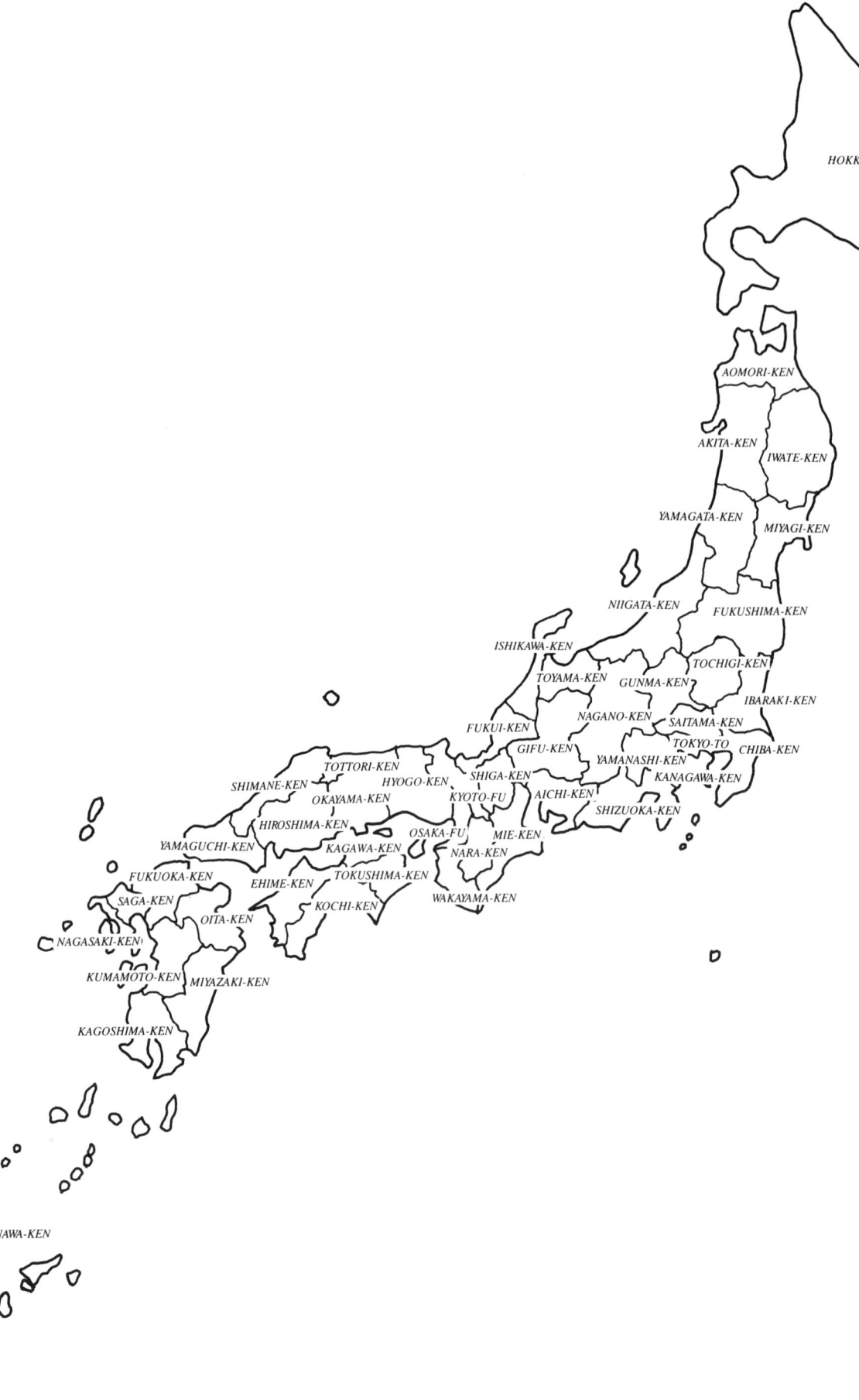

Japanese for Young English Speakers

Volume II

John Young and Yuriko Uchiyama Rollins

Published for
Kawai Institute for Culture and Education

Georgetown University Press
Washington, D.C.

Georgetown University Press, Washington, D.C. 20007
© 1997 by Gakko Hojin Kawaijuku. All rights reserved.
Printed in the United States of America
10 9 8 7 6 5 4 3 2 1   1997
THIS VOLUME IS PRINTED ON ACID-FREE OFFSET BOOK PAPER.

Library of Congress Cataloging-in-Publication Data

Young, John, 1920 -
    Japanese for young English speakers / John Young and Yuriko Uchiyama Rollins.
        p.   cm.
    ISBN 0-87840-351-5
      1. Japanese language — Textbooks for foreign speakers — English.
    I. Rollins, Yuriko Uchiyama.   II. Title.
    PL535. Y598   1994
    495. 6' 82421 — dc20   94-31793

CONTENTS

Acknowledgments viii

Introduction ix

Lesson 1: Thank you letter 2
       I. PERSPECTIVE   II. PREPARATION   III. PARTICIPATION

      2: Souvenirs 10
       I. PERSPECTIVE   II. PREPARATION   III. PARTICIPATION

      3: Review & Application 16
       IV. PERFORMANCE
         1. Application
         2. Actualization
         3. Enrichment

      4: Peter's trip to Japan 24
       I. PERSPECTIVE   II. PREPARATION   III. PARTICIPATION

      5: Leaving for Japan 32
       I. PERSPECTIVE   II. PREPARATION   III. PARTICIPATION

      6: Review & Application 40
       IV. PERFORMANCE
         1. Application
         2. Actualization
         3. Enrichment

      7: Summer festival 50
       I. PERSPECTIVE   II. PREPARATION   III. PARTICIPATION

      8: Traveling around Japan 60
       I. PERSPECTIVE   II. PREPARATION   III. PARTICIPATION

      9: Review & Application 68
       IV. PERFORMANCE
         1. Application
         2. Actualization
         3. Enrichment

    10: Calling home 80
       I. PERSPECTIVE   II. PREPARATION   III. PARTICIPATION

11: A farewell dinner 86
        I. PERSPECTIVE   II. PREPARATION   III. PARTICIPATION

12: Review & Application 92
    IV. PERFORMANCE
        1. Application
        2. Actualization
        3. Enrichment

13: At Narita Airport 104
        I. PERSPECTIVE   II. PREPARATION   III. PARTICIPATION

14: Videotapes of Peter's trip 112
        I. PERSPECTIVE   II. PREPARATION   III. PARTICIPATION

15: Review & Application 120
    IV. PERFORMANCE
        1. Application
        2. Actualization
        3. Enrichment

16: New Year's cards 130
        I. PERSPECTIVE   II. PREPARATION   III. PARTICIPATION

17: Photographs of Japan 138
        I. PERSPECTIVE   II. PREPARATION   III. PARTICIPATION

18: Review & Application 144
    IV. PERFORMANCE
        1. Application
        2. Actualization
        3. Enrichment

19: Geography class 152
        I. PERSPECTIVE   II. PREPARATION   III. PARTICIPATION

20: Valentine's Day chocolate 158
        I. PERSPECTIVE   II. PREPARATION   III. PARTICIPATION

21: Review & Application 164
    IV. PERFORMANCE
        1. Application
        2. Actualization
        3. Enrichment

22:	Basketball game 172	
	I. PERSPECTIVE II. PREPARATION III. PARTICIPATION	
23:	An accident during the game 178	
	I. PERSPECTIVE II. PREPARATION III. PARTICIPATION	
24:	Review & Application 184	
	IV. PERFORMANCE	
	1. Application	
	2. Actualization	
	3. Enrichment	
25:	Health checks 192	
	I. PERSPECTIVE II. PREPARATION III. PARTICIPATION	
26:	Thermometer 198	
	I. PERSPECTIVE II. PREPARATION III. PARTICIPATION	
27:	Review & Application 204	
	IV. PERFORMANCE	
	1. Application	
	2. Actualization	
	3. Enrichment	
28:	Social studies class 210	
	I. PERSPECTIVE II. PREPARATION III. PARTICIPATION	
29:	The day before the exam 216	
	I. PERSPECTIVE II. PREPARATION III. PARTICIPATION	
30:	Review & Application 222	
	IV. PERFORMANCE	
	1. Application	
	2. Actualization	
	3. Enrichment	

ACKNOWLEDGMENTS

We would like to express our sincere appreciation to the following people who have participated in the compilation of this textbook: Melanie K. Bush, Yoshiyuki Kataoka, Takashi Kawabe, Victor Jungham Lee, Miyuki Kawada, Shoko Miwa, Hiromi Mizuma, Shigefumi Murata, Yoshimi Nakamura, Makiko Shinjo, Junko Sugiyama, and graduate assistants from Seton Hall, Hunter, and Georgetown University.

Despite the fact that many creative and pioneering new designs have been incorporated into our compilation endeavor, Mr. Ayato Kawai and Mr. Hiroto Kawai of Kawaijuku were willing to sponsor this project. We would like to thank them for their foresight.

The University of Maryland University College has given us permission to quote certain segments of *Learn Japanese, New College Text* for this textbook.

John Young and Yuriko Uchiyama Rollins

INTRODUCTION

JAPANESE FOR YOUNG ENGLISH SPEAKERS is a proficiency-based and participation-oriented text compiled specifically for young, English-speaking students with particular relevance to North America to help them interact with people from around the world in a culturally appropriate manner.

A **proficiency-based text** helps students to learn interpersonal and cross-cultural communicative skills built upon a series of necessary functions in context to perform various tasks. Objectives are set in terms of functions needed to carry out those tasks; language forms necessary to perform those functions; and culture notes that exist to help students to communicate with and to understand others appropriately. The Intermediate – Mid Level of the "ACTFL Proficiency Guidelines for Japanese" is used as the target level for Volumes One and Two.

A **participation-oriented text** helps students to become engaged in meaningful and task-oriented interaction among themselves. Therefore, the majority of learning time should be devoted to interactive and task-based communicative activities designed to encourage student participation. Recognizing that the learning process should be exciting and productive, we had as our goal in compiling this text to make it interesting and stimulating so that students enjoy themselves and have fun while learning. The majority of class time should be devoted to activities. Ample illustrations, photos, and sketches are included to facilitate activities and to stimulate interest.

In addition to developing communicative skills in context with cultural consideration, the authors have also attempted to help students strengthen their cognitive capacities as well as to achieve curricular goals at the secondary school level. While the communicative approach serves as the most important basis for this text, there are other intentions, such as encouraging critical thinking; broadening student awareness through cross-cultural understanding; developing students' interest in math, science, and social studies ("sheltered content studies"); and helping students develop strategies for faster and surer learning.

The lessons in Volume Two have been arranged in such a way that students, depending on their age, gender, level, personality, motivation, learning style, and purpose, may follow different tracks: listening and speaking track, four-skills track, subject/discipline-centered track, or shortcut track. This multitrack arrangement enables teachers to satisfy students' needs, purposes, and interests.

LESSON ARRANGEMENTS

There are thirty lessons in Volume Two. Each lesson can be completed in one week of five 45-minute class periods. Every third lesson is a review lesson.

The modified Hepburn romanization was used in Volume One. However, *Hiragana*, *Katakana* and some *Kanji* were introduced in review lessons as enrichment elements preparing students for Volume Two where *Kanji/Kana* orthography is used along with the modified Hepburn romanization.

(A) REGULAR LESSONS (R)

There are twenty regular lessons: 1, 2, 4, 5, 7, 8, 10, 11, 13, 14, 16, 17, 19, 20, 22, 23, 25, 26, 28, 29.

I. PERSPECTIVE

1. Objectives

The **Objectives** – Function, Language and Culture – provide the overall framework and guide for each lesson. They include what the authors intend the student to learn both actively and passively.

II. PREPARATION

1. Context

Context provides the setting of the lesson – situation, time, place, characters, and events. From the Context several dialogue situations could be produced; the dialogue given is only one such sample.

2. Sample Conversation

Sample Conversation is an authentic, communicative encounter among characters reflecting one situation in the Context and incorporating the Objectives. It serves as a model to demonstrate the cumulative elements of the structural points to be learned, the cultural points to be covered, and the functions to be performed.

The Sample Conversation also shows how strongly Japanese discourse is affected by context: items can be omitted or added, and topics can be changed. The Sample Conversation also illustrates the finer points of communication: knowing what to say, what not to say, and when to speak, all of which are skills requiring thought and caution.

3. Language and Culture Notes

Cultural and other useful information has been presented here. Notes elucidating the structures implicit in the Sample Conversation have been presented. Neither the Sample Conversation nor the notes are the center of focus of the text. The PARTICIPATION component is the core.

III. PARTICIPATION

1. Vocabulary

1) From Sample Conversation
2) Useful for Activities, Practice, and Exercise

Only vocabulary from Sample Conversation and some necessary vocabularies are required for both recognition and production. Others are not required for mastery. The scope of required vocabulary will be designated by the teacher.

2. Activity, Practice, & Exercise (APE)

The emphasis of this textbook is on development of communication skills. The core feature of the Japanese-YES approach is a heavy dose of activities, practice, and exercises. APE is the centerpiece of the learning experience in this approach. Students are expected to achieve each lesson's objectives through participation in the activities. Therefore, most of the class time should be spent on APEs.

Games, role-plays, word-puzzles, and native Japanese games have also been incorporated. Such diverse activities will keep student interest high and reduce distractions.

(B) REVIEW AND APPLICATION (RA)

There are ten review lessons that are designed to advance from learning through participation to learning through performance. They contain activities that include objectives from the previous two lessons. In addition, these lessons offer ample opportunity to review the combined skills developed up to that point. Together with all previous lessons, this review constitutes a snowballing (*yukidaruma*) process or recycling/spiral process. This process will enable the student to apply learned language behavior to new situations (Application). The goal here is to internalize not only the language in the learner, but also to allow the learner to creatively communicate in a different, real-life situation (Actualization). The final section (Enrichment) has been devoted to the study of *Kanji* and learning strategies.

IV. PERFORMANCE

1. Application

Ample activities based on new situations are presented here.

2. Actualization

This section will help students to reinforce their knowledge of other disciplines, such as math, science, music, social studies, and physical education, through the use of the Japanese language.

3. Enrichment

For this section, we have introduced *Kanji* exclusively to enable students to read and write Japanese native writing (not romanized.) The Japanese native writing system was introduced in the review lessons of Volume One. Students who did not previously study the native writing system should review Volume One to be introduced to authentic Japanese writing.

Lesson 1: Thank you letter[1]

I. PERSPECTIVE

1. Objectives

1 Function:

(1) Expressing appreciation: *Zuibun osewa ni narimashita.*

2 Language:

(1) *(Nihon) e (it)ta toki wa, (zuibun osewa ni) narimashita.*
(2) *(Jisaboke) ni narimashita.*   (3) *(Shashin ga deki)mashita node, (doofuu) shimasu.*

3 Culture:

(1) Japanese thank you letters and other types of letters
(2) Seasonal greetings   (3) Expressing thanks

II. PREPARATION

1. Context

お礼の手紙

夏休みを利用して日本旅行から帰ってから一週間もたった。ピーターはお礼の手紙を書きながら、日本で会った人達のことを考えた。ペンパルのあきらと、その家族、みんなで食べたすきやきはとても美味しかった。あきらの友達と夏祭りに行って、盆踊りをした。飛行機の中で会った夏目さんには広島を案内してもらった。ピーターは日本で多くの人に会えて喜んだ。みんなに「ありがとう」を言わなければならない。

One week has passed since Peter returned to the United States from his trip to Japan during summer vacation. While writing thank you notes, he thought about the people he met there. He ate delicious sukiyaki with Akira, his pen pal, and Akira's family. Peter went to the summer festival and danced bon'odori with Akira. Mr. Natsume, who he met on the plane, guided Peter around Hiroshima. He was glad that he met so many people in Japan. He has to thank everyone.

2. Sample Conversation

夏がもうすぐ終わります。
みなさん、お元気ですか。
ぼくが日本へ行った時は、ずいぶんおせわになりました。
ありがとうございました。
ぼくは元気です。
時差ボケになりましたが、今はもう大丈夫です。
日本がなつかしくて、また行きたくなりました。
しゃしんができましたので同封します。
また、手紙を書きます。
さようなら。

ピーター　スミス　より
九月三日

Natsu[2] ga moo sugu owarimasu. Summer is almost over.
Minasan, ogenki desu ka? How is everybody?
Boku ga Nihon e itta toki wa, zuibun osewa ni narimashita.[3] Thank you for your help and hospitality while I was in Japan.
Arigatoo gozaimashita.[3] Thank you so much.
Boku wa genki desu. I am fine.
Jisaboke ni narimashita ga, ima wa moo daijoobu desu. I had jet lag, but I'm all right now.
Nihon ga natsukashikute, mata ikitaku narimashita. I miss Japan so much. I wish I could visit again.
Shashin ga dekimashita node[4], doofuu shimasu. I have enclosed the pictures that I developed.
Mata tegami o kakimasu. I will write again.
Sayoonara. Good bye.

Piitaa Sumisu yori   kugatsu mikka. From, Peter Smith   September 3rd

3. Language & Culture Notes

1 In Japan, it is common to send thank you letters to show gratitude and appreciation. Such letters are sent to thank someone for a birthday present or a gift brought back from somewhere, for an invitation to a party or event, or for a visit while one was in the hospital. It is appropriate to write and send the letter immediately after receiving the gift or invitation or returning home from the hospital. The style of the letter is similar to how one would write a thank you letter in English.

Japanese write for other purposes as well. Letters are written to wish someone a happy birthday or congratulations on their marriage or getting accepted into college. People also write letters just to keep in touch. However, with advances in technology, people are writing less and less. Telephone, fax machine, and e-mail are becoming the major modes of communication. It is not uncommon for teenagers to spend hours on the telephone talking to friends in the same town or in a city 200 miles away.

2 The seasons are very important to Japanese people in everyday life. Each season has its own meaning and significance. Japan is a group-oriented society, and the season is one thing that everyone shares at the same time. People discuss the season in conversations and even in letters. On an August morning, a man may greet his coworkers by commenting on how hot it is. A woman in Kyoto may write a letter to her friend in Nagasaki in January commenting on the amount of snow that has fallen. Seasons promote unity by placing people on a common ground.

3 Expressing gratitude is an extremely important social code. Saying thanks is always appropriate, even if someone did something simple. There are, of course, varying degrees of thanks. The most polite is *arigatoo gozaimashita*, "thank you very much," in English. This is usually the most appropriate expression in letters. In speaking, there are many ways to say "thank you." To one's superiors, the polite *arigatoo gozaimashita* is the best choice. To friends or family, simply saying *arigatoo*, "thanks," is suitable. The expression *osewa ni narimashita* is a formal way of saying "Thank you for taking care of me." One would use this when leaving a homestay family, no matter how long or short the stay, or even upon leaving an inn or small hotel where one has stayed.

4 *node*, a clause function word, means "since" or "because." This sentence could also be translated as "Since the pictures are ready, I have enclosed them."

III. PARTICIPATION

1. Vocabulary

1 From sample conversation:

doofuu shimasu (enclose)
jisaboke (jet lag)
kugatsu mikka (September 3rd)
natsukashiku (miss, long for, think fondly of)
owarimasu (end, be over)
tegami (letter)
zuibun (very much, extremely)

itta (went, was in)
kakimasu (write, will write)
natsu (summer)
osewa (hospitality, care, help, kindness)
shashin (pictures, photos)
toki (time, when, while)

2 Useful for activities:

aida (between, during)
kankookyaku (tourist)
Mata aimashoo. (See you again.)
Osewa ni narimashita. (Thank you very much for taking care of me.)
otona (adult)
sotsugyoosei (a graduate)

ganbaru (to persist in)
ki o tsukeru (be careful)
Ohisashiburi desu. (It's been a long time.)
shootai suru (to invite)
zettai (ni) (absolutely, definitely)

2. Activity, Practice, & Exercise

1 Listening comprehension

Individually: Listen to the following conversations between two people. Write A if the situation is about parting with someone, or write B if the situation is about meeting someone again.

1. Tomu: *Sensei, nagai aida osewa ni narimashita.*
    (Thank you very much for helping me for such a long time.)
   Sensei: *Tomu san, yoku benkyoo shimashita ne.* (Tom, you've studied really hard.)
   Tomu: *Hai, sensei no okage desu.* (Thanks to you.)
   Sensei: *Korekara mo ganbatte kudasai ne. Karada ni ki o tsukete.*
    (I hope you keep on trying hard. Take care of yourself.)
   Tomu: *Hai, sensei mo dooka ogenki de.* (You, too.)

2. Keiko: *Maa, Tomu san. Genki datta?* (Oh! Tom. How have you been?)
   Tomu: *Hai, okagesama de. Nihon e itta toki wa, taihen osewa ni narimashita.*
    (I've been fine, thank you. I appreciate what you did for me when I was in Japan.)
   Keiko: *Iie. Tomu san ga uchi ni ita toki wa, hontoo ni tanoshikatta wa ne. Hiroshi mo Ayako mo Tomu san o hontoo no kyoodai no yoo ni omotte ita wa.*
    (My pleasure. When you were at our house, we had a very good time. Both Hiroshi and Ayako think of you as a real brother.)
   Tomu: *Boku mo hontoo ni tanoshikatta desu. Nihon de wa iroiro arigatoo gozaimashita.*
    (I had a good time, too. Thank you for everything in Japan.)

3. An: *Sensei, ohisashiburi desu.* (It's been a long time.)
   Sensei: *An san, sukkari otona ni narimashita ne.* (Ann, you have really grown up.)
   An: *Kookoo no toki wa, osewa ni narimashita.*
   (I appreciate what you did for me when I was in high school.)
   Sensei: *An san, nihongo ga joozu ni narimashita ne.* (Ann, your Japanese has gotten much better.)
   An: *Sensei no okage de nihongo ga suki ni natta n desu. Dakara ima no daigaku de nihongo o benkyoo shiteimasu.*
   (Thanks to you, I became fond of Japanese. So, I'm now studying Japanese at college.)
   Sensei: *Sore o kiite ureshiku omoimasu.* (I'm glad to hear that.)

4. Yooko: *An, arigatoo. Anata ni wa osewa ni natte . . .*
   (Ann, thank you. I appreciate what you did . . .)
   An: *Iie. Yooko, genki de ne.* (My pleasure. Yoko, take care.)
   Yooko: *Anata mo ne. Iroiro oshiete moratta koto, wasurenai wa. Itsuka Nihon e asobi ni kite ne.*
   (You, too. I won't forget what you taught me. Please come to Japan someday.)
   An: *Ee, zettai ni iku wa. Mata aimashoo ne.* (I definitely will. See you again.)

Answers:
  1. ( )   2. ( )   3. ( )   4. ( )

2 Reuniting and parting

In pairs: Each pair is given a card with a specific situation. Write a dialogue between two people using the situation. Include the sentence *Osewa ni narimashita* in the dialogue.
Examples of situations:
1. A teacher and a high school student at a graduation ceremony.
2. A host-mother and a student parting (with each other.)
3. A tour guide and a tourist parting (with each other.)
4. A person who invited and a person who was invited to a camp parting.
5. A high school teacher and a graduate meeting again.
6. A Japanese host-father and an American student meeting again in America.

3 Matching

In class: Divide the class into two groups. Each student in Group A gets a card with a reason for something written on it. Each student in Group B gets a card with a sentence that should follow Group A students' cards. Each student has to find a student in the other group who holds a card that matches his/her card. Student A should approach student B by asking, "*Sumimasen. Anata no kaado wa nan desu ka?*" Report to the teacher after finding the match.

Example: A's card → *Atama ga itakatta node,*   B1's card → *Keeki o kaimashita.*
                  (Because I had a headache)   (I bought a cake.)
                                                    B2's card → *Gakkoo o yasumimashita.*
                                                          (I was absent from school.)

A: *Sumimasen. Anata no kaado wa nan desu ka?* (Excuse me. What's your card?)
B1: *"Keeki o kaimashita" desu. Anata no wa nan desu ka?*
    (It's "I bought a cake." What's yours?)
A: *"Atama ga itakatta node" desu.* (It's "Because I had a headache.")
B1: *Jaa, aimasen ne. Hoka no hito ni kikimashoo.* (We don't match. Let's ask someone else.)
A: *Soo shimashoo.* (OK. [Literally: Let's do that.])
A: *Sumimasen. Anata no kaado wa nan desu ka?* (Excuse me. What's your card?)
B2: *"Gakkoo o yasumimashita" desu.* (It's "I was absent from school.")
A: *Watashi no kaado wa "Atama ga itakatta node" desu. Aimasu ne.*
    (My card is "Because I had a headache." We match.)
B2: *Soo desu ne.* (That's right.)
A: *Sensei, paatonaa o mitsukemashita.* (I found my partner.)
T: *Ja, sono bun o itte mite kudasai.* (Please tell me the sentence.)
B2: *Atama ga itakatta node, gakkoo o yasumimashita.*
    (Because I had a headache, I was absent from school.)
T: *Hai, OK desu.* (You're right.)

4 Making sentences with *-ta node*

In three groups: The teacher writes five incomplete sentences on the blackboard using *-ta node*. The leaders from each group will *jan ken* to decide which one phrase each group will use. The object is to make as many complete sentences as possible using the given phrase. The students should be given a time limit of about ten to fifteen minutes. Afterward, the leader from each group reads two or three of their sentences to the class. The teacher then works with the students as a class to complete the remaining two phrases.

Examples of phrases:
1. *Kinoo gakko o yasunda node* ...
2. *Kuruma ga kowareta* (broken) *node* ...
3. *Shukudai o wasureta node* ...
4. *Kinoo no yoru osoku neta node* ...
5. *Kyoo wa ame ga futta node* ...

5 Completing sentences with *-ta node*

In groups of three: Students work together to complete sentences using *-ta node*. For sentences 1–4, students must complete the second half of the sentence; for sentences 5–8, students complete the first half. In 9 and 10, students create their own unique sentences using *-ta node*. Each group should read at least two of their sentences to the class.

Lesson 1   7

1. *Kyoo wa yuki ga <u>futta node</u>* ...
2. *Ashita nihongo no tesuto ga <u>aru node</u>* ...
3. *Kinoo wa otoosan ga osoku ie ni <u>kaetta node</u>* ...
4. *Tanjoobi purezento o <u>kaitai node</u>* ...
5. ... *<u>node</u> toshokan e ikimasu.*
6. ... *<u>node</u> isshookenmei benkyoo shimasu.*
7. ... *<u>node</u> arubaito o sagashimasu.*
8. ... *<u>node</u> denwa shimasu.*
9. ... *<u>node</u>* ...
10. ... *<u>node</u>* ...

6 John became a teacher because ...

In two groups: The students sit around the classroom in two separate circles. If the class is small, one circle would be better. Following the example below, students practice --- *ni narimashita*. Students go in order around the circle taking the part of A, stating what someone has become. Names of classmates, friends, family members, or famous people may be used. The sentences, however, should be true. Anyone may call out with B's response: *Dooshite desu ka?* The person taking the part of A should always use (person's name) *wa* --- *ni narimashita* to state their fact and --- *(da)kara desu* to answer B's question.

Example: A: *Jon san wa sensei <u>ni narimashita</u>.* (John became a teacher.)

B: *Dooshite desu ka?* (Why?)

A: *Kodomo ga suki <u>dakara desu</u>.* (Because he likes children.)

7 Seasonal greetings

In pairs: Japanese people often greet each other and proceed to talk about the weather. In pairs, write seasonal greetings for summer, autumn, and winter in which two Japanese people meet each other. Decide the relationship of the two people and where they are meeting. Each pair presents one of their greeting dialogues to the class. Use the following dialogue for spring as an example.

Example: Spring → Two friends, Emi and Yumi, are meeting in the park on a beautiful spring afternoon.

Emi: *Yumi san! Ie ni kaeru no?* (Yumi! Are you going home?)

Yumi: *Aa, Emi. Konnichi wa.* (Oh, Emi. Good afternoon.)

Emi: *Kyoo wa atatakai wa nee!* (It's really warm out today.)

Yumi: *Soo ne. Kotoshi no sakura wa totemo kirei ne.*

(Yeah. This year's cherry blossoms are so pretty.)

Emi: *Kion mo choodo ii wa.* (The temperature is just right, too.)

8 Letter to a pen pal

Individually: Write a letter to a pen pal in Japan. The following are some suggestions of what to include in the letter.

1. Self introduction (*jikoshookai*)
    a. name, age, birthday, gender
    b. hobby, sports/music you like/dislike, part-time job
    c. what you would like to do next summer, next year
    d. why you want to have a pen pal
2. Family introduction
    a. about your parents, brothers, sisters (occupations, hobbies, what they like/dislike)
    b. anyone else who lives with you (aunt, uncle, grandparents)
    c. pets
3. School information
    a. subjects you take, subjects you like/dislike
    b. club activities or after-school activities that you do
    c. plans for after graduation
4. Area information
    a. state where you live
    b. any big city near by
    c. environment (big city/countryside)
    d. famous products
    e. well-known history

Lesson 2: Souvenirs

I. PERSPECTIVE

1. Objectives

1 Function:

(1) Making sure someone already knows something: *Shitte iru daro?*
(2) Confirming agreement: *Daro.*
(3) Inviting someone to do something together with a reason: *(Boku mo ... katte kita) kara (... kookan) shiyoo.*
(4) Stating something is fit for or looks good on someone: *(Neesan) ni wa (sore kurai) ga niau yo.*
(5) Thinking about whether or not to do something: *(Tsuka)oo ka na.*
(6) Stating that something is just right for someone or something: *(Pinku no doresu) ni pittari yo.*

2 Language:

(1) *(Shit)te iru daro?*   (2) *(Katte kita) kara, (tokidoki kookan) shiyoo.*
(3) *(Neesan) ni wa (sore kurai) ga (niau) yo.*

3 Culture:

(1) *Omiyage*: Japanese souvenirs and the gift-giving concept
(2) Hobbies of Japanese teenagers   (3) Popular Japanese postcards
(4) Japanese arts and crafts   (5) High school dance parties

II. PREPARATION

1. Context

おみやげ

スミス一家、団らんの時。お母さんが焼いたチーズケーキを食べながら、ピーターの日本旅行を話題にして盛り上がる。ピーターの買ってきたお土産と出来上がった写真。そして、昨日届いたばかりの日本からの絵はがき。みんな好き勝手なことを言う。ピーターはそれぞれについて説明をする。でも、お姉さんのお土産を買い忘れそうになった事がわかったら、お姉さんが怒るから秘密だ。お姉さんへのお土産は、お母さんと柄違いの扇子だが、気に入ったようだ。

Everyone is sitting around together at the Smiths' house. While eating the cheesecake that Mother baked, everyone is excited to hear about Peter's trip to Japan. Peter has the souvenirs that he brought back, pictures, and the postcard that arrived from Japan yesterday. Everyone comments on the souvenirs that Peter has brought back for them, and Peter explains the souvenirs. It is a secret that he almost forgot to buy a souvenir for his sister. If she finds out, she'll get angry. The souvenir for his sister is a folding fan; it is the same as his mother's but with a different pattern. His sister seems to like it.

2. Sample Conversation

A: 僕のおみやげ、こいのぼりじゃなかったの。
P: 何だよ。きせつはずれだよ。知っているだろ。
A: じょうだんだよ。このファミコンソフト、本当はとっても嬉しい。
P: だろ。僕も自分のを買ってきたから、時々こうかんしよう。
B: このせんす、ちょっとはでじゃない。
P: 姉さんにはそれくらいがにあうよ。
B: そうかなあ。ダンスパーティーの時に使おうかな。
L: あなたのピンクのドレスにぴったりよ。
B: そう言われてみれば、そうかも・・・。
P: ほら、僕ってセンスあるでしょう。
B: 何よ。写真も見せて。
V: 何だ、こいつ。自分あてにえはがきを送って。
P: だって、その写真気に入っているんだ。

A: *Boku no omiyage¹, koinobori ja nakatta no?*
P: *Nan da yo. Kisetsuhazure da yo. Shitte iru daro²?*
A: *Joodan da yo. Kono famikonsofuto, hontoo wa tottemo ureshii.*
P: *Daro. Boku mo jibun no³ o katte kita kara, tokidoki kookan shiyoo⁴.*
B: *Kono sensu⁵, chotto hade ja nai?*
P: *Neesan ni wa sore kurai ga niau yo.*
B: *Soo ka naa⁶. Dansu paatii⁷ no toki ni tsukaoo ka na.*
L: *Anata no pinku no doresu ni⁸ pittari yo.*
B: *Soo iwarete mireba, soo kamo⁹.*
P: *Hora, boku tte sensu aru deshoo.*
B: *Nani yo. Shashin mo misete¹⁰.*
V: *Nan da, koitsu. Jibun ate ni ehagaki¹¹ o okutte . . .*
P: *Datte¹², sono shashin ki ni itte iru n da.*

A: Wasn't my souvenir supposed to be a *koinobori*?
P: What are you talking about? You know it's out of season.
A: I'm just kidding. I'm really happy with this TV game.
P: Sure. I bought myself a different one, so let's trade sometimes.
B: Isn't this fan a little showy?
P: I think it suits you.
B: Really? Maybe I'll bring it with me to the dance party.
L: It goes well with your pink dress.
B: You may be right.
P: See, I have excellent taste.
B: Come on, show me the pictures.
V: What's this? You sent the postcard to yourself.
P: Well, I really liked the picture.

P: ピーター　スミス　　　　　*Piitaa Sumisu*　　　　Peter Smith
A: アラン　スミス（弟）　　　*Aran Sumisu (otooto)*　Alan Smith (younger brother)
B: ベティ　スミス（お姉さん）　*Betii Sumisu (oneesan)*　Betty Smith (elder sister)
L: リリー　スミス（お母さん）　*Ririi Sumisu (okaasan)*　Lily Smith (mother)
V: ビクター　スミス（お父さん）*Bikutaa Sumisu (otoosan)*　Victor Smith (father)

3. Language & Culture Notes

1 The gift-giving concept is one of the basic fundamentals of Japanese society, which has been built on harmonious human relationships. Expressing gratitude by more than just saying *arigatoo gozaimasu* is as important as it is appreciated. Japanese by nature go out of their way for others without really expecting any favors in return. To give someone a gift in return for a favor is a way of maintaining the stability of human relationships. One does not have to, but one should give gifts, even for the smallest favor. For example, a family goes on vacation for a week. Before leaving, they ask a neighbor to collect their mail while they are gone. To show their appreciation, the family will bring the neighbor back a gift. The quality or type of gift doesn't count as much as the fact that a gift is given.

There is a wide range of Japanese souvenirs, or *omiyage*. The most common types of gifts or souvenirs are chocolate, Japanese sweets, and fruit. *Omiyage* bought in Japan is packaged for the purpose of gift-giving, neatly organized in perfectly wrapped boxes. Japanese who travel abroad may bring back a box of chocolates with a picture of the place they visited on the box or something specific from that country. Japanese do a lot of their *omiyage* shopping at duty free shops at the airport just before they return home.

2 *Daro* serves the same function as *daroo*. Only males use this expression.

3 *Jibun no famikonsofuto* is shortened omitting the object, which follows *no*. Another example is *Yamada san no (kamera) o tsukatta*, "I used Yamada's (camera)."

4 *Shiyoo* in *kookan shiyoo* is the *oo* form of *suru* (to do). The Japanese created hundreds of new vocabulary words by attaching *suru* to nouns, such as *benkyoo* (study), *ryokoo* (travel), and *kekkon* (marriage).

5 Japanese people take pride in their arts and crafts because they are an important part of Japanese culture. There are, of course, specific arts native to particular parts of Japan, but there are plenty of creative works that represent the culture of Japan as a whole. *Origami*, familiar to many Americans, is the art of folding paper into various shapes and designs. *Sensu* are handheld folding fans made of different kinds of paper, some of which are hand painted. *Yakimono* is known in English as ceramics. Works varying from plates and bowls to vases and sculptures are found throughout Japan. Other artistic works are carvings made from wood and baskets made from bamboo.

6 *Soo ka naa* means "Really?" "Is that so?" or "Maybe so." It expresses uncertainty; the speaker is not sure.

7 In America, high school students attend social functions like theme dances and proms. However, dances like these do not occur in Japan simply because it is not a part of Japanese culture. Japanese teens would rather go to a disco or a dance club with their friends when the mood suits them. The only kinds of school-related social functions in Japan are the various annual school festivals.

8 *ni* is a reference function word that refers the description following it to the preceding noun.

9 *Iwarete* is the *-te* form of the passive verb *iwareru*, derived from *iu*, "to say." *Mireba* is the *-ba* form of the verb *miru*. Normally, the *-te* form of a verb plus *miru* means "try to do something." Therefore, *iwarete mireba* means "If you say so" or "When it is said so." When *shirenai* is omitted from *soo kamo shirenai*, it means "It might be said that way."

10 *Kudasai* is omitted from *misete kudasai*, which means "Please show me."

11 Japanese people are very fond of postcards. There are some that are so popular that they can be found at almost any tourist location. Japan's highest, most sacred mountain, Mt. Fuji, is probably the most popular. Pictures of Japanese gardens, *maiko* in Kyoto, Japan's flag, and a map of Japan are other common images on postcards. These postcards symbolize Japan.

12 *Datte* is a discourse function word indicating the speaker's wish to offer reason or explanation.

III. PARTICIPATION

1. Vocabulary

1 **From sample conversation:**

- *ate* (addressed to)
- *hade* (showy, flamboyant, gaudy, loud)
- *iwarete* (to be told)
- *joodan* (joke, be kidding, tease)
- *ki ni itte* (be a favorite with, favor)
- *koinobori* (a carp streamer)
- *misete* (let me see, show me)
- *Nan da yo.* (What?, What are you talking about?)
- *neesan* ([one's own] elder sister)
- *okutte* (sent/send)
- *pittari* (exactly, suitable, fit)
- *shitte iru* (know)
- *tsukaoo* (will use, will bring ... to)
- *ehagaki* ([picture] postcard)
- *hontoo wa* (in fact, actually, really)
- *jibun* (oneself)
- *katte kita* (bought)
- *kisetsuhazure* (out of season)
- *kookan shiyoo* (let's trade, let's exchange)
- *Nan da.* (Oh boy!, What's the matter?)
- *Nani yo.* (What?, Excuse me?, Come on.)
- *niau* (to suit, fit, complement, match well, go well)
- *omiyage* (souvenir, gift)
- *sensu* (Japanese folding fan)
- *tokidoki* (sometimes, occasionally)
- *ureshii* (be glad, be happy)

2 **Useful for activities:**

- *amimono* (knitting)
- *datte* (they say, I hear)
- *eiga* (movie)
- *hajimete kiita* (never heard of that before)
- *igo* (go [a game])
- *iku* (to go)
- *kafeteria* (cafeteria)
- *kondo no* (next)
- *nomu* (to drink)
- *ryuugaku suru* (to study abroad)
- *taiikukan* (gymnasium)
- *benkyoo suru* (to study)
- *Doo suru?* (What shall/should we do?)
- *Gomen ne.* (I'm sorry.)
- *hirugohan* (lunch)
- *ii yo* (OK)
- *jettokoosutaa* (roller coaster)
- *kaku* (to write)
- *miru* (to look)
- *noru* (to get on, to ride)
- *shoogi* (chess)
- *yakusoku* (a promise, appointment)

Lesson 2   13

2. Activity, Practice, & Exercise

1 **Verb conjugation: volitional *-oo* form**

In pairs: Make cards of verbs in the dictionary form. Place the cards face down. Students take turns drawing cards and changing the verbs into the volitional *-oo* form.

Example: *kaku* → *kakoo*   *miru* → *miyoo*   *benkyoo suru* → *benkyoo shiyoo*

2 **Giving invitations**

In class: Divide the class into two groups. Each student in Group A draws a verb card. Using the verb on each card, the student asks a Group B student to do something. The Group B students can either accept or refuse the request. The Group A students should try to get as many acceptances as possible within the time limit, about seven or eight minutes. Then the two groups reverse the roles and repeat the same process. Verbs should be limited to those concerned with invitations: go, watch, eat, drink, play, and so on.

Example: *Iku*

 A: *B san, "Dorakyura" o mi ni ikoo.* (B, let's go see <u>Dracula</u>.)
 B: *Itsu?* (When?)
 A: *Kondo no nichiyoobi.* (Next Sunday.)
 B: *Un, ii yo./Kondo no nichiyoobi wa yakusoku ga aru n da. Gomen ne.*
  (Um, OK./I have an appointment next Sunday. I'm sorry.)

3 **Confirming information**

In pairs or small groups: Students ask each other if they know about someone else's plan.

Example: Etsuo: *Nee, Takashi kun ga ryuugaku suru koto, shitteru/shitte iru daroo?*
      (Did you know that Takashi is going to study abroad?)
    Shino: *Iie, shiranai wa. Hajimete kiita. Doko e ryuugaku suru no.*
      (No, I didn't. That's news to me. Where will he go?)
    Etsuo: *Igirisu datte.* (To Britain, I hear.)

4 **Verb conjugation: *-oo* form**

In pairs: Make verb cards. Each student draws a card, changes the form of the verb into the *-oo* form, and makes a sentence. Follow the example.

Example: *nomu* (to drink) → *Ocha o no<u>moo</u>.* (Let's drink tea.)
    iku (to go)   → *Kafeteria ni i<u>koo</u>.* (Let's go to the cafeteria.)
    noru (to ride) → *Jettokoosutaa ni no<u>roo</u>.* (Let's ride a roller coaster.)
    miru (to see) → *Eiga o mi<u>yoo</u>.* (Let's see a movie.)
    taberu (to eat) → *Hirugohan o tabe<u>yoo</u>.* (Let's eat lunch.)
    suru (to do) → *Nihongo o benkyoo shi<u>yoo</u>.* (Let's study Japanese.)

5 **Does Mary look good in red?**

In groups of three: Make a list of five male and five female classmates. For each person on the list, write a question that asks if something suits or looks good on that person. The questions may ask about what they are presently wearing or something else. Use the form (classmate's name) *ni wa --- ga niaimasu ka?* in making sentences. Next, as a class, students take turns asking one of their group's questions to the rest of the class. Students may answer the questions randomly. Follow the example, paying attention to the differences between male and female speech.

Example questions:
1. *Mearii san <u>ni wa</u> akai seetaa <u>ga niaimasu ka?</u>* (Does a red sweater suit Mary?)
2. *Maiku san <u>ni wa</u> yakyuu no booshi <u>ga niaimasu ka?</u>* (Does Mike look good in a baseball hat?)

Example conversation:
A: *Mearii san <u>ni wa</u> akai seetaa <u>ga niaimasu ka</u>?*
B: (male) *Un. Niau yo./Iie. Niawanai yo.*
B: (female) *Un. Niau wa; Niau wa yo; Niau wa ne./Iie. Niawanai wa; Niawanai wa yo.*

6 Making conversations

In groups of three: Japanese teens' hobbies are similar to those of American teenagers. First, as a class, discuss popular hobbies among Japanese teenagers. As students call out guesses, the teacher writes them on the blackboard. Then students form groups of three and write dialogues in which two Japanese teenage friends are trying to decide what to do one day after school. The friends decide what to do depending on the weather. Following the example below, write dialogues for two of the following: sunny, rainy, or cloudy weather. The first line of the example may be used to start the dialogues.

Example: A: *Kyoo, gakkoo ga owattara, doo suru?* (What should we do after school today?)
B: *Sakkaa o shiyoo ka?* (Shall we play soccer?)
A: *Demo ame ga furisoo da yo.* (But it looks like it might rain.)
B: *Soo ne. Ja, taiikukan de basuketto o shiyoo ka?*
   (Oh. So, should we play basketball in the gym?)
A: *Un. Soo shiyoo.* (OK. Sure.)

Examples of popular hobbies among Japanese teenagers:

amimono (knitting)	*badominton* (badminton)	*bareebooru* (volleyball)
basukettobooru (basketball)	*daatsu* (darts)	*furisubii* (frisbee)
geemusofuto (computer games)	*haikingu* (hiking)	*igo* (*igo*)
maajan (mahjong)	*nuimono* (sewing)	*osero* (Othello)
ryoori (cooking)	*sakkaa* (soccer)	*shoogi* (chess)
sofutobooru (softball)	*suiei* (swimming)	*takkyuu* (table tennis)
tenisu (tennis)	*terebi* (TV)	*terebigeemu* (Video games)
yakyuu (baseball)		

7 Substitution

In pairs: Substitute the underlined expression with other appropriate expressions that indicate that something is just right for someone or something.

<u>*Pinku no doresu*</u> *ni pittari desu.*

8 Substitution

In pairs: Substitute the underlined words with other appropriate words that indicate that one is thinking about whether or not to do something.

<u>*Gohan o tabeyoo*</u> *ka?*

Lesson 3: Review & Application

IV. PERFORMANCE

1. Application

1 **Thank you letter**

In small groups: Create a thank you letter by putting the following sentences in the appropriate order.

a. *Moo sugu natsu ga owarimasu. Minasan, ogenki desu ka?*
   (Summer is coming to an end. How is everybody?)

b. *Minasan to totta shashin ga dekimashita. Sono shashin o mite Nihon o natsukashiku omoimasu.*
   (I developed the pictures that we took together. These pictures make me miss Japan.)

c. *Watashi wa kuni e kaette kita bakari no toki wa, jisaboke ni narimashita ga, ima wa moo genki desu.*
   (I got jet lag shortly after coming back home, but I'm fine now.)

d. *Mata tegami o kakimasu. Ogenki de.* (I will write to you again. Take care.)

e. *Sono shashin o doofuu shimasu. Watashi no koto o omoidashite kudasai ne.*
   (I enclosed the pictures. I hope you remember me.)

f. *Nihon de wa iroiro osewa ni narimashita. Doomo arigatoo gozaimashita.*
   (You helped me in many ways while I was in Japan. I am really grateful to you.

2 **Conversation completion**

In small groups: The following is a conversation between Jim (J) and his brother (B), sister (S), mother (M), and father (F). From the list of sentences below, choose the correct sentences for Jim.

B: *Jim, Nihon no famikon arigatoo.* (Jim, thanks for the Japanese computer game.)
J: (   ). (I also got one for myself, so let's trade once in a while.)
B: *Un.* (OK.)
S: *Watashi no sensu, chotto hade ja nai?* (Isn't my fan a little too loud?)
J: (   ). (It suits you.)
S: *Ja, dansu paatii no toki ni motte iku wa.* (Well, I'll bring it with me to the dance party.)
M: *Kono yukata suteki da wa.* (This yukata is so nice.)
J: (   ) (It's very easy to put on.)
M: *Soo ne. Momen dakara, suzushii soo da shi.* (Yeah. It's cotton, so it should be cool.)
F: *Kono Nihon no yama no shashinshuu mo subarashii ne.*
   (This picture book of Japanese mountains is great, too!)
J: (   ). (You're so fond of mountains, so ...)
F: *Kondo, watashi mo Nihon e itte, Fujisan ni noboritai ne.*
   (I would like to go to Japan and climb Mt. Fuji some day.)
J: (   ). (When you go, I'll go with you.)

   1. *Otoosan wa yama ga suki dakara ne.*
   2. *Kantan ni kirareru n da yo.*
   3. *Sono toki wa, boku mo issho da yo.*
   4. *Neesan ni wa sore gurai ga niau yo.*
   5. *Boku mo jibun no o katte kita kara, tokidoki kookan shiyoo yo.*

3 Verb conjugation: *-nakereba naranai*

In pairs: Using verb cards or a list of verbs, change verbs from the dictionary form into *-nakereba naranai*.

Example: *kaku* → *kakanakereba naranai*
okiru → *okinakereba naranai*
benkyoo suru → *benkyoo shinakereba naranai*
kuru → *konakereba naranai*

4 Verb conjugation: *-te wa ikenai*

In pairs: In the same manner as APE 3, change verbs from the dictionary form into *-te wa ikenai*.

Example: • *kaku* → *kaite wa* (*-ku* → *-ite*),
oyogu → *oyoide wa* (*-gu* → *-ide*),
au → *atte wa*; *matsu* → *matte wa*; *noru* → *notte wa* (*-u*; *-tsu*; *-ru* → *-tte*),
hanasu → *hanashite wa* (*-su* → *-shite*),
shinu → *shinde wa*; *tobu* → *tonde wa*; *nomu* → *nonde wa* (*-nu*; *-bu*; *-mu* → *-nde*),
iku → *itte wa* (exception)
• *miru* → *mite wa*; *kakeru* → *kakete wa* (*-iru*; *-eru* → *-te*),
• *benkyoo suru* → *benkyoo shite wa* (*-suru* → *-shite*),
• *kuru* → *kite wa* (*kuru* → *-kite*)

5 Team competition

In class: Make cards with the name of a place written on each. Divide the class into two or three groups, depending on the size of the class. One person from each group goes to the front of the room and draws a different card. The students have to say what one must do or what one must not do at the place written on the card. Use the expression *-shinakereba naranai* or *-te wa ikenai*. The faster the students say the sentence, the more points their team will get; however, sentences must be correct and appropriate to earn points. The first student to answer correctly will get 5 points for the team, the second 3 points, and the third 1 point. The teacher will judge the sentences.

Example: *Toshokan* → *Shizuka ni <u>shinakereba naranai</u>.* (Library → One must be quiet.)
Gakkoo → *Chikoku shi<u>te wa ikenai</u>.* (School → One must not come late.)

6 Gesture game

In class: Divide the class into two teams. Each team makes six or seven sentences using the form *-nagara -masu* and writes them on a piece of paper. One person from Team A performs a gesture for Team B for one of their sentences. Team B must guess the gesture by saying the sentence in the correct form. Set the time limit at two or three minutes for each sentence and gesture. Teams take turns doing a gesture and guessing the sentence. Teams get a point for each correct sentence.

Example: *Otoosan wa tabako o <u>suinagara</u>, shinbun o <u>yomimasu</u>.*
(My father smokes while reading the newspaper.)
Watashitachi wa poppukoon o <u>tabenagara</u>, eiga o <u>mimasu</u>.
(We eat popcorn while watching a movie.)

7 Collecting information

In class:

① Divide the class into six groups. Each group chooses one of the topics given below and asks all classmates one by one if they do the topic action, and why they do it.

Arubaito o shite iru. (have a part-time job)

Jogingu o shite iru. (go jogging)

Borantia katsudoo o shite iru. (do volunteer activities)

Yoku toshokan e iku. (often go to the library)

Yoku _____ (a place) *e iku.* (often go to ____)

Yoku tomodachi no uchi e iku. (often go to a friend's house)

Example: A: *Anata wa arubaito o shite imasu ka?* (Do you have a part-time job?)

B: *Hai, shite imasu.* (Yes, I do.)

A: *Nan no tame ni arubaito o shite imasu ka?* (Why are you working?)

B: *Kuruma o kau tame ni arubaito o shite imasu.* (I'm working so I can buy a car.)

② Each group combines the results from the information that they received in ①. A representative from each group reports the results to the class.

Example: *Watashitachi no guruupu wa "arubaito" ni tsuite kikimashita. Kono kurasu de arubaito o shite iru hito wa 10 nin, shite nai hito wa 8 nin desu. Arubaito o suru mokuteki wa iroiro desu. Daigaku e iku tame ni arubaito o shite iru hito ga 4 nin, ryokoo ni iku tame ni arubaito o shite iru hito ga 3 nin, nani ka o kau tame ni arubaito o shite iru hito ga 3 nin imasu. Minasan, arubaito ganbatte kudasai.*

(Our group asked about part-time jobs. There are ten people in this class who have part-time jobs and eight who do not. There are various reasons why they are working. Four people work to go to college, three to go on a trip, and three to buy something. Good luck with your part-time jobs, everybody.)

8 Verb conjugation: *-oo* form

In pairs: Using verb cards or a list of verbs, change verbs from the dictionary form into the volitional form.

Example: *iku → ikoo* (*-u* verbs)

miru → miyoo (*-iru*; *-eru* verbs)

renshuu suru → renshuu shiyoo (*suru*)

kuru → koyoo (*kuru*)

9 Invitations

① In class: Ask your classmates to do something with you at a specific time and place. You may ask different questions to different people. Boys use the volitional form *-yoo* and girls use the *-mashoo* form to ask. Keep track of the responses on a task sheet by marking an X if someone decides to do something with you and an O if they don't.

Example: 1) A: *B san, kin'yoobi no yoru, uchi de issho ni bideo o miyoo.*
 (B, let's watch a video together on Friday evening.)
 B: *Donna bideo?* (What kind of video?)
 A: *"13 nichi no Kin'yoobi" no shiriizu.* (One of the Friday the 13th movies.)
 B: *Ii ne. Kowai eiga wa daisuki da./Uun, kowai eiga wa chotto ...*
 (Sounds good. I like horror movies./Well, I really don't like horror movies.)
 2) A: *B san, kin'yoobi no yoru, uchi de issho ni bideo o mimashoo.*
 (B, let's watch a video together on Friday evening.)
 B: *Donna bideo?* (What kind of video?)
 A: *"Goddo Faazaa" no shiriizu.* (One of the Godfather movies.)
 B: *Ii wa ne. Watashi, Aru Pachiino ga daisuki na no./Uun, mafia no eiga wa chotto.*
 (Sounds good. I love Al Pacino./Well, I really don't like Mafia movies.)

Example task sheet

Sasotta hito	*Naiyoo*	*Henji*
An	*Doyoobi, issho ni booringu o suru.*	O
Tomu	*Kin'yoobi no yoru, issho ni kowai eiga o miru.*	X

② Students count the numbers of Xs and Os. The teacher may then show a chart like the following just for fun.

Three types of personality:
1. Os outnumber Xs → Amiable, but possibly a little unreliable.
2. Xs outnumber Os → Cautious, but possibly a little difficult to please.
3. Os and Xs are about the same in number. → Normal, having clear likes and dislikes.

10 Male and female speech

In small groups: Determine whether the following sentences are spoken by men or women, and discuss why you think so.

1. *Anata ni aete, ureshii wa.* (I'm glad to see you.)
2. *Boku wa natsuyasumi ni ryokoo shitai.* (I want to go on a trip during summer vacation.)
3. *Kon'ya wa yuki ga furu daroo na.* (It will snow tonight.)
4. *Chichi wa asu hima na no.* (My father will be free tomorrow.)
5. *Nichiyoobi wa tsuri ni iku n da.* (I will go fishing on Sunday.)
6. *Issho ni tabeyoo.* (Let's eat together.)
7. *Ano booshi, suteki ne.* (That hat is nice, isn't it?)
8. *Nomo wa kakkoii ne.* (Nomo is cool, isn't he?)
9. *Kono kooen, shizuka da ne.* (This park is quiet, isn't it?)
10. *Kono okashi, oishii wa ne.* (This cake is delicious, isn't it?)

2. Actualization

1 Practice the following conversation and develop your own dialogue on a similar subject with your partners.

Suiyoobi no 4jikanme, taiiku no jugyoo desu. 4 nen 5 kumi no seito wa, tobibako no renshuu o shite imasu.

(Fourth period on Wednesday is physical education. The 4th grade, class 5 students are practicing *tobibako*, or the horse vault.)

Tanaka san:	*Sensei, watashi, 3 dan wa tobemasen.* (Ms. Oyama, I can't do it with three stands.)
Oyama sensei:	*Moo ichido, yatte goran.* (Try it again.)
Tanaka san:	*Takasugite, kowai n desu.* (It's so high. I'm scared.)
Suzuki kun:	*Tanaka no yowamushi. Boku nanka 5 dan datte heiki da yo.* (Tanaka, you're a coward. I can do it with five stands.)
Tanaka san:	*Suzuki kun no ijiwaru. Suzuki kun wa watashi yori zutto se ga takai kara.* (Suzuki, you're mean. You're much taller than me, that's why.)
Oyama sensei:	*Hora, futari tomo kenka shinai no. Tanaka san, moo sukoshi ushiro kara ikioi-yoku hashittara kitto toberu wa.* (You two, stop arguing. Tanaka, you'll be able to make it if you run faster from farther back.)
Tanaka san:	*Hai.* (OK)
	[Tanaka san 3 dan o tobu.] (Tanaka makes it with three stands.)
Oyama sensei:	*Hora, dekita deshoo.* (See. You made it.)
Tanaka san:	*Sensei, arigatoo gozaimashita.* (Thank you very much.)

2 Practice the following conversation and develop your own dialogue on a similar subject with your partners.

Kin'yoobi no 3jikanme, taiiku desu. 4 nen 3 kumi no seito wa matto undoo no renshuu o shite imasu.

(Third period on Friday is physical education. The 4th grade, class 3 students are practicing floor-mat exercises.)

Nakamura sensei:	*Minasan, zenten wa daijoobu na yoo na node, kondo wa kooten no renshuu o shimasu.* (You all seem to be all right with forward rolls. Next we'll do backward rolls.)
Zen'in:	*Hai.* (OK)

Hirota san:	*Kobayashi kun wa undoo ga tokui de ii wa ne. Watashi mo Kobayashi kun mitai ni umaku kooten ga dekitara ii noni.*
	(Kobayashi, I envy you because you're good at sports. I wish I could do backward rolls as well as you.)
Kobayashi kun:	*Moo sukoshi tsuyoku te de matto o oshitara, umaku dekiru yo.*
	(It would help if you pushed harder on the mat with your hands.)
Hirota san:	*Hontoo?* (Really?)
Kobayashi kun:	*Un.* (Yes.)
	[*Hirota san kooten o suru.*] [Hirota does it better.]
Hirota san:	*Ureshii wa. Sakki yori umaku dekita wa. Arigatoo.*
	(I'm happy. I did it better than before. Thank you.)
Kobayashi kun:	*Yokatta ne.* (Good for you.)

3 In small groups: The following is a conversation between an American student (A) and a Japanese student (J) who is studying in America. They are talking about sports. Fill in the underlined parts with the appropriate sport for the American student.

J: *Nihon de dentooteki na supootsu tte nan da to omou?*
(What do you think are traditional sports in Japan?)

A: *Eeto, _____ toka _____ toka.* (Well, _____ and _____.)

J: *Soo. Ninki wa maa maa dakedo, amari kodomo ga yaritagaru supootsu ja nai yo. Nihon de ninki ga aru supootsu tte nan da to omou?*
(Yes. They are popular, but not the kind of sports that children would enjoy. What do you think are popular sports in Japan?)

A: *_____ toka _____ toka.* (_____ and _____.)

J: *Soo. Ninki no chiimu ya jimoto no chiimu no shiai ga aru toki wa, chiketto ga urikireru yo.*
(Yes. Tickets are sold out when popular or local teams have games.)

A: *Amerika de wa _____ toka _____ toka _____ da na. Puro mo ama mo ooi kara.*
(In America, _____, _____, and _____ are popular sports. There are many professional and amateur sports.)

J: *Amerika wa puro supootsu ga takusan aru ne.* (There are a lot of professional sports in America.)

4 Choose a Japanese traditional sport from the following. Research the topic, and then discuss it in English and Japanese.

sumoo, kendoo, juudoo, aikidoo, karate, kyuudoo

3. Enrichment

In Volume One, under the Enrichment sections of the review lessons, students were introduced to the authentic Japanese writing conventions of *katakana*, *hiragana*, and *kanji*. For students who may not have covered the Enrichment sections, it is recommended that the following pages of Volume One be reviewed: 21~23, 45, 70~71, 92, 138~140, 167~170, 193, 216~217.

Since 1984, the Japan Foundation, a Japanese government supported organization, has been conducting annual proficiency examinations for non-native speakers of Japanese. Volume Two attempts to introduce about 250 *kanji* that are necessary to pass Level 3 (intermediate) of this exam. (Levels range from 1 to 4, 1 being the most difficult.)

The Enrichment sections of the Review & Application lessons list the *kanji* learned in previous regular lessons as well as other related *kanji*. These sections also include strategies for learning *kanji*.

1 *Kanji* for Lesson 1

夏	終わる	元気	僕	日本
行く	時	時差	今	大丈夫
同封	手紙	書く	九月	三日

2 *Kanji* for Lesson 2

| 何 | 知る | 本当 | 嬉しい | 自分 |
| 買う | 時々 | 姉 | 使う | 写真 |

3 Other useful *kanji*

Numbers:	一、二、三、四、五、六、七、八、九、十、百、千、万
Days of the week:	日、月、火、水、木、金、土、曜
Time:	年、週、分、時間、朝、昼、夕、夜、晩
Family:	家族、私、子、父、母、兄、妹
Seasons & climate:	季節、秋、冬、春、寒、涼、暖、暑

4 **Strategies**

K*anji* formation: Part one

Each *kanji* represents a word and involves three elements: form or symbol, meaning, and pronunciation. After *kanji* was introduced from China, the Japanese began using *kanji* to write their own language. Most *kanji* were formed on the basis of one of six types of arrangements. This lesson covers two types.

(1) Shapes of visual objects: These *kanji* convey original, concrete meanings. 日 (sun), 月 (moon), 木 (tree), 川 (river), 水 (water), 田 (field), 火 (fire), 竹 (bamboo), 羊 (sheep), 馬 (horse), 鳥 (bird), 魚 (fish), 目 (eye), 耳 (ear), 手 (hand), 井 (well), 門 (gate), 車 (wheel), 口 (mouth), 刀 (knife)

(2) Symbols representing abstract concepts: Abstract concepts such as "up" or "down" cannot be visualized because they are shapeless. Symbols such as lines or dots are used to represent abstract concepts. 上 (up), 下 (down), 一 (one), 二 (two), 三 (three), 大 (big), 小 (small), 北 (north), 比 (compare).

Sometimes a *kanji* with a concrete meaning, such as 木 (tree), is used to form *kanji* with abstract concepts. It loses its original meaning by adding one or two symbols. 本 (foundation), 末 (tip).

Two strategies can easily be discerned from the above information.

Strategy A

Learning the historical process of *kanji* formation may be helpful in recognizing cultural features.

Strategy B

Cognitive skills may be used to form some abstract concepts by identifying symbols, such as lines and dots, that are placed in a contrastive way (such as 上 and 下) or signs of visual objects used in forming abstract concepts (such as 本).

5 Exercise

Try to identify the *kanji* listed in 1, 2, and 3 that might have been formed from strategies A and B.

Lesson 4: Peter's trip to Japan

I. PERSPECTIVE

1. Objectives

1 Function:
(1) Stating someone had finally experienced something: *Tootoo (Nihon e itte ki)mashita.*
(2) Replying with a bit of surprise: *Maa, soo desu ka?*
(3) Expressing comparisons: *(Amutorakku) yori (hayai) to omoimashita.*
(4) Asking how something was: *(Omatsuri) wa doo deshita ka?*
(5) Confirming one's desire to do more: *Motto (ohanashi) ga/o (kiki)tai desu ne.*
(6) Proposing to do something next: *Tsugi no (jugyoo) wa, ...ni shimashoo ka?*

2 Language:
(1) *(Amutorakku) yori (haya)i to (omoi)mashita.*   (2) *(Omatsuri) wa doo deshita ka?*
(3) *Motto (ohanashi) ga (kiki)tai desu ne.*
(4) *(Tsugi) no (jugyoo) wa, (Piitaa kun) no (Nihon taiken) ni shimashoo ka?*

3 Culture:
(1) School year schedule, entrance ceremonies, and graduation
(2) *Shinkansen* (bullet train) vs. Amtrak   (3) *Yukata* and *kimono*
(4) Summer festivals

II. PREPARATION

1. Context

ピーターの日本旅行

ピーターは新学期が始まって学校へ行ったら、校舎の入り口のところで、はやし先生に出会った。早速はやし先生に話しかけた。夏休みの日本旅行のことを話したくて、ウズウズしている。はやし先生は、ピーターの話を聞いて驚いた。ピーターが日本へ行ったことを、全く知らなかったからだ。ピーターがどんな生活を日本で経験したか、いろいろ質問してくれた。ピーターは興奮して話し続けた。はやし先生は、次の授業のテーマを提案した。それは、夏休みの体験だった。
(第4課から第13課迄が、ピーターの日本での体験談だ。)

On the first day of school, Peter saw his teacher Hayashi *sensei* at the entrance of the school. Peter started talking to her immediately. He was anxious to talk about his summer vacation trip to Japan. Hayashi *sensei* was surprised to hear about Peter's trip because she had no idea that he went to Japan. She asked many questions about his experiences. Peter continued to talk with excitement. Hayashi *sensei* suggested talking about Peter's experiences in Japan in the next class.
(Lessons 4 through 13 cover Peter's experiences in Japan.)

2. Sample Conversation

P: はやし先生、とうとう日本へ行ってきました。
K: まあ、そうですか。それはいつのこと。
P: 夏休みの時です。3週間の日程で。
K: 新幹線に乗りましたか。
P: はい。アムトラックより速いと思いました。
K: 夏祭りは行きましたか。
P: はい。ペンパルの家のそばでお祭りがありました。
K: お祭りはどうでしたか。
P: 楽しかったです。
K: 浴衣は着ましたか。
P: いいえ。でも、盆踊りをしました。
K: もっとお話が聞きたいですね。
次の授業は、ピーターくんの日本体験にしましょうか。

P: *Hayashi sensei, tootoo Nihon e itte kimashita.*
K: *Maa[1], soo desu ka. Sore wa itsu no koto?*
P: *Natsuyasumi[2] no toki desu. 3shuukan no nittei de . . .*
K: *Shinkansen[3] ni norimashita ka?*
P: *Hai. Amutorakku yori[4] hayai to omoimashita.*
K: *Natsumatsuri wa ikimashita ka?*
P: *Hai. Penparu no ie no soba de omatsuri ga arimashita.*
K: *Omatsuri wa doo deshita ka?*
P: *Tanoshikatta desu.*
K: *Yukata[5] wa kimashita ka?*
P: *Iie. Demo, bon'odori[6] o shimashita.*
K: *Motto ohanashi ga[7] kikitai desu ne. Tsugi no jugyoo wa, Piitaa kun no Nihon taiken ni shimashoo ka.*

P: Hayashi *sensei*, I finally went to Japan.
K: Is that so! When did you go?
P: For about three weeks during summer vacation.
K: Did you ride on the bullet train?
P: Yes, I did. I thought it was faster than Amtrak.
K: Did you go to the summer festival?
P: Yes, I did. The festival was held near my pen pal's house.
K: How was the festival?
P: I enjoyed it a lot.
K: Did you wear a *yukata*?
P: No, I didn't. But I joined the *bon'odori*.
K: I'd like to hear more about your trip to Japan. Shall we talk about your experiences in the next class?

P: ピーター　スミス　　　*Piitaa Sumisu*　　　Peter Smith
K: はやし　かおり先生　　*Hayashi Kaori Sensei*　　Kaori Hayashi (teacher)

3. Language & Culture Notes

1 *Maa* is a discourse function word indicating the speaker's surprise (Really?) or serving as a softener (Well . . .). *Maa* is generally used by females.

2 The Japanese school year schedule is nothing like the American academic calendar. In Japan, the school year begins the second week of April and ends in mid-March. The year is divided into trimesters. The first ends July 20, followed by a summer vacation of about 40 days. The second trimester runs from September 1 until December 22 and the third from the second week of January until the end of the academic year. American students go to school for 180 days; Japanese students attend classes for 240 days. Japanese students have longer winter and spring vacations than their American peers, but their summer vacation is much shorter.

Compared to American schools, the Japanese procedures for graduation and the first and last days of each term may seem quite elaborate. There are mandatory opening and closing ceremonies for the first and last day of each term. There is also an entrance ceremony for first-year students entering junior high or high school as well as graduation for those moving on to the next level of education. The atmosphere of a Japanese graduation ceremony does not share the same festive spirit as one in the United States. In the United States, opening, closing, and entrance ceremonies are very relaxed, if they exist at all.

3 The *shinkansen*, or the bullet train, is the fastest land mode of transportation in Japan. Reaching speeds up to 160 miles per hour, the fastest *shinkansen* can go from Tokyo to Hiroshima (about 500 miles) in four hours. Women in uniforms walk down the train aisles pushing carts and selling drinks from beer to cola and food from ice cream to Japanese boxed lunches. The *shinkansen*, directly translated as "new trunk line," is both faster and more expensive than America's Amtrak, although there aren't nearly as many routes.

4 *yori*, a function word, indicates comparison.

5 *Kimono* and *yukata* are two similar types of traditional Japanese clothing worn by both men and women. A *kimono* is a full-length robe tied with a wide sash called an *obi*. *Kimono* are handmade with beautiful and intricate patterns, designs, and colors. A *kimono* involves several layers of material, all of which are worn together. Today, *kimono* are not worn very often. They are usually reserved for weddings, festivals, or other special occasions.

A *yukata* differs from a *kimono* in that it consists of only one lightweight layer of cotton and is less formal. It replaces *kimono* in the summer. Most *yukata* have a geometric or floral pattern on a white or deep blue background. Originally it was a garment worn after a bath; however, during the 19th century, people began to wear *yukata* during the hot summer months outdoors as well as indoors. It is common for people to wear *yukata* to *obon*. *Yukata* are sometimes worn as pajamas as well. Most *ryokan* (Japanese-style inns) lay out *yukata* for guests to wear.

6 Most towns and villages throughout Japan celebrate the spirit of their ancestors in a summer festival known as *obon*. The festival is celebrated in July or August, depending on the town. *Obon* and the worshiping of ancestors' spirits are important parts of Japanese culture. Family members who have moved from the villages to the big cities usually return home for the festival as families and neighborhoods celebrate together. People sometimes dress in traditional Japanese clothes, and everyone joins in a spiritual dance called *bon'odori*. During *obon*, the town streets come alive with culture, spirit, and laughter.

7 *ga* is used instead of *o* when followed by the potential form of a transitive verb. The potential form is used to imply the meaning of "be possible to." Recently, however, people have had a tendency to use *o* instead of *ga*.

III. PARTICIPATION

1. Vocabulary

1 From sample conversation:

amutorakku (Amtrak)
hayai (fast)
itte kimashita (have been to, went to)
kikitai (would like to hear)
maa, ... (well, ...)
natsuyasumi (summer vacation)
nittei (schedule, program)
ohanashi (story; about ..., on ...)
omoimashita (thought)
sanshuukan (three weeks)
tanoshikatta (was fun, was enjoyable, enjoyed)
tsugi (next)

bon'odori (Bon Festival dance)
ikimashita (went)
jugyoo (class)
kimashita (wore, put on)
natsumatsuri (summer festival)
Nihon taiken (experiences in Japan)
norimashita (took, went by, rode)
omatsuri (festival)
penparu (pen pal)
shinkansen (bullet train)
tootoo (finally)
yukata (Japanese summer kimono)

2 Useful for activities:

basho (place)
bunkasai (cultural festival)
chotto (a little)
Fujisan (Mt. Fuji)
--- gawa (... River)
hitori (one person)
Igirisu (England)
12 gatsu 10ka (December 10th)
kimatsushiken (term examination)
nichiji (the date and time)
nyuugakushiken (entrance examination)
okashi (Japanese sweets, candy)
paatii (party)
rokku (rock music)
shussekisha (participants)
shuugakuryokoo (school excursion)
tabemono (food)
too (ten)
yosan (a budget)

boonenkai (year-ending party)
chirashizushi (a type of sushi)
denkiseihin (electrical appliances)
fuyuyasumi (winter vacation)
haruyasumi (spring vacation)
hoshii (want)
issho ni (together)
kakkoii (cool [as in style, personality])
kyooshitsu (classroom)
nomimono (beverages)
nyuugakushiki (entrance ceremony)
oshoogatsu (New Year's Day)
poppusu (pop music)
seinoo (performance, quality)
--- shuu (state)
sotsugyooshiki (graduation ceremony)
tawaa (tower)
undookai (sports festival, competition)
zen'in (all members, everyone)

2. Activity, Practice, & Exercise

1 Planning a party

In groups of four or five: Each group plans to hold a party. First, decide the kind of party, the time, place, and participants or guests. Then discuss what is necessary for the party, such as food, drinks, music, and so on. Then estimate the budget. Use the expression *-ni shiyoo/shimashoo (ka)* in the discussion.

Examples of parties: *Tanjoo paatii, Sotsugyoo paatii, Kurisumasu paatii.*

Example:
Paatii:	*boonenkai* (year-ending party)
Basho:	*kyooshitsu* (classroom)
Nichiji:	*12 gatsu 10 ka gogo 6 ji* (December 10th, 6 p.m.)
Shussekisha:	*kurasu zen'in* (the whole class)
Tabemono:	*sandoitchi, chirashizushi, piza, okashi*
	(sandwiches, chirashizushi, pizza, Japanese sweets and candy)
Nomimono:	*koohii, koocha, ocha, koora, juusu*
	(coffee, tea, green tea, cola, juice)
Ongaku:	*rokku no teipu, Nihon no poppusu no teipu*
	(tapes of rock music and Japanese pop music)
Yosan:	*hitori 5 doru* ($5 per person)

2 Making comparisons

In groups of three or four: Compare the following pairs in size. Describe which is bigger or taller or which is smaller or shorter. Use reference books if necessary.

Example: *Jiyuu no Megami → Nara no Daibutsu* (Statue of Liberty → Great Buddha in Nara)
  Jiyuu no Megami wa Nara no Daibutsu yori ookii desu.
  (The Statue of Liberty is bigger than the Great Buddha in Nara.)
  Nara no Daibutsu wa Jiyuu no Megami yori chiisai desu.
  (The Great Buddha in Nara is smaller than the Statue of Liberty.)

1. *Eberesutozan → Fujisan* (Mt. Everest → Mt. Fuji)
2. *Amerika → Igirisu* (America → England)
3. *Mishishippiigawa → Amazongawa* (Mississippi River → Amazon River)
4. *Tookyoo tawaa → Efferutoo* (Tokyo Tower → Eiffel Tower)
5. *--- san → --- san* (Mr. --- → Mr. ---)
6. *Nyuu Jaajii shuu → Kariforunia shuu* (New Jersey → California)

3 Buying electrical appliances

In pairs: Bring in advertisements or mail-order catalogs of electrical appliances. Tell your partner what you want to buy from the ads or catalogs using the expression *--- ga hoshiku natta*.

Example: A: *Denkiseihin ga takusan aru ne/wa. Aa, Sonii no bideokamera mo aru.*
  (There are a lot of electrical appliances. Oh, they have Sony video cameras, too.)

B: *Atarashii bideokamera ga <u>hoshiku natta</u> no?* (You've wanted to buy a new video camera?)
A: *Un. Seinoo ga yokute, dezain mo kakkoii mono ga <u>hoshii</u> yo/wa.*
   (Yes. I want a good quality one with a good design.)
B: *Demo, chotto takai naa/wa ne.* (But, it's a little expensive, isn't it?)
A: *Soo da ne/ne.* (Yeah.)
B: *Shaapu no hoo ga yasui yo/wa yo.* (Sharp's is cheaper.)
A: *Un, demo yappari Sonii ga ii naa/wa.* (Yes, but Sony is still good.)

4 How was Kyoto?

In pairs: Each student makes three cards with the name of a place on each, such as a city, a country, the beach, zoo, park, circus. The teacher collects the cards and then randomly gives three cards back to each student. Students pair up and ask each other about the places on their cards. For example, student A draws one of his/her own cards and asks student B about what he/she did there. Students A and B then change roles and repeat the activity. Then they find new partners. Students should be given enough time to work in three different pairs. Follow the example.

Example conversation:

A: *Kyooto <u>wa doo deshita ka</u>?* (How was Kyoto?)
B: *(Watashi wa) tanoshikatta desu.* (I had a good time.)
A: *Soo desu ka? <u>Motto hanashi o kikitai desu</u>.* (Really? I'd like to hear more about it.)
B: *Kazoku to issho ni, Kinkakuji to Ginkakuji to Kiyomizudera o mi ni ikimashita.*
   (I went with my family. We saw Kinkakuji Temple, Ginkakuji Temple, and Kiyomizudera Temple.)

5 Calendar events

In pairs: The teacher makes a set of cards for each pair with a school or calendar event written on each card. The cards should be scrambled. The teacher also gives each pair a piece of paper with the months written in Japanese down the left side of the paper. In pairs, partners take turns drawing cards and asking each other when the event on the card takes place. Then they place the card on the paper next to the appropriate month. There may be more than one event for some months, and some events may take place over consecutive months. Afterward, to check the answers, the teacher asks the whole class when each event takes place, and the students answer. Follow the example.

Example: A: *Obon wa itsu desu ka?* (When is *obon*?)
 B: *Obon wa hachi gatsu desu.* (It's in August.)

Examples of events:
- 1 *gatsu*: *oshoogatsu* (New Year's Day); *fuyuyasumi* (winter vacation)
- 2 *gatsu*: *daigaku nyuugakushiken* (college entrance examinations)
- 3 *gatsu*: *3 gakki no kimatsushiken* (third-term final examinations) [first & second grade only]; *sotsugyooshiki* (graduation ceremony); *haruyasumi* (spring vacation)
- 4 *gatsu*: *haruyasumi* (spring vacation); *nyuugakushiki* (entrance ceremony)
- 5 *gatsu*: Golden week
- 6 *gatsu*:
- 7 *gatsu*: *1 gakki no kimatsushiken* (first-term final examinations); *natsuyasumi* (summer vacation)
- 8 *gatsu*: *natsuyasumi* (summer vacation); *obon* (Bon Festival)
- 9 *gatsu*: *shuugakuryokoo* (school trip or excursion)
- 10 *gatsu*: *undookai* (sports festival)
- 11 *gatsu*: *bunkasai* (culture festival)
- 12 *gatsu*: *2 gakki no kimatsushiken* (second-term final examinations); *fuyuyasumi* (winter vacation)

6 Use of *tootoo*

In groups of three or four: Use *tootoo* to write five different sentences.
Example: *Tootoo byooki ni narimashita.*

7 Use of *maa*

In groups of three or four: Use *maa* to write five different sentences.
Example: *Maa, soo desu ka?*

Lesson 5: Leaving for Japan

I. PERSPECTIVE

1. Objectives

1 Function:

(1) Saying good-bye to someone who is leaving (but returning): *Ki o tsukete itte koi yo.*
(2) Stating opinions with reasons: *(Chian ga ii) kara (daijoobu) da yo.*
(3) Recalling roughly (approximately): *(Juunijikan) gurai ja nakatta kana?*
(4) "Please be careful so that ...": *(Jisaboke ni nara) nai yoo ni na.*
(5) Suggesting that it is OK for someone to do something: *(Shikkari nemu)ru to ii yo.*
(6) Expressing one's first time doing or experiencing something: *... wa hajimete na n da.*
(7) Suggesting something might happen: *... kamo shirenai wa ne.*
(8) Changing or concluding the topic with smooth transition ("anyway," "in any case"): *Maa tonikaku.*

2 Language:

(1) *Ki o tsukete.*
(2) *(It)te koi yo.*
(3) *(Juunijikan) gurai ja nakatta kana.*
(4) *(Jisaboke) ni naranai yoo ni na.*
(5) *(Daijoobu) da yo.*
(6) *(Hikooki) no (naka) de (shikkari nemu)ru to ii yo.*
(7) *(Hikooki) wa (hajimete) nan da.*
(8) *(Koofun)shite (nemure)nai kamo shirenai wa.*
(9) *Tonikaku (ii tabi o).*

3 Culture:

(1) Expressing concern
(2) Time difference

II. PREPARATION

1. Context

日本に向けて旅立ち

ピーターがいよいよ日本へ行く。1週間の予定で、京都にあるペンパルの家にホームステイをしたり、観光地などを旅行したりする。空港までは友達が車で送ってくれた。ピーターにとって初めての海外旅行なので、よしこは少し心配している。チェックインをすませ、ゲートに入るピーターに、友達は旅行中の健康や安全についての話をする。ピーターは明るく「行ってきます。」と言って、ゲートの中へ消えて行った。

Peter is finally going to Japan. His plan is to stay at his pen pal's house in Kyoto for one week and then travel to tourist places. His friends drove him to the airport. This is Peter's first overseas trip, so Yoshiko is a little worried about him. As Peter finishes checking in and walks toward the gate, his friends tell him to have a safe and healthy trip. Peter says cheerfully, "I'm off," and disappears through the gate.

2. Sample Conversation

N: 気を付けて行ってこいよ。
P: 日本は治安がいいから、大丈夫だよ。
Y: 無理をしないで、という意味よ。
P: うん。気を付けるよ。
N: 何時間、飛行機に乗る。
P: １２時間ぐらいじゃなかったかな。
N: 時差ボケにならないようにな。
P: 大丈夫だよ。
Y: 飛行機の中でしっかり眠るといいよ。
P: 僕、飛行機ははじめてなんだ。
Y: こうふんして、眠れないかもしれないわね。
N: まあ、とにかくいい旅を。
P: はい。行ってきます。

N: *Ki o tsukete[1] itte koi[2] yo.*
P: *Nihon wa chian[3] ga ii kara daijoobu da yo.*
Y: *Muri o shinai de to iu imi yo.*
P: *Un[4]. Ki o tsukeru yo.*
N: *Nanjikan hikooki ni noru[5]?*
P: *Juunijikan gurai ja nakatta kana[6].*
N: *Jisaboke[7] ni naranai yoo ni[8] na.*
P: *Daijoobu da yo.*
Y: *Hikooki no naka de[9] shikkari nemuru to[10] ii yo.*
P: *Boku, hikooki wa hajimete na n da[11].*
Y: *Koofun shite nemurenai kamo shirenai[12] wa ne.*
N: *Maa, tonikaku ii tabi o.*
P: *Hai. Itte kimasu[13].*

N: Be careful.
P: Japan is a safe place, so I'll be all right.
Y: He means, take it easy.
P: I'll be careful.
N: How many hours is the flight?
P: It's about twelve hours, isn't it?
N: I hope you don't get jet lag.
P: I'll be all right.
Y: It will be good if you sleep well on the plane.
P: It's my first time on a plane.
Y: Since you're so excited, you might not be able to sleep.
N: Well, anyway, have a good trip.
P: I will. I'm off!

N: きのした　のぶお　　*Kinoshita Nobuo*　　Nobuo Kinoshita
P: ピーター　スミス　　*Piitaa Sumisu*　　Peter Smith
Y: やまだ　よしこ　　*Yamada Yoshiko*　　Yoshiko Yamada

3. Language & Culture Notes

1 The Japanese language has several ways of expressing concern or care for other people. *Ki o tsukete* has a couple of meanings, depending on how the expression is used. It is used casually as one would say in English "Take care," in ending a letter or parting with a friend. It also means "Be careful," perhaps to one venturing off alone into a big city or to one driving home in the rain.

Miokuri means to see someone off. When people go on a trip, it is customary for their friends to see them off, offer advice, and wish the travelers well. A traditional going-away gift of money may be given to the person, and, in return, the traveler will usually bring back a souvenir or gift.

2 *Koi* is the informal imperative form of *kimasu* (in contrast to the formal *kite kudasai*). Nobuo can use this rather intimate expression with Peter because he is a male and because they are close friends.

3 A very positive feature of Japan is the amount of concern for public safety. There are many examples of this throughout the country. For example, signs or flags are posted on the streets urging people to obey traffic laws and to drive safely and slowly. "Traffic safety weeks" are held a couple of times a year to reinforce awareness. Also, automobile drivers may not make turns while traffic lights are red.

There are several safety measures for pedestrians. Since elementary school children are so small, they wear yellow hats so that they can be seen more easily by automobile drivers. Crosswalks at intersections are striped with white lines. There are even diagonal crosswalks at busy crossings. At many intersections there is music or bird chirping sounds to let the blind know when traffic has stopped and it is safe to cross the street. At busy intersections in the big cities, there may be two different kinds of music – one to cross in one direction and another to cross in the other direction. Many streets in Tokyo and Osaka are too busy to cross, so footbridges have been built across the streets so that people may cross safely.

4 *Un* is a function word and is much less formal than *hai*.

5 It is common in Japanese speech simply to raise one's pitch at the end of a statement to indicate a question rather than adding *ka*.

Nanjikan hikooki ni <u>noru?</u> /   (How many hours will you ride on the plane?)

6 *kana* in *ja nakatta kana* is used as a function marker meaning "isn't it?" or "wasn't it?"

Juunijikan gurai ja nakatta kana.   (Well, around twelve hours, isn't it?)

7 What time is it now? It may already be tomorrow in Japan. Japan's time is fourteen hours ahead of New York and seventeen hours ahead of Los Angeles. For example, when it is noon in New York, it is 2:00 a.m. the next day in Tokyo. The U.S. spans seven of the earth's twenty-four time zones from Alaska and Hawaii to the east coast; Japan's long chain of islands is in only one. Traveling across time zones in an airplane interrupts one's "internal clock" – the body's natural rhythms that determine when it is time to go to sleep and time to wake up. Jet lag, or *jisaboke*, results from crossing time zones faster than the body can adjust. After a very long flight, one may suffer several days of *jisaboke* fatigue before getting back on schedule. (Note: These calculations are based on world standard time.)

8 The expression *yoo ni* may be followed by verbs such as *iu* (to tell), *tanomu* (to ask), *onegai suru* (to request), or *meirei suru* (to order/command) and means "to ask someone to do" or "to request that someone do something."

    Denwa suru yoo ni itte kudasai.   (Please tell him/her to call me.)
    Yameru yoo ni tanomimashita.   (I asked him/her to quit.)
    Moo okurenai yoo ni iimashita.   (I told him/her not to be late anymore.)

9 *de* in *-no naka de* means "among," in defining scope.

10 *to* means "when," "if," or "whenever."

11 *-na n da* in *hajimete na n da* applies more emphasis to the statement.

12 *Kamo shirenai* follows informal verbs, adjectives, and nouns (without the copula) to mean "may" or "might." (*Da* never precedes *kamo shirenai*.)

    Nemurenai kamo shirenai wa ne. (You might not be able to sleep.)
    Sono hito wa Indo kara kita kamo shirenai. (That person may have come from India.)
    Chotto shoppai kamo shirenai. (It might be a little salty.)

13 *Itte kimasu* is a common expression that literally means, "I will go and come." One often says it when departing, even from one's own home, for a short period of time. Those remaining behind respond with *itte irasshai* or *itterasshai*, literally meaning "go and come."

III. PARTICIPATION

1. Vocabulary

1 **From sample conversation:**

chian (public peace and order)	*hajimete* (first time)
hikooki (airplane)	*imi* (meaning, sense)
itte (go)	*juunijikan* (twelve hours)
Ki o tsukete. (Take care. Pay attention.)	*ki o tsukeru* (to pay attention, be careful)
koofun (exciting, be excited)	*muri* (over strain, overwork, force)
naka (inside)	*nanjikan* (how many hours)
nemurenai (cannot sleep)	*nemuru* (to sleep)
noru (to go by, to ride)	*shikkari* (well)
tabi (trip)	*tonikaku* (anyway)

Lesson 5

2 Useful for activities:

binboo (poor)	*Doitsu* (Germany)
furafura (be dizzy)	*furui* (old)
fuyu (winter)	*hipparidako* (be in great demand)
hitori de (alone)	*ippai* (many, full)
Itsumo osewa ni natte imasu. (Thank you for taking care of me.)	
Ittekimasu. (I'm off, I'll be back.)	*Itterasshai.* ([literally] "Go and come back.")
ja nakatta (not, was not)	*jiko* (accident)
jinkoo (population)	*kaette kita* (came back)
kakaru (to take [period of time])	*kamo shirenai* (maybe, may, might)
karakara (be very thirsty)	*... kara ... made* (from ... to ...)
kashu (singer)	*kaze o hiku* (to catch a cold)
kinchoo suru (be strained, stressed, nervous)	*konbiniensu sutoa* (convenience store)
kotoshi (this year)	*kowagaru* (be afraid)
mensetsu o uke ni (be interviewed)	*nani mo* (not ... anything)
ninki (popularity)	*nodo* (throat)
nyuuin (hospitalization)	*odoru* (to dance)
Okaeri(nasai). (Welcome home.)	*ryokoo suru* (to travel)
shiawase (happiness)	*shinpai* (anxiety, worry)
sorekara (then)	*Tadaima.* (I'm home.)
tera (temple)	*tobu* (to fly)
ugoku (to move)	*undoo* (exercises)
yaru (to do)	*yoku* (well)

2. Activity, Practice, & Exercise

1 Giving advice

In pairs or small groups: Give advice to a person in the following situations using the expression *-nai yoo ni ki o tsukete kudasai* and *--- to ii desu yo*. Present it to the class later.

Example: *Hikooki de gaikoku ni iku hito ni* (To a person who is going abroad by airplane)
- *Jisaboke ni <u>naranai yoo ni</u> ki o tsukete kudasai.* (Be careful not to get jet lag.)
- *Hikooki no naka de yoku <u>nemuru to ii desu yo</u>.*
  (It would be good if you sleep well on the airplane.)

1. *Afurika ni iku hito ni* (To a person who will go to Africa)
2. *Fuyu, Arasuka ni iku hito ni* (To a person who will go to Alaska in the winter)
3. *Fune de ryokoo suru hito ni* (To a person who will travel by ship)

2 The first time I went to ...

In pairs: Talk to your partner about the first time that you went to a particular place. (When, where, what you did, etc.)

Example: A: *Watashi wa kotoshi no 8 gatsu ni Nihon e ikimashita.* (I went to Japan this August.)
B: *Nihon wa <u>hajimete deshita ka</u>?* (Was it the first time?)
A: *Hai.* (Yes, it was.)

B: *Nihon wa tanoshikatta desu ka?* (Did you have a good time?)

A: *Hai. Watashi wa penparu ni aimashita. Issho ni Kyooto no furui tera o mimashita. Sorekara, matsuri ni itte, bon'odori o shimashita.*

(Yes. I met my pen pal. We visited old temples in Kyoto together. Then I went to a festival and joined the bon'odori.)

B: *"Bon'odori" tte nan desu ka.* (What's *bon'odori*?)

A: *Nihon no natsumatsuri no dansu desu. Minna issho ni odorimasu. Tanoshii dansu desu yo.*

(It's a dance at a Japanese summer festival. Everybody dances together. It's fun.)

3 Matching

In pairs: Match scenarios 1 – 3 with the most appropriate expression from below.
1. The night before the day you are going to take a very important examination.
2. You are invited to the White House and have an opportunity to talk to the President.
3. When your cat sees a big, wild dog on the street.

A. *Kowagatte nigeru kamo shirenai.*
B. *Shinpai shite nemurenai kamo shirenai.*
C. *Kinchoo shite hanasenai kamo shirenai.*

4 Question

Individually: When does *jisaboke* or jet lag occur? Circle the correct answers.
1. *Amerika kara Nihon e hikooki de tobu toki.*
2. *Amerika kara Peruu e hikooki de tobu toki.*
3. *Amerika kara Nihon e fune de iku toki.*
4. *Doitsu kara Amerika e hikooki de tobu toki.*

5 Matching

Small groups: The teacher divides the class into groups of three or four, depending on the size of the class. The teacher makes about 10 sentences in the form --- *kara* --- *da yo/desu* and divides each sentence after *kara*. Each half should be written on a separate card. Make a set for each group of students. Within the group, students have to correctly match the sentences. The teacher gives the correct answers.

Examples of sentences:
1. *Ano kashu wa ninki ga aru <u>kara</u>*
2. *Chian ga warui <u>kara</u>*
3. *Shikkari benkyoo shita <u>kara</u>*
4. *Takusan tabeta <u>kara</u>*
5. *Kimi ga iru <u>kara</u>*
6. *Okane ga nai <u>kara</u>*
7. *Yoku neta <u>kara</u>*
8. *Asa kara nani mo tabete inai <u>kara</u>*
9. *Undoo shita <u>kara</u>*
10. *Kyoo wa ame ga futte iru <u>kara</u>*

a. *binboo da yo.*
b. *daijoobu deshoo.*
c. *furafura da yo.*
d. *genki desu.*
e. *hipparidako da yo.*
f. *nodo ga karakara desu.*
g. *onaka ga ippai desu.*
h. *shiawase da yo.* .
i. *shinpai desu.*
j. *yakyuuu no shiai o yaranai yo.*

Lesson 5

6 Using common expressions

In pairs: The teacher makes copies of the chart below and assigns one of the following sentences to each student. If possible, each student should have a different situation. Students should write their statement at the top of the chart where indicated. Students then pair up and read their statements to each other. In the chart, write down the name of the partner and their response, then change roles with your partner. Next find a new partner. Continue to change partners until the chart is completed. The idea is to get a variety of responses for each statement. Afterwards, the teacher calls on a few students to read their statement and some of the responses that they got. Finally, the teacher should make sure that the students understand the meanings and uses of the following expressions.

Examples of statements:

1. *Hitori de Nihon e ikimasu.*
2. *Mensetsu o uke ni ikimasu.*
3. *Konbiniensu sutoa e ittekimasu.*
4. *Hisashiburi desu.*
5. *Ashita wa kimatsushiken ga arimasu.*
6. *Kaze o hikimashita.*
7. *Mata aimashoo.*
8. *Ima kaerimashita.*
9. *Ima kaette kita yo.*
10. *Mikka kan nyuuin shite imashita.*
11. *Ja, sayoonara.*
12. *Kuruma de ikimasu yo.*
13. *Shukudai wa takusan arimasu.*
14. *Kuruma no jiko ni atta yo.*
15. *Iroiro arigatoo gozaimasu.*

Examples of expressions:

Ittekimasu	*Itterasshai*	*Tadaima*	*Okaeri(nasai)*
Ki o tsukete	*Ogenki desu ka?*	*Ganbatte*	*Daijoobu desu ka?*
O genki de	*Konnichi wa*	*Oisogashii desu ka?*	*Doo itashimashite*
Itsumo osewa ni natte imasu			

Statement:	
Name	Response
1.	
2.	
3.	
4.	
5.	
6.	
7.	
8.	
9.	
10.	

7 Giving advice

In pairs: Give advice to a friend who is going to travel to Africa.

Example: A: *Afurika ni iku n da.*
You: *Kono kusuri o motte iku to ii yo.*
A: *Arigatoo. Ja, itte kimasu.*
You: *Ki o tsukete itte koi yo. Jisaboke ni naranai yoo ni.*

8 Expressing uncertainty

Individually: You are worrying about your picnic for next weekend. Say what you are worrying about using the expression *-kamo shirenai*.

Example: *Ame ga furu kamo shirenai*. (It might rain.)

You are worried that
1. your friends may not come.
2. it may be very cold.
3. you might have a lot of homework to do during that weekend.
4. your yard may be too small.

9 What would you say ...?

In pairs: What would you say
1. when you see off someone who is about to take a trip?
2. to a traveler who is worrying about safety in a foreign country?
3. when you want to express that you are going on an airplane for the first time?
4. when you change the topic and tell the traveler to have a good trip?

10 Japanese goods in U.S. dollars

In class: The teacher makes a chart like the one below and gives a copy to each student. In the *shoohin* (item) column, the students make a list of various items. Be sure to leave a few spaces blank. One by one, students ask the teacher how much an item costs in Japan, in U.S. dollars, and write the price in the US$ column. If a student asks about the price of an item also on your own list, write down the price. If it is not on your list, add the item and the price in the extra spaces. After each student has asked about an item, the teacher makes the same chart on the blackboard, asks students about prices of items and fills in the chart. When answering questions, the teacher and students should use --- *doru gurai ja nakatta kana*. Follow the example.

Example: Student: *Sensei, Nihon de atarashii terebi o kau to ikura gurai desu ka?*
Teacher: *400 doru gurai ja nakatta kana*.

shoohin	US$	shoohin	US$
1.		8.	
2.		9.	
3.		10.	
4.		11.	
5.		12.	
6.		13.	
7.		14.	

Lesson 6: Review & Application

IV. PERFORMANCE

1. Application

1 Conversation completion

In small groups: The following is a conversation between a high school student (S) who went to Japan during summer vacation and his high school teacher (T). Guess what the teacher would say in the conversation. Choose the most appropriate answer from the sentences below.

S: *Sensei. Nihon e itte kimashita.* (I went to Japan.)

T: ( ) (Did you? When?)

S: *8 gatsu desu. Nihon ni hantsuki gurai taizai shimashita.*
   (In August. I stayed for about half a month.)

T: ( ) (Really? Where?)

S: *Saitama ken no chiisai machi desu. Penparu no Yamada san no ie ni hoomusutei shimashita.*
   (A small town in Saitama Prefecture. I stayed at my pen pal's house.)

T: *Sore wa yokatta desu ne.* (That's great.)
   ( ) (Did you go to a summer festival?)

S: *Mochiron. Yukata o kite, minna to issho ni odorimashita.*
   (Of course. I wore a yukata and danced with everyone.)

T: ( ) (Did you go anywhere else?)

S: *Hai. Shinkansen de Kyooto e ikimashita.* (Yes. I went to Kyoto by *shinkansen*.)

T: ( ) (How did you like it?)

S: *Totemo omoshirokatta desu. Furui ie ya otera nado, iroiro na mono o mimashita.*
   (It was very interesting. I saw various things, such as old houses and temples.)

T: *Motto kuwashiku kikitai desu ne. Kurasu de nihonryokoo no hanashi o shite kudasai.*
   (I would like to hear more about it. Please talk about your trip during class.)

   1. *Soo desu ka? Doko ni?*
   2. *Doo deshita ka?*
   3. *Natsumatsuri wa ikimashita ka?*
   4. *Hee, itsu desu ka?*
   5. *Hoka no tokoro e mo ikimashita ka?*

2 Conversation completion

In small groups: The following is a conversation between a student (S) who is leaving for Japan and his father (F) who is seeing him off. Guess what they would say in the underlined parts in the conversation. After completing them, each group presents their dialogue to the class.

F: *Ki o tsukete itte koi yo.* (Have a safe trip.)
S: _____ *kara, daijoobu da yo.* (I'll be OK because _____ .)
F: *Tonikaku, muri o shinai yoo ni.* (Anyway, don't push yourself too much.)
S: *Un. Ki o tsukeru yo.* (I'll be careful.)
F: _____ ? (_____ ?)
S: *9 jikan gurai ja nakatta kana.* (I guess it's about 9 hours.)
F: *Jisa ga aru kara, karada no chooshi ga okashiku naru kamo shirenai na.*
   (You may get jet lag because of the time difference.)
   _____ *to ii yo.* (You should _____ .)
S: *Un. Demo hikooki wa hajimete dakara,* _____ .
   (Yeah. But, since this is my first time on an airplane, _____ .)
F: *Soo da na. Tonikaku genki de na.* (I see. Anyway, take care.)
S: *Un. Ja,* _____ . (Well, _____ .)
F: *Ii tabi o.* (Have a good trip.)

3 Verb conjugation: *-ta/da* form

In pairs: Using verb cards or a list of verbs, change the verbs from the dictionary form into the *-ta/da* form (past tense).

Example: • *kaku → kaita* (*-ku → -ita*); *oyogu → oyoida* (*-gu → -ida*)
 au → atta; *matsu → matta* (*-u; -tsu → -tta*),
 hanasu → hanashita (*-su → -shita*),
 shinu → shinda; *tobu → tonda*; *nomu → nonda* (*-nu; -bu; -mu → -nda*)
 iku → itta (exception)
• *miru → mita*; *kakeru → kaketa* (*-iru; -eru → -ta*)
• *benkyoo suru → benkyoo shita* (*-suru → -shita*)

4 I went swimming, camping, skiing ...

In pairs: Think about what you did during summer and winter vacations. Did you travel, do sports, have a part-time job, or study? Talk with your partner about what you did. Use the expression *-tari, -tari shimashita*.

Example: A: *B san, kyonen no natsuyasumi ni nani o shimashita ka?*
   (B, what did you do during summer vacation last year?)

 B: *Tozan o <u>shitari</u>, umi de <u>oyoidari</u>, yuuenchi e <u>ittari shimashita</u>. A san wa?*
   (I went mountain climbing, swimming in the sea, to an amusement park, and other things like that. How about you?)

 A: *Resutoran de arubaito o <u>shitari</u>, kazoku to kyanpu ni <u>ittari shimashita</u>. Fuyuyasumi wa doo deshita ka?*
   (Well, I worked part-time at a restaurant and went camping with my family. How was your winter vacation?)

 B: *Sukii o <u>shitari</u>, sukeeto o <u>shitari shimashita</u>. Tanoshikatta desu. A san wa doo deshita ka?*
   (I went skiing, skating, and so on. I had a good time. How about you?)

 A: *Watashi mo sukii o tanoshimimashita. Sorekara, ie de ryoori o <u>tsukuttari</u>, seetaa o <u>andari</u>, hon o <u>yondari shimashita</u>.*
   (I enjoyed skiing, too. I also cooked at home, knitted a sweater, and read a book.)

 B: *Soo desu ka?* (Did you?)

5 Team competition

In class: Make cards with the name of a place written on each. Divide the class into two or three teams. One student from each group goes to the teacher's desk and draws a card. Using the form *-tari, -tari suru*, the students will make sentences stating what one usually does at the place on the card. The teacher will judge the sentences and give points accordingly. Students take turns within their group. Set the time limit at 10 to 20 minutes.

Example: *Toshokan* → *Hon o <u>yondari</u>, hon o <u>karitari suru</u>.*

(Library → We do such things as reading and borrowing books.)

Gakko → *Benkyoo <u>shitari</u>, supootsu o <u>shitari suru</u>.*

(School → We do such things as studying and doing sports.)

6 I was surprised ...

In small groups: Within the group, each member talks about something surprising that they recently saw, heard or even a false tale that they created. Each person should explain why they were surprised. The sentence pattern to be used is *-te, odorokimashita*. Normal sentence + *kara desu*.

Example: *Watashi wa Tookyoo no chikatetsu sarin jiken no nyuusu o terebi de <u>mite</u>, totemo <u>odorokimashita</u>. Chian ga ii Nihon de, osoroshii tero ga okotta <u>kara desu</u>.*

(I was very surprised to see the news on TV about the sarin poison gas attack on the Tokyo subway because I never thought terrorism would happen in a safe country like Japan.)

7 Did you know ...?

In small groups: After completing APE 6, everyone changes groups. Ask the new group members if they know about your piece of news. If they have heard about it, they should comment on it. If no one knows about it, repeat what you had said in APE 6.

Example: 1) A: *Tookyoo no chikatetsu de sarin jiken ga okotta koto o <u>shitte imasu ka</u>?*

(Do you know about the sarin poison gas attack on the subway in Tokyo?)

B: *Iie.* (No.)

A: *Watashi wa sono nyuusu o terebi de <u>mite</u>, totemo <u>odorokimashita</u>. Chian ga ii Nihon de tero ga okotta <u>kara desu</u>.*

(I was very surprised to see the news on TV because I never thought terrorism would happen in a safe country like Japan.)

2) A: *Koobe de ookii jishin ga atta koto o <u>shitte imasu ka</u>?*

(Did you know that there was a big earthquake in Kobe?)

B: *Hai, <u>shitte imasu</u>. Shinbun de yomimashita. 5,000 nin ijoo no hito ga nakunari mashita. Hontoo ni hidoi jishin deshita ne.*

(Yes, I did. I read it in the paper. More than 5,000 people died. It was a really terrible earthquake.)

A: *Soo desu ne. Koobe no hito wa taihen desu ne.*

(Yeah. People in Kobe must be having a hard time.)

8 Be careful not to ...

In small groups: In what situation would you use each of the following sentences? Think about the reason why it is used in each situation.

Example: *Jisa boke ni naranai yoo ni ki o tsukete kudasai.* (Be careful not to get jet lag.)
→ *Hikooki de gaikokuryokoo o suru hito ni tsukaimasu. Jisa ga ookii to, karada no chooshi ga okashiku natte, taihen tsukareru kara desu.*
(We say this to a person who is taking a trip abroad. If there is a big time difference, one may feel strange and very tired.)

1. *Muri o shinai yoo ni ki o tsukete kudasai.* (Be careful not to push yourself too much.)
2. *Kaze o hikanai yoo ni ki o tsukete kudasai.* (Be careful not to catch a cold.)
3. *Inemuri shinai yoo ni ki o tsukete kudasai.* (Be careful not to doze off.)
4. *Yosomi o shinai yoo ni ki o tsukete kudasai.* (Be careful not to take your eyes off/look away.)
5. *Otosanai yoo ni ki o tsukete kudasai.* (Be careful not to drop it.)

9 Making selections

In three groups: The teacher brings in a restaurant menu, a movie rental catalog, and a travel pamphlet or guidebook and gives one to each group. Each person chooses an item from the group's list. Within the group, each person says what item they chose and why they have chosen it. Use the sentence pattern Noun + *ni suru*.

Example: Using a movie rental catalog

A: *Boku wa "Dai Haado" ni suru yo. Akushon ga suki dakara ne.*
(I'll rent *Die Hard*. I like action movies.)

B: *"Dai Haado" wa ii ne. Demo, moo mita kara, chigau eiga ga ii na. Boku wa "Taamineetaa 2" ni suru yo. Shuwarutsunegaa wa boku no suki na haiyuu dakara.*
(*Die Hard* is good, but I would like a different one because I've already seen it. I'll watch *Terminator 2*. Schwarzenegger is my favorite actor.)

10 Giving advice

In pairs: On a card, each student writes about something that is troubling them. Then students ask their partners for advice about their problems. Use the sentence pattern Verb (in dictionary form) + *to ii*.

Examples of problems:
- *Ka ga ooi.* (There are a lot of mosquitoes.)
- *Inu ga totemo futotte iru.* (My dog is very fat.)
- *Tonari no musuko ga yoru doramu no renshuu o shite urusai.*
  (The boy next door practices the drums at night and makes a lot of noise.)
- *Asobu okane ga nai.* (I don't have any spending money.)
- *Suugaku no seiseki ga warui.* (My grade in math is bad.)

Example: A: *Kinjo ni ka ga ooi kara, komatte imasu/iru n da/iru no.*
(I am troubled because there are a lot of mosquitoes in my neighborhood.)
B: *Nihon no katorisenkoo o tsukau to ii desu yo/ii yo/ii wa yo.*
(You should use a Japanese *katorisenkoo*.)
Tsukai yasui shi, nedan mo yasui desu yo/yo/wa yo. (It's cheap and easy to use.)
A: *Soo?/ Soo desu ka?* (Really?)

11 Fast reading practice

Individually: Read the following passage and answer the questions. Time how long it takes to finish the entire activity.

アリスは夏休みに日本へ行きます。2週間、京都の田中さんの家にホームステイをする予定です。田中さんの家族は5人です。お父さん、お母さん、おばあさん、お兄さん、そしてアリスと同じ高校生のさとみさん。さとみさんはアリスに電話してくれました。さとみさんはアリスと一緒に東京ディズニーランドへ行きたいと言いました。アリスも東京に興味があります。大変大きい都市だからです。成田空港に、さとみさんが迎えに来てくれます。その日はさとみさんと一緒に東京のホテルに泊まります。そして次の日に東京ディズニーランドへ行きます。そして、また東京に泊まって、少し東京見物をしてから、新幹線で京都へ行きます。アリスは飛行機も新幹線も初めてですから、とても楽しみです。京都でさとみさんの家に滞在します。京都は古い町ですから、見る物がたくさんあります。アリスとさとみさんは夏祭りに行く予定です。

アリスのお母さんは、アリスが一人で日本へ行くので、ちょっと心配しています。お母さんは「日本で健康と安全に十分気を付けて。」と言います。お父さんはあまり心配していません。お父さんは「アリスはもう高校生だから、何でも自分でできるよ。」と言います。弟は「日本へ行けて、いいなあ。うらやましいなあ。必ずお土産買って来てよ。」と言います。アリスは早く日本へ行きたくて、うずうずしています。きっといい旅行になるでしょう。

Arisu wa natsuyasumi ni Nihon e ikimasu. 2shuukan, Kyooto no Tanaka san no ie ni hoomusutei o suru yotei desu. Tanaka san no kazoku wa 5nin desu. Otoosan, okaasan, obaasan, oniisan, soshite Arisu to onaji kookoosei no Satomi san. Satomi san wa Arisu ni denwa shite kuremashita. Satomi san wa Arisu to issho ni Tookyoo Dizuniirando e ikitai to iimashita. Arisu mo Tookyoo ni kyoomi ga arimasu. Taihen ookii toshi dakara desu. Narita kuukoo ni, Satomi san ga mukae ni kite kuremasu. Sono hi wa Satomi san to issho ni Tookyoo no hoteru ni tomarimasu. Soshite tsugi no hi ni Tookyoo Dizuniirando e ikimasu. Soshite, mata Tookyoo ni tomatte, sukoshi Tookyoo kenbutsu o shite kara, shinkansen de Kyooto e ikimasu. Arisu wa hikooki mo shinkansen mo hajimete desu kara, totemo tanoshimi desu. Kyooto de Satomi san no ie ni taizai shimasu. Kyooto wa furui machi desu kara, miru mono ga takusan arimasu. Arisu to Satomi san wa natsumatsuri ni iku yotei desu.

Arisu no okaasan wa, Arisu ga hitori de Nihon e iku node, chotto shinpai shite imasu. Okaasan wa "Nihon de kenkoo to anzen ni juubun ki o tsukete" to iimasu. Otoosan wa amari shinpai shite imasen. Otoosan wa "Arisu wa moo kookoosei dakara, nan demo jibun de dekiru yo" to iimasu. Otooto wa "Nihon e ikete, ii naa. Urayamashii naa. Kanarazu omiyage katte kite yo" to iimasu. Arisu wa hayaku Nihon e ikitakute, uzuuzu shite imasu. Kitto ii ryokoo ni naru deshoo.

Alice is going to Japan during summer vacation. She is going to stay with the Tanaka family in Kyoto for two weeks. There are five people in the Tanaka family: father, mother, grandmother, older brother, and Satomi, who is a high school student like Alice. Satomi called Alice and told her that she would like to go to Tokyo Disneyland with her. Alice, too, is interested in Tokyo because it is a very big city. Satomi will go to Narita Airport to meet Alice. The day Alice arrives, they will stay at a hotel in Tokyo. The next day they will go to Tokyo Disneyland and stay in Tokyo again. After doing some sightseeing in Tokyo, they will go to Kyoto by *shinkansen*. It will be Alice's first time on both a plane and the *shinkansen*, so she is really looking forward to it. They will stay at Satomi's house in Kyoto. Kyoto is an old city, and there are many things to see. Alice and Satomi are planning to go to a summer festival.

Alice's mother is a little worried because Alice is going to Japan by herself. Her mother says, "Take care of yourself and be safe." Her father is not so worried. He says, "Alice is a high school student, so she can take care of herself." Her brother says, "I wish I could go to Japan. I'm jealous. Be sure to get a souvenir for me." Alice is anxious to go to Japan. This will surely be a good trip for her.

Questions:
Write O if the sentence is true, and X if it is false.

1. ( ) *Arisu wa Tookyoo de hoomusutei shimasu.* (Alice will stay with a family in Tokyo.)
2. ( ) *Tanaka san no ie ni wa ojiisan ga imasu.* (There is a grandfather in the Tanaka family.)
3. ( ) *Satomi san mo Arisu mo kookoosei desu.* (Both Satomi and Alice are high school students.)
4. ( ) *Arisu wa mada hikooki ni notta koto ga arimasen.* (Alice has never been on an airplane.)
5. ( ) *Kyooto wa furui machi desu.* (Kyoto is an old city.)
6. ( ) *Arisu no otoosan wa Arisu no ryokoo o taihen shinpai shite imasu.*
   (Alice's father is really worried about her.)
7. ( ) *Arisu wa hitori de ryokoo suru koto o shinpai shite imasu.*
   (Alice is nervous about going on a trip by herself.)

Time spent: (   ) minutes

12 Summary practice

In small groups: After reading the passage in APE 11, discuss the following questions in groups. A representative from each group presents the group's answers to the class.

1. *Arisu wa itsu Nihon e ikimasu ka?* (When will Alice go to Japan?)
2. *Tanaka san wa doko ni sunde imasu ka?* (Where does Mr. Tanaka live?)
3. *Arisu wa saisho ni Nihon de nani o shimasu ka?* (What will Alice do first in Japan?)
4. *Sono ato doo shimasu ka?* (What will Alice do after that?)
5. *Arisu no kazoku wa Arisu no ryokoo ni tsuite doo omotte imasu ka?*
   (What do Alice's family think about her trip?)
6. *Arisu wa ryokoo ni tsuite doo omotte imasu ka?* (What does Alice think about her trip?)

13 Research and discussion

In groups of three: Follow the directions for the following three problems. Discuss and record the group's responses or answers in Japanese.

① Time differences:
- Find out the time differences between your area and major cities in America, such as New York, Chicago, Los Angeles, and Denver. Say what time it is now in your area and in those cities.
- Find out the time difference between your area and Japan. Say what time it is in Japan now.
- Find out the time differences between your area and countries other than Japan. Say what time it is now in those countries.

② Jet lag:
- Describe the symptoms of jet lag.
- Are there good ways to cope with jet lag? If any of the group members have experienced jet lag, they should talk about their situation. Some English may be used to answer this question.

③ Talk about what one should be careful of when going on a trip abroad. A representative from each group makes a presentation to the class.

2. Actualization

1 Practice the following conversation and develop your own dialogue on a similar subject with your partners.

Getsuyoobi no 2jikanme, ongaku no jugyoo desu. 4 nen 1 kumi no seito wa fue no renshuu o shite imasu.
(Second period on Monday is music. The 4th grade, class 1 students are practicing the flute.)

Yamada sensei:	*Tanaka kun, oto ga yoku dete inai wa yo. Motto tsuyoku fukanai to.* (Tanaka, you are playing too softly. Blow it harder.)
Tanaka kun:	*Hai.* (All right.)
Yoshida san:	*Sensei, re no oto ga yoku demasen.* (Ms. Yamada, I can't play the D note well.)
Yamada sensei:	*Motto, chanto yubi de fue no ana o osaete.* (Hold the holes tighter with your fingers.)
Yoshida san:	*Hai.* (I see.)
Yamada sensei:	*Soo, sono chooshi yo. Suzuki kun umaku natta wa ne.* (Good. That's it. Suzuki, you have improved.)
Suzuki kun:	*Kinoo ie de takusan renshuu shimashita.* (I practiced it a lot at home yesterday.)
Yamada sensei:	*Soo, erai wa ne.* (Did you? That's great.)

2 Practice the following conversation and develop your own dialogue on a similar subject with your partners.

Mokuyoobi no 5jikanme, ongaku no jugyoo desu. Minna de uta no renshuu o shite imasu.
(Fifth period on Thursday is music. Everyone is practicing a song.)

Suzuki sensei:	*Tanaka san hazukashigaranai de, motto kuchi o ookiku akete.*
	(Tanaka, don't be shy. Open your mouth wider.)
Tanaka san:	[*Unazuku*] [She nods.]
Suzuki sensei:	*Nakamura kun sonna ni kinchoo shinai de, kata no chikara o nuite.*
	(Nakamura, don't be so nervous. Take it easy.)
Nakamura kun:	[*Unazuku*] (He nods.)
Suzuki sensei:	*Yamada san, sakki, amari utatte inakatta wa ne. Dooshita no?*
	(Yamada, you weren't singing before. What's the matter?)
Yamada san:	*Gomennasai. Kashi o wasurete shimaimashita.* (I'm sorry. I forgot the words.)
Suzuki sensei:	*Ie de chanto renshuu shita?* (Did you practice it at home?)
Yamada san:	*Ie de wa umaku iku n desu kedo ...* (It went well at home, but ...)
Suzuki sensei:	*Mata, renshuu shite kudasai ne.* (Practice it again, please.)
Yamada san:	*Hai.* (Yes.)

3 **Listing examples**

① In groups: Each group is assigned one of the topics written below. Each student gives a few examples of their topic. The first person in the group uses the expression --- *to ieba* --- *toka* --- *toka*. Everyone else uses *Sorekara* --- *deshoo*, --- *deshoo*.

Topics: music, vegetables, fruits, drinks, electric appliances, European countries, Asian countries, sports, occupations

Example: music

        A: *Ongaku to ieba, rokku toka, jazu toka.* (Speaking of music, there is rock and jazz.)
        B: *Sorekara kurashikku deshoo, poppusu deshoo.* (There's classical and pop music.)
        C: *Sorekara regee deshoo, rappu deshoo.* (And reggae and rap.)
        D: *Sorekara min'yoo deshoo, dooyoo deshoo.*
           (There's *min'yoo* [Japanese folk music] and *dooyoo* [nursery rhymes].)

② A representative from each group presents the examples given by the group members to the class.

Example: *Ongaku to ieba, rokku toka jazu toka kurasikku toka poppusu desu. Sorekara regee toka rappu toka min'yoo toka dooyoo mo arimasu.*

    (Speaking of music, there are many kinds, such as rock, jazz, classical, and pop music. There are also reggae, Japanese folk music, and nursery rhymes.)

4 Choose a Japanese traditional musical instrument from the following list and discuss it in both English and Japanese.

    shakuhachi, shamisen, koto, biwa, tsuzumi

3. Enrichment

1 *Kanji* for Lesson 4

先生	休む	週間	日程	新幹線
乗る	速い	思う	祭り	家
楽しい	浴衣	着る	盆踊り	話し
聞く	次	授業	体験	

2 *Kanji* for Lesson 5

付ける	治安	無理	意味	飛行機
中	眠る	旅		

3 Other useful *kanji*

Colors: 色、赤、青、黒、白、茶色
The body: 体、目、耳、手、口、頭、顔、足、心
Directions: 方、東、西、北、南
At the library: 図書館、貸、借、読、返

4 Strategies

Kanji formation: Part two

Lesson 3 named two types of *kanji* formation, (1) shapes of visual objects and (2) symbols representing abstract concepts. This lesson covers the remaining four types of *kanji* formation.

(3) Adding one or two symbols to a *kanji* whose original meaning is concrete indicates specific location of an object or places emphasis on the object.

　刀 (knife, sword) → 刃 (blade)

The difference between 本 and 刃 is that the original meaning of 木 is lost but 刀 is not.

(4) Combining two or more *kanji* or *kanji* components gives a new but related meaning.

　日 (sun)　+　月 (moon)　=　明 (bright)
　木 (tree)　+　木 (tree)　=　林 (woods)
　火 (fire)　+　火 (fire)　=　炎 (flame)

(5) Combining two *kanji* components in which one represents the meaning or concept and the other represents the pronunciation of the new *kanji*.

semantic part	phonetic part	combination	pronunciation	meaning
言 [say]	吾 [go]	語	[go]	word, a language
忄 [mind]	吾 [go]	悟	[go]	realization
言 [say]	寺 [ji]	詩	[shi]	poetry
日 [sun]	寺 [ji]	時	[ji]	time
扌 [hand]	寺 [ji]	持	[ji]	to hold
亻 [person]	寺 [ji]	侍	[ji]	to attend to

(6) Transformation and borrowing creates new *kanji*. For example, the *kanji* 楽 was originally created to represent a wooden musical instrument. Since music is enjoyable, the meaning of 楽 has come to mean enjoyable as well.

From the above information, several more strategies can be established in addition to strategies A and B in Lesson 3.

Strategy C
  Since the majority of *kanji* were formed on the basis of a *kanji* representing meaning or concept plus a *kanji* representing pronunciation, it should not be too difficult to pronounce other *kanji* with similar pronunciation components.
  語 (go) → 悟 (go)

Strategy D
  Since each *kanji* represents a word (meaning or concept), the original meaning or concept can be extended with some modification to other composite *kanji*.
  日 (sun) + 月 (moon) = 明 (bright)

Strategy E
  Using cognitive abilities, such as generalization, analysis, precision, evaluation, and making analogies, comparisons, and inferences, can help one to relate, regroup, and reinterpret the relationships between various *kanji* in order to expand skills in pronouncing, recognizing, and reproducing *kanji*.

5 Exercise
Try to group the *kanji* listed in 1, 2, and 3 and guess the general meaning of each group.

Lesson 7: Summer festival

I. PERSPECTIVE

1. Objectives

1 Function:

(1) Asking what someone has done: *Nani shiteta?*
(2) Asking permission to do something: *(Mi ni it)te ii?*
(3) Giving permission: *Ii yo.*
(4) Expressing failure or regret: *Shimatta.*
(5) Asking what has happened: *Dooshita n dai?*
(6) Suggesting that someone do something: *(Tsukaisute kamera) o (kat)tara?*
(7) Indicating hesitancy in a response: *Demoo.*
(8) Confirming or sticking to one's original thought or idea: *Yappari (tori ni iku) yo.*

2 Language:

(1) *(Oso)katta ne. (Nani shi)teta?*
(2) *(Mado) no (soto) o (mi)teta.*
(3) *(Mini it)te ii?*
(4) *(Boku) mo (iroiro mi)tai kara.*
(5) *(Motte kuru) no o (wasure)chatta.*
(6) *(Kameraya) de (tsukaisute kamera) o (kat)tara?*
(7) *Yappari (tori ni iku) yo.*

3 Culture:

(1) *Yatai*: food and game stands
(2) *Watagashi*, *ringoame*, and *kingyosukui*
(3) Disposable goods

II. PREPARATION

1. Context

夏祭り

花火の音が聞こえる。今日はあきらの住んでいる町の夏祭りだ。近くにある神社に屋台がたくさん出ている。盆踊りをする場所もある。ピーターは日本のお祭りについて全く知らなかった。2階の窓から外を見たら、浴衣を着た女の人達が町を歩いている。外がだんだんにぎやかになってくる。今日は何があるのだろう。下で、あきらが「お祭りに行こう。」とピーターを呼んだ。ピーターは急いで外に出た。

One can hear the sound of fireworks. Today is the summer festival in the town where Akira lives. There are a lot of stands at a nearby shrine. There's a place to do *bon'odori*, too. Peter doesn't know anything about Japanese festivals. Looking out the second-floor window, Peter sees women wearing *yukata* walking down the street. The street gradually becomes more and more lively. Peter wonders what's going on today. Akira calls to Peter from below, "Let's go to the festival!" Peter hurries outside.

2. Sample Conversation

MA: 遅かったね。何してた。
P: 窓の外を見てた。浴衣を着た女の人がとても多いなあ。あっ、屋台が沢山ある。
MA: わたがし、りんごあめ、金魚すくい・・・。
P: 見に行っていい。
MA: いいよ。僕もいろいろ見たいから。
P: しまった。
MA: どうしたんだい。
P: カメラ持ってくるのを忘れちゃった。
MA: 近くのカメラ屋で、使い捨てカメラを買ったら。
P: でもー。やっぱり取りに行くよ。

MA: *Osokatta ne. Nani shiteta[1]?*
P: *Mado no soto o miteta. Yukata o kita onna no hito ga totemo ooi naa[2]. A! Yatai[3] ga takusan aru.*
MA: *Watagashi, ringoame, kingyosukui[4] ...*
P: *Mi ni[5] itte ii?*
MA: *Ii yo. Boku mo iroiro mitai kara.*
P: *Shimatta[6].*
MA: *Dooshita n dai[7]?*
P: *Kamera motte kuru no[8] o wasurechatta[9].*
MA: *Chikaku no kameraya de tsukaisute[10] kamera o kattara[11]?*
P: *Demoo. Yappari tori ni iku[12] yo.*

MA: You're late. What were you doing?
P: I was looking out the window. There are so many women wearing *yukata*! Oh! There are lots of *yatai* stands.
MA: Cotton candy, candy apples, goldfish-catching.
P: Can we go see?
MA: Sure. I want to see some things, too.
P: Darn it!
MA: What's the matter?
P: I forgot to bring my camera.
MA: How about buying a disposable camera at a nearby camera shop?
P: Well ... I guess I'll just go back and get it.

MA: もり あきら   *Mori Akira*   Akira Mori
P: ピーター スミス   *Piitaa Sumisu*   Peter Smith

3. Language & Culture Notes

1 The object marker *o* has been omitted here. Among close friends or intimate family members, this kind of omission or informal speech is common.

2 *naa*, like *nee*, is a sentence function word used to make a statement emphatic or exclamatory. However, only *naa* is used to seek agreement or a response from the listener. *Naa* is used mainly by men.

3 *Yatai*, food and game stands, are a major part of Japanese festivals. There are stands selling various kinds of food, drinks, and toys, as well as stands offering different kinds of games. It is similar to what would be found at an American carnival. Japanese food such as *yakisoba*, *okonomiyaki*, *takoyaki*, *manjuu*, and tea as well as hot dogs, hamburgers, cotton candy, candy apples, and soda are sold at *yatai*. Goldfish-catching is one of the more popular games. Most of the toys sold at *yatai*, such as slinkies and noisemakers, are for young children. *Yatai* are usually set up side by side in a line, circle, or semicircle.

4 *Watagashi*, *ringoame*, and *kingyosukui* are traditional festival attractions among the various *yatai* stands. *Watagashi* is cotton candy. Another popular treat is *ringoame*, or candy apples, which are

similar to the American counterpart. In Japan, this treat may be made from apricots as well. *Kingyosukui* is a game in which players attempt to catch goldfish from a large aquarium with a spoon. The spoon is made of very thin paper framed by wire that is about the same thickness as a paper clip. The wire extends to form a handle. The paper breaks very easily after being submerged in water. Players that fail to catch any fish are often given a small goldfish as a consolation prize. Like American carnival games, people must pay to play.

5 *ni* in *mi ni itte ii* indicates the purpose or reason for doing something.

6 *Shimatta* literally means "closed up" or "shut." As an expression, it corresponds to "Oh, darn!," "Darn it!," or other similar expressions which convey that one is disappointed or annoyed.

7 *dai* is a more informal and intimate equivalent of *da*.

8 Recall that the dependent noun *no*, when attached to an informal style verb, functions as a nominalizer and transforms that verb into a noun (equivalent to a gerund or infinitive in English.) This construction is often the object of a verb.
   Kamera o motte kuru no o wasureta n desu. (I forgot to bring my camera.)
   Kuruma o unten suru no wa hajimete desu. (This is my first time driving a car.)

9 *Wasurechatta* is a more informal and intimate equivalent of *wasurete shimatta*.

10 In recent years, disposable goods have become a popular trend in Japan. For example, disposable cameras are sold, bought, and used all over the country. They are relatively inexpensive, lightweight, and easy to use. Disposable cameras are convenient for people who don't own a camera and don't want to buy one and for those who don't want to risk losing their camera at a field trip or a crowded festival. Another disposable item is *kairo*, or "warmers." In a country without central heating, winter can seem much colder than it really is, so *kairo* become a necessity. They are like a cloth bag that, when opened, becomes warm. They are made to stick to one's shirt (but never directly on the skin), inside shoes, or just to hold in one's hands. In the United States, *kairo* are often sold at ski shops and sporting goods stores.

11 *Kattara* is the *-tara* form of the verb *kau*, "to buy." It is made by adding *ra* to the *-ta* form of a verb or an adjective copula. This is a conditional form that corresponds to "If ---." This form is often used to make a suggestion or recommendation.
   Tsukaisute kamera o kattara. (How about/What if you buy a disposable camera?)
   Atatakai uchi ni tabetara. (How about/Why don't you eat it while it's still warm?)
   Mise ni kaeshitara. (Why don't/What if you return it to the store?)

12 *Tori ni iku* means "to go to get." The functional marker *ni* indicates the purpose of one's action. It is used with the pre-*masu* form of a verb and is most often followed by a verb of motion, such as *kuru* (to come), *iku* (to go), or *kaeru* (to return). *Ni* followed by a verb in this form may correspond to "in order to" or "for the purpose of" (doing something.)

III. PARTICIPATION

1. Vocabulary

1 **From sample conversation:**

chikaku (near, close to)
kingyo (goldfish)
mado (window)
mitai (want to see)
motte kuru (to bring, to carry)
ooi (many, large number of)
shimatta (darn)
tori ni --- (--- to take, --- to get)
wasurechatta (forgot)
yatai (food or game stand)

kameraya (camera shop)
kita (wore, wearing)
mi ni --- (--- to see)
miteta (was looking)
Nani shiteta? (What were you doing?)
osokatta (was late)
soto (outside)
tsukaisute (disposable)
yappari (as expected)

2 **Useful for activities:**

akusesarii (accessories)
bangohan (dinner, supper)
erabu (to choose)
hayaku (quickly, in a hurry)
hiruyasumi (lunch break, recess)
kagi o kakeru (to lock)
kawaii (cute, pretty)
kyookasho (textbook)
modoru (to go back, to return)
nemui (sleepy)
oyashirazu o nuku (to get ones wisdom teeth pulled out)
sashimi (sliced raw fish)
suteki (cool, neat)
Tetsudatte kureru? (Could you help me?)
tsukeru (to turn on)
yatte miru (to try)

asobi ni iku (go to play)
denwa o kakeru (to make a telephone call)
furansugo o toru (to take French [language])
heya (room)
itai (hurt, be painful)
kakanakereba (has/have to write)
kusuri (medicine)
mattete (wait)
moo --- nai (not --- anymore)

suru hoo ga ii (would be better to)
taikutsu (bored)
tsukareru (be tired)
tsuri (fishing)

2. Activity, Practice, & Exercise

1 **Describing illustrations**

In pairs: The teacher will bring in several illustrations or pictures from magazines or other sources. Based on the pictures, students tell their partner what one has forgotten to do. Partners take turns explaining the pictures. Use the expression *Shimatta. --- o wasurechatta.*

(1) Forgot to bring a camera.
(2) Forgot to bring a textbook.
(3) Forgot to do homework.
(4) Forgot to make a telephone call.
(5) Forgot to write a letter.

2 Making suggestions

In pairs: Make appropriate suggestions to the people in each of the following situations.

Example: Patrick forgot to bring his camera. → *Tsukaisute kamera o kattara.*
(How about buying a disposable camera?)

(1) Stephen just got his wisdom teeth pulled out and cannot eat hard food.

(2) Debbie has no plans for the weekend and is very bored.

(3) Marianne wants to try some Japanese food.

(4) Lucy is sleepy but cannot go to sleep right now.

3 Making suggestions

In pairs: Write an appropriate suggestion for each situation. Use the expression *-tara* or *-dara*.

Example: A: *Un, atama ga itai naa.* (Oh, I have a headache.)
B: *Kusuri o <u>nondara</u>?* (Why don't you take some medicine?)

1. A: *Aa, tsukareta naa.* (Oh, I'm so tired.)
   B: _____ ?
2. A: *Aa, samui.* (Oh, it's cold.)
   B: _____ ?
3. A: *A! Terebi ga tsukanai.* (Oh, the TV won't turn on.)
   B: _____ ?
4. A: *A! Moo kaeri no basu ga nai.* (Oh, the last bus has left.)
   B: _____ ?

4 One goes to the sea to ...

In pairs: Make several cards with the name of a place written on each. Each pair gets the same set of cards. Partners take turns drawing cards and thinking about why one usually goes to that place. Use the sentence structures Verb + *ni ikitai kara* --- and Noun (indicating an activity) + *ni ikitai kara* ---.

Example: *Umi* (sea) → *Asobi ni ikitai kara.* (One would like to have fun.)
Shashin o tori ni ikitai kara. (One would like to take pictures.)
Oyogi ni ikitai kara. (One would like to go swimming.)
Tsuri ni ikitai kara. (One would like to go fishing.)

5 Detectives and suspects

In class: In this activity, six students will act as detectives, and the rest of the class will be suspects. Each of the detectives asks all of the suspects what they were doing yesterday at a specific time by asking *Kinoo no --- ji goro nani o shite imashita ka?* Each detective will be looking for a different response. Detectives should not tell the suspects the response that they are expecting. The detectives should keep track of how many suspects were doing the specific action around the specific time. Afterward, each of the detectives will report their results to the class.

Tantei 1: Kinoo no gogo 5ji goro (tomodachi to asonde ita.) (spending time with friends)
Tantei 2: Kinoo no gogo 6ji goro (shukudai o shite ita.) (doing homework)
Tantei 3: Kinoo no gogo 7ji goro (bangohan o tabete ita.) (eating dinner)
Tantei 4: Kinoo no gogo 8ji goro (ongaku o kiite ita.) (listening to music)
Tantei 5: Kinoo no gogo 9ji goro (terebi o mite ita.) (watching TV)
Tantei 6: Kinoo no gogo 10ji goro (hon o yonde ita.) (reading a book)

Example: *Kinoo no gogo 5ji goro, tomodachi to asonde ita hito wa 5 nin desu.*
(There are five people who were with friends around 5 p.m. yesterday.)

6 Refusing suggestions

In pairs: Refuse your friend's suggestion by saying what you would rather do.

Example: A: *Chikaku no kameraya de tsukaisute kamera o kattara.*
(How about buying a disposable camera at a nearby camera shop?)
B: *Demo, yappari tori ni kaerimasu.* (I'll just go back and get it.)

(1) *Atarashii jisho o kattara?*
(2) *Kono sashimi o tabetara?*
(3) *Kongakki, furansugo o tottara?*
(4) *Denwa o kaketara?*

7 Listening comprehension

Individually: Listen to the following conversation between two people. Write down what the person has forgotten to do.

Example: A: *Aa, wasureteta.* (Oh! I forgot!)
B: *Dooshita no?* (What's the matter?)
A: *Kyoo repooto o dasanakereba ikenakatta n da.*
(I just remembered that I have to hand in a paper today.)
B: *Repooto wa moo kaita no?* (Have you already written it?)
A: *Mada nan da. Hiruyasumi ni kakanakereba.*
(Not yet. I have to finish it during lunch.)
B: *Ee, hiruyasumi ni? Dekiru no?* (During lunch? Can you finish it?)
A: *Wakaranai kedo, tonikaku kaite miru yo.* (I'm not sure, but I'll try.)
Answer:
→ *Repooto o kaku* no o wasurete imashita. (He/She has forgotten to write a paper.)

1. A: *Aa, wasureteta.* (Oh! I forgot!)
   B: *Dooshita no?* (What's the matter?)
   A: *Heya ni kagi o kakenakatta!* (I didn't lock my room!)
   B: *Ara, taihen.* (That's not good.)
   A: *Chotto heya ni modotte, kagi o kakete kuru. Mattete.*
   (I'm going back to my room to lock it. Just wait.)
   B: *Ee.* (Sure.)
   → He/She has forgotten to lock his/her room.

2. A: *Aa, wasurete imashita.* (Oh! I forgot!)
   B: *Dooshita n desu ka?* (What's the matter?)
   A: *Kyoo 2ji ni tomodachi ni au koto ni natte ita n desu.*
   (I was supposed to meet a friend at 2 o'clock today.)
   B: *Ee, moo 2ji han desu yo.* (Really? It's already 2:30.)
   A: *Chotto denwa o kakete mimasu.* (I'll go call him/her.)
   B: *Hayaku shita hoo ga ii desu yo.* (You'd better hurry.)
   → He/She has forgotten to meet his/her friend.

3. A: *Aa, wasureteta.* (Oh! I forgot!)
    B: *Dooshita no?* (What's the matter?)
    A: *Kyoo wa imooto no tanjoobi datta. Doo shiyoo? Mada purezento o kattenai n da.*
       (I remembered that today is my sister's birthday. I haven't bought her a present yet.)
    B: *Ima kara kai ni ittara.* (Why don't you buy one now?)
    A: *Nani ga ii ka naa?* (What should I get her?)
    B: *Suteki na hon ka, kawaii akusesarii ka ...* (A nice book or some pretty accessories ...)
    A: *Issho ni kite, purezento o erabu no o tetsudatte kureru?*
       (Can you come with me and help me pick out something?)
    B: *Ii wa yo.* (Sure.)
    → He/She has forgotten to buy a birthday present for his/her sister.

Answers:
1. _____ *no o wasurete imashita.*
2. _____ *no o wasurete imashita.*
3. _____ *no o wasurete imashita.*

8 Games using *hashi*

Hashi, or chopsticks are the most important item of tableware in Japanese cuisine. As children grow up and learn how to feed themselves, their parents teach them the correct way to use *hashi*. However, some Japanese use *hashi* in an incorrect or unnatural way. In this activity, students will play two different games that will give them a fun way to practice using *hashi*.

Game 1. *Hashi* relay race
Three teams: (The number of teams and team size will depend on the number of students in the class.) Each team is given a pair of hashi and a piece of candy. Each team's *hashi* and candy should be the same size. The teacher puts one chair in the front of the room for each team. Each team lines up single-file, about 10 to 15 feet away from their team's chair. The person in the front of each line starts the game by picking up the candy from their own hand with the *hashi*. Then they have to walk toward and around the chair and back to their team. The runner puts the candy in the next runner's hand, and that person must pick it up from their hand with the *hashi*. If anyone drops the candy while running around the chair, they must pick it up with their hands and start again from the front of the team line. The first team to have everyone run around the chair with the *hashi* and candy is the winner.

Game 2. Bean placing
Individually: For this game, each student needs a pair of *hashi* and 16 small beans. The teacher also gives each student a 4 x 4 grid of 16 squares, each square 1 cm x 1 cm. At the teacher's signal, the students race to be the first one to get all of their beans into the squares in the grid. Students may not touch the beans with their hands. Anyone caught touching the beans with their hands by the teacher or a classmate has to remove one bean from their grid as a penalty.

9 Disposable goods

Groups of five: In the United States, people use a variety of disposable goods (*tsukaisute shoohin*) without even realizing it because they are taken for granted. This activity gives students the opportunity to think about what types of disposable goods are commonly used. Each group needs a copy of the chart below. Under the "Disposable Goods" column, students should make a list in English of disposable goods used in the United States. Under the "*Tsukaisute Shoohin*" column, students should write the Japanese translation of the English words. Some may be derived from English and written in *katakana;* others may require standard Japanese. Afterward, if there is time, the teacher should try to get the whole class to discuss these disposable goods and whether or not they are harmful to the environment (*kankyoo*).

Disposable Goods	*Tsukaisute Shoohin*
1.	1.
2.	2.
3.	3.
4.	4.
5.	5.
6.	6.
7.	7.
8.	8.
9.	9.
10.	10.

10 Asking permission

In pairs: You are sick, but there are some things that you might want to do. Ask your doctor whether or not you can do the following things. Partners should alternate in taking the part of the patient and the doctor.

Example: You want to swim.

    Patient: *Suiei o shite mo (Oyoide mo) ii desu ka?*

    Doctor: *Sore wa chotto ... Suiei o shite (Oyoide) wa ikenai yo.*

(1) You want to drink coffee.
(2) You want to eat a lot.
(3) You want to go hiking.
(4) You want to play basketball.

Lesson 8: Traveling around Japan

I. PERSPECTIVE

1. Objectives

1 Function:
(1) Asking if someone is going to go somewhere: *(Kyooto) e ikimasen ka?*
(2) Discovering or asking with surprise (female): *Ara,*
(3) Asking if someone is not going to do something: *(Nara) ni wa (ika)nai no?*
(4) Stating something does not exist in a certain place: *(Kyooto) ni wa (--- wa) nai wa yo.*
(5) Asking how big something is: *Dore gurai ookii (n) desu ka?*
(6) Indicating that one is considering something: *Soo ne,*
(7) Indicating approximate size with doubt (female): *(Juugo meetoru) gurai kashira.*

2 Language:
(1) *(Kyooto) e (iki)masen ka?* (2) *(Nara) ni wa (ika)nai no?*
(3) *(Kyooto) ni wa (daibutsu) wa nai wa yo.* (4) *(Sekai) de ichiban (ooki)i.*
(5) *Dore gurai (ooki)i (n) desu ka?* (6) *(Juugo meetoru) gurai kashira.*
(7) *(Jiyuu no megami) yori (chiisa)i kedo.* (8) *(Hasseiki) datta kana.*
(9) *(Hoka) de wa (mi)rare nai.* (10) *(Nara) wa (Kyooto) to (chika)i kara,*
(11) *(Tsuide ni itte mi)tara?*

3 Culture:
(1) Traditional cities (2) Popular tourist spots

II. PREPARATION

1. Context

観光地選び

ピーターはアメリカを出発する前から決めていた。京都、広島、箱根の3ヶ所は絶対行こう。京都では、金閣寺や清水寺を見たい。広島では原爆資料館。箱根では富士山。できれば、富士山に登ってみたい。夕食の時間に、ピーターは観光地についてあきらの家族にたずねた。いろいろなところを紹介された。時間があれば、全部行きたい。

Before he left America, Peter decided that he would definitely go to Kyoto, Hiroshima, and Hakone. In Kyoto he wants to see Kinkakuji Temple and Kiyomizudera Temple. In Hiroshima he wants to see the atomic bomb museum. Peter would also like to go to Hakone and then try to climb Mt. Fuji. During dinner, Peter asks Akira's family about the tourist places, and they tell him about the cities. If he has time, he thinks he would like to go to all of those places.

2. Sample Conversation

MA: あした京都へ行きませんか。
P: うん。そこへは絶対行きたい。
MF: あら、奈良には行かないの。
P: 時間がないからだめです。
MF: でも、京都には大仏はないわよ。
P: 大仏は絶対見たいですね。
MF: ええ、世界で一番大きい仏様です。
P: どれぐらい大きいですか。
MF: そうね、１５メートル位かしら。自由の女神より小さいけど。
P: いつ出来たんですか。
MA: ８世紀だったかな。確か。
MF: とにかく、大きくて、古いのよ。他では見られないわよ。
MA: 奈良は京都と近いから、ついでに行ってみたら。

MA: *Ashita Kyooto[1] e ikimasen ka?*
P: *Un. Soko e wa zettai ikitai.*
MF: *Ara[2], Nara[1] ni wa ikanai no?*
P: *Jikan ga nai kara dame desu.*
MF: *Demo, Kyooto ni wa daibutsu[1] wa nai wa yo.*
P: *Daibutsu wa zettai mitai desu ne.*
MF: *Ee, sekai de[3] ichiban[4] ookii hotokesama desu.*
P: *Dore gurai ookii desu ka?*
MF: *Soo ne[5], juugo meetoru gurai kashira[6]. Jiyuu no megami yori[7] chiisai kedo[8].*
P: *Itsu dekita n desu ka?*
MA: *Hasseiki datta ka[9] na, tashika...*
MF: *Tonikaku ookikute furui no yo. Hoka de wa mirare nai[10] wa yo.*
MA: *Nara wa Kyooto to chikai kara, tsuide ni itte mitara?*

MA: Aren't you going to Kyoto tomorrow?
P: Yeah. I definitely want to go!
MF: Oh. Aren't you going to Nara?
P: I don't have time.
MF: But, there's no *daibutsu* in Kyoto.
P: I really want to see the Great Buddha.
MF: It's the largest Buddha in the world.
P: About how big is it?
MF: Well, it's about fifteen meters, I think. It's smaller than the Statue of Liberty, though.
P: When was it built?
MA: The eighth century, if my memory is correct.
MF: Anyway, it's big and old. There isn't anything else like it.
MA: Since Nara and Kyoto are close, you could try to go while you're in Kyoto.

MA:	もり あきら	*Mori Akira*	Akira Mori
P:	ピーター スミス	*Peter Sumisu*	Peter Smith
MF:	もり ふみこ（あきらのお母さん）	*Mori Fumiko (Akira no okaasan)*	Fumiko Mori (Akira's mother)

Lesson 8

3. Language & Culture Notes

1 The cities of Kyoto and Nara are almost as old as Japan itself. They are both full of authentic examples of traditional art and architecture. Nara is considered the cradle of culture and civilization in Japan. In 710 A.D., the capital of Japan was established in this city, making it the political and cultural center of Japan. The government remained there for 74 years. This period is now referred to as the Nara Period. It was during this time that Japan adopted Buddhism, art, and architecture from the Chinese. It was also during this period that one of the greatest statues of Buddha was built. The political and economic systems were at their strongest. Today Nara is no longer a political center, but it remains as a major cultural center of Japan. Nara's industry consists mainly of traditional crafts such as carved wooden dolls, lacquerware, and ceramics. Nara's wealth of historic sites, including the famous Todaiji and Horyuji temples and art treasures, attract around 10 million visitors each year.

Kyoto became the capital of Japan in 794 A.D., and was originally known as Heiankyoo, "City of Peace." Kyoto remained the seat of government until the 16th century, but it was the home of the Emperor until 1868. Kyoto was the principal cultural center of Japan for over 1,000 years. During this period, court life reached its highest state of refinement as architecture, painting, sculpture, and literature flourished. Some of Japan's most beautiful treasures can be seen in Kyoto's many museums, Buddhist temples, Shinto shrines, castles, and parks. Though Kyoto has more industry than Nara, the city is still well-known for such traditional pursuits as silk weaving, embroidery, porcelain, and lacquerware.

There are certain popular tourist places in Japan that draw hundreds of thousands of visitors every year. In Kyoto, Kinkakuji and Kiyomizudera temples are two of the oldest in Japan. In Nara, people go to see the *daibutsu*, or Great Buddha, and other ancient shrines and temples. The Atomic Bomb Memorial in Hiroshima is a reminder of Japan's situation in World War II. Of course, one cannot forget snowcapped Mt. Fuji, the highest point in Japan. Every summer, thousands of climbers reach the summit of this inactive volcano. These are only a few examples of the many cultural spots that Japan has to offer. These places are of interest to foreigners as well as to Japanese people.

2 *Ara* shows some degree of surprise or an unexpected situation. It means "Oh!," " Why!," " Dear me!," or "My goodness!" and is used predominantly by women.

3 The function marker *de* is used to show the scope or area to which some statement is applicable. Its usage corresponds to "among," "in," or "of." *De* is sometimes used with --- *no naka*.
   sekai de (in the world)
   gakusei no naka de (among the students)
   kono naka de (among these, of these)

4 *Ichiban* literally means "number one," and is also used to indicate the superlative (most ---, -est) degree of an adjective or adjectival noun.

   ichiban ookii (biggest)   *ichiban kirei (na)* (prettiest)
   ichiban joozu (na) (most skillful, the best at)   *ichiban atarashii* (newest)
   ichiban aji ga ii (best tasting)   *ichiban suki (na)* (most favorite, most liked)

5 *Soo ne* is a discourse function word meaning "Let me see ..."

6 *kashira* is a sentence function word that indicates some doubt or uncertainty. It is usually used when speaking to oneself, as in "I wonder if --- " or " I wonder what ---" *Kashira* follows the informal style of verbs, adjectives, and adjectival nouns. *Kashira* is used mainly by women.

7 *yori* is used to describe things in comparison (more ---, -er.) It corresponds to "than."
   Daibutsu wa jiyuu no megami yori chiisai desu.
   (The Great Buddha is smaller than the Statue of Liberty.)
   Kita Nihon wa minami Nihon yori samui desu. (Northern Japan is colder than the South.)

8 *kedo* is a function word that serves the purpose of reversing the previous statement or clause. It means "but," "although," or "however."

9 *datta ka* in this example is not used to ask a question, but is uttered to oneself when trying to recall something (Was it ...?).

10 *Mirarenai* means "cannot see." *Mirareru* is the potential form (can ---, able to ---, possible to ---) of *mimasu*. Vowel verbs (base form ends in a vowel) are made into the potential form by replacing the *ru* ending of the dictionary form with *rareru*.

tabe(ru)	(eat)	*taberareru*	(can eat)
mi(ru)	(see)	*mirareru*	(can see)
kangae(ru)	(consider)	*kangaerareru*	(can consider)
shinji(ru)	(believe)	*shinjirareru*	(can believe)
ne(ru)	(sleep)	*nerareru*	(can sleep)

Consonant verbs (base form ends in a consonant) are made into the potential form by replacing the *u* ending with *eru*.

iku	(go)	*ikeru*	(can go)
asobu	(play)	*asoberu*	(can play)
kau	(buy)	*kaeru*	(can buy)
kaeru	(return)	*kaereru*	(can return)
omou	(think)	*omoeru*	(can think)
iu	(say)	*ieru*	(can say)

There are two exceptions to these verbs:
   shimasu (do) → *dekiru* (can do) and *kimasu* (come) → *korareru* (can come.)

Generally speaking, if the dictionary form of a verb does not end in either *-eru* or *-iru*, then that verb belongs to the consonant verb group. When the dictionary form of a verb ends in *-eru* or *-iru*, that verb belongs to the consonant verb group if the pre-*nai* form ends in *a* [e.g. *kaeru* → *kaera(nai)*]. But if the pre-*nai* form ends in *e* or *i*, then that verb belongs to the vowel verb group. [e.g. *neru* → *ne(nai)*].

III. PARTICIPATION

1. Vocabulary

1 **From sample conversation:**

chikai (close)
dekita (built, established)
gurai/kurai (about)
hoka de wa (elsewhere, other places)
ichiban (the best, the most, the first)
ikanai, ikimasen (do not go; What/How about going to ...?)
jiyuu (liberty, freedom)
megami (goddess)
ookikute (big and ...)
tashika (be sure, surely)
zettai (absolutely, definitely)

daibutsu (Great Buddha)
furui (old)
hasseiki (the 8th century)
hotokesama (Buddha)

jiyuu no megami (Statue of Liberty)
mirarenai (cannot see)
sekai (the world)
tsuide (at the same time)

2 **Useful for activities:**

akeru (to open)
dame (not good, no use)
hakken suru (to discover)
kabe (wall)
kotaeru (to answer)
naraberu (to arrange)
--- ni naru (to become ...)
okiru (to get up)
renshuu suru (to practice)
se (height)
Shiaazu Tawaa (Sears Tower)
shiraseru (to inform)
tsukuru (to make)

bakari (just)
dono/dore kurai (how much/many)
ireru (to put something in)
kariru (to borrow)
miseru (to show)
neru (to sleep)
oboeru (to remember, to memorize)
penki o nuru (to paint)
Roshia (Russia)
seiki (century)
shimeru (to close)
shitai (want to [do])

2. Activity, Practice, & Exercise

1 **Estimating**

In groups of three or four: Each group is given a sheet with three questions about the sizes of things. Find out the exact size of each. Use reference books such as encyclopedias, atlases, geography textbooks, town and state guidebooks, and so on.
Example:
1. _____ *shuu wa* <u>*dore kurai*</u> *ookii desu ka?* (How big is [the state of] _____ ?)
2. _____ *san (yama) wa* <u>*dore kurai*</u> *takai desu ka?* (How tall is Mt. _____ ?)
3. _____ *san wa* <u>*dore kurai*</u> *se ga takai desu ka?* (How tall is Mr./Ms. _____ ?)

Before starting, the teacher should give examples by asking the following questions.
- *Amerika wa dono kurai ookii desu ka? - Yaku 900 man heihoo kiromeetoru desu.*
  (About how big is America? - It is about 9 million square kilometers.)

- *Eberesutozan wan dore kurai takai desu ka? - Yaku 8,800 meetoru desu.*
  (About how tall is Mt. Everest? - It is about 8,800 meters tall.)
- *Jiyuu no megami wa dono kurai ookii desu ka? - 46 meetoru desu.*
  (About how big is the Statue of Liberty? - It is about 46 meters tall.)

2 Substitution

In pairs: In this activity, students change the underlined parts of the example sentence into things with which they are familiar. Student A substitutes *Kyooto* with the name of a store and *daibutsu* with a product or merchandise. Student B replies by saying *soo desu* (correct) or *chigaimasu* (wrong). Pairs should try to make as many new sentences as they can in about 10 minutes. Afterwards, each pair will present one sentence to the class.

Example: <u>Kyooto</u> *ni wa* <u>daibutsu</u> *wa nai yo/wa yo.*

    A: <u>Suupaa</u> *ni wa* <u>terebi</u> *wa nai yo/wa yo.*
       (There aren't TVs at supermarkets.)
    B: *Soo desu.* (That's right.)

3 Sentence completion

In pairs: Describe what you want to say after the following clauses.

1. *Ima okita* <u>bakari desu kara</u> (Since I have just gotten up), _____ .
2. *Gohan o tabeta* <u>bakari desu kara</u> (Since I have just eaten a meal),_____ .
3. *Kabe ni penki o nutta* <u>bakari desu kara</u> (Since I have just painted the wall), _____ .
4. *Kono ryoori wa tsukutta* <u>bakari desu kara</u> (Since this meal has just been cooked), ____ .
5. *Sensei ni natta* <u>bakari desu kara</u> (Since I have just become a teacher), _____ .

4 Is that a fact?

In pairs: Students take turns asking each other about different factual information. Student A makes a statement and expresses that they aren't sure if the information is accurate. Student B will either confirm A's statement or give the correct information. Students should try to discuss four different facts within their pair. They should take turns asking and answering questions. Follow the example.

Example: A: *Koronbusu ga Amerika o hakken shita no wa 15 seiki* <u>datta ka naa/kashira</u>?
       (Columbus discovered America in the 15th century, didn't he?)
    B: *Soo desu.* (That's right.)
    or
    A: *Koronbusu ga Amerika o hakken shita no wa 12 seiki* <u>ka naa/kashira</u>?
       (Columbus discovered America in the 12th century, didn't he?)
    B: *Chigaimasu. 15 seiki desu.*

5 Verb Conjugation

In pairs: Write sentences using the *-rare nai* or *-re nai* forms of the following verbs.
Example: *Hoka de wa mirarenai yo.*

neru (to sleep)	*oboeru* (to memorize)	*shimeru* (to close)
okiru (to get up)	*akeru* (to open)	*oshieru* (to teach)
ireru (to insert)	*shiraseru* (to notify)	*kariru* (to borrow)
taberu (to eat)	*kiru* (to wear)	*kotaeru* (to answer)
miseru (to show)	*naraberu* (to line up)	

6 Aren't you going to ...?

In pairs: Students tell their partner that they plan to go somewhere. The partner asks what they will do at that place, and the others name two or three things that they plan to do there. The partner then suggests something in addition. Students may choose any country or city in the world. Change roles, and then do the activity again with a different partner. Try to think of a different place for the new partner, but the same place may be used if necessary. Students should do the activity with three different partners. Follow the example conversation below.

Example: A: *Kyooto e ikimasu.* (I am going to Kyoto.)

B: *Kyooto de <u>nani o shimasu ka</u>?* or *Kyooto no <u>doko e ikimasu ka</u>?*
(What will you do in Kyoto? or Where in Kyoto are you going?)

A: *Kinkakuji to Kiyomizudera o <u>mi ni ikimasu</u>.*
(I'll see Kinkakuji and Kiyomizudera temples.)

B: *Ara! Ginkakuji o mi ni <u>ikanai no</u>?* (Aren't you going to see Ginkakuji Temple?)

A: *Soo ne. Ginkakuji mo mi ni ikimashoo.* (Well. Let's go to see Ginkakuji Temple also.)

7 Where is Tokyo?

In groups of three:

① The teacher makes a copy of the list below and the map of Japan on the inside cover of the textbook, or another map, for each group. The teacher then labels big or important cities on the map with numbers only. Without a matching list, the students must identify the cities on the map by writing the name of each city next to the corresponding number in the list below. Take turns asking each other in Japanese where each city is.

Example: A: *Tookyoo <u>wa dore desu ka</u>?* (Which is Tokyo?)

B: *Tookyoo wa 3 <u>da to omoimasu</u>.* (I think it's 3.)

or

A: *3 <u>wa nan to iu toshi desu ka</u>?* (What city is 3?)

B: *3 wa Tookyoo <u>da to omoimasu</u>?* (I think it's Tokyo.)

② The students must then match their list of cities with the given list of tourist, historic, or significant places. Take turns asking each other in Japanese where each famous place is.

Example: A: *Kinkakuji wa <u>doko ni arimasu ka</u>?* (Where is Kinkakuji Temple?)

B: *Kinkakuji wa Kyooto <u>ni aru to omoimasu</u>.* (I think it's in Kyoto.)

Use the following chart and list of places, or create a new one that may be more suitable to what the students have learned.

	① CITY	② CITY NUMBER	FAMOUS PLACE
1.	_____	_____	A. *Heiwakooen* (1)
2.	_____	_____	B. *Kinkakuji*
3.	_____	_____	C. *Daibutsuden*
4.	_____	_____	D. *Meijijingu*
5.	_____	_____	E. *Kiyomizudera*

6. _____	_____	F. *Heiwakooen* (2)
7. _____	_____	G. *Kenrokuen*
8. _____	_____	H. *Ginkakuji*
9. _____	_____	I. *Shinjukueki*
10. _____	_____	J. *Meijimura*
	_____	K. *Kookyo*
	_____	L. *Miyajima*
	_____	M. *Ijinkan*
	_____	N. *Tokeidai*
	_____	O. *Uenokooen*

Suggested cities: Tokyo, Kyoto, Osaka, Nara, Hiroshima, Kobe, Nagoya, Nagasaki, Sapporo, Kanazawa

8 The biggest in the world

In pairs: Complete each sentence using an adjective in the superlative form to describe the following places in the world.

Example: *Nara no daibutsu* → *Nara no daibutsu wa sekai de <u>ichiban ookii</u> hotokesama desu.*
(The Great Buddha in Nara → The Great Buddha in Nara is the biggest Buddha in the World.)

(1) *Eberesuto zan* → *Eberesuto wa _____ yama desu.*
(2) *Amazon gawa* → *Amazon gawa wa _____ kawa desu.*
(3) *Shiaazu tawaa* → *Shiaazu tawaa wa _____ biru desu.*
(4) *Roshia*: → *Roshia wa _____ kuni desu.*

9 Making comparisons

In pairs: Write comparative sentences for each of the following.
 (1) Sears Tower → Empire State Building
 (2) ---'s car → ---'s car
 (3) new house → old house
 (4) expensive watch → cheap watch
 (5) interesting book → boring book

10 I can't because . . .

In pairs: Your friend Patrick has asked you to go to Japan with him this summer. However, you cannot or do not want to go this summer. Give Patrick at least two reasons why you will not go with him.

Example: *Jikan ga nai <u>kara dame desu</u>.* (I can't because I don't have time.)

Lesson 8   67

Lesson 9: Review & Application

IV. PERFORMANCE

1. Application

1 Conversation completion

In small groups: The following is a conversation between a Japanese (J) and an American (A) high school student at a summer festival. Guess what the American student would say in the conversation. Choose the most appropriate sentences from the list below.

J: *Koko ga watashitachi no machi no natsumatsuri no basho yo.*
(This is the place where our town's summer festival is.)
A: ( ) (There's a jungle gym over there. This place looks like a park.)
J: *Soo. Fudan wa shiminkooen na no.* (Right. It's actually a public park.)
A: ( ) (Oh, there are many *yatai* stands.)
J: *Watagashi, ringoame, yooyoo, kingyosukui ...*
(Cotton candy, candy apples, yo-yos, goldfish catching ...)
A: ( ) (I want to eat *ikayaki*.)
J: *Demo sakki gohan o tabeta bakari yo.* (But we just ate dinner.)
A: ( ) (*Ikayaki* is a snack, not dinner.)
J: *Jaa, doozo. Watashi wa aisukyandii ni suru wa.* (Well, go ahead. I'm going to have ice candy.)
A: ( ) (Oh, *bon'odori* has begun.)
J: *Issho ni odorimashoo yo.* (Let's dance together.)
A: ( ) (I'm not good at dancing, so ...)
J: *Daijoobu yo. Kodomo datte dekiru n dakara. Kantan yo.*
(No problem. Even children can do it. It's easy.)

1. *Boku, ikayaki ga tabetai na.*
2. *Boku, dansu wa tokui ja nai kara, chotto ...*
3. *Aa, bon'odori ga hajimatta.*
4. *Asoko ni jangurujimu ga aru ne. Koko kooen mitai da ne.*
5. *Ikayaki wa gohan ja nai. Oyatsu da yo.*
6. *Aa, yatai ga ippai aru.*

2 Conversation completion

In small groups: The following is a conversation between a Japanese (J) and an American (A) student who are talking about a trip to Kyoto. Guess what the American student would say in the underlined parts in the conversation. Each group will present their conversation to the class.

J: *Asu wa iyoiyo Kyooto da ne.* (Tomorrow we're finally going to Kyoto.)
A: *Un. _____ , kon'ya wa nemurenai kamo shirenai na.*
(Yeah. _____, we may not be able to sleep tonight.)

J: *Honto? Moshi nemurenakattara, asu basu no naka de nenakya ne.*
(Really? If we can't sleep, we'll have to sleep on the bus tomorrow.)

A: *Basu da to, _____ .* (If we take a bus, _____.)

J: *Nagoya kara daitai 3 jikan gurai da yo.* (It takes about three hours from Nagoya.)

A: *Shinkansen yori _____ .* (_____ than the *shinkansen*.)

J: *Sore wa toozen da yo ne. Demo, unchin wa shinkansen no hanbun ika da yo.*
(It certainly is. But the fare is less than half the price of the *shinkansen*.)

A: *Yasui n da ne. Demo, boku _____ .* (It's cheap. Still, I _____ .)

J: *Jaa, kaeri wa shinkansen de kaeroo. Chotto takai kedo.*
(Then let's take the *shinkansen* on the way back, even though it's a little expensive.)

A: *Soo shiyoo. Tokorode, Kyooto wa _____ ?* (OK. By the way, is Kyoto _____ ?)

J: *Iya, Nara no hoo ga furui yo. Nara ga "miyako," tsumari shuto datta Narajidai wa Kyooto ga miyako datta Heianjidai yori mae dakara ne.*
(No, Nara is older than Kyoto. The Nara Period, when Nara was the capital, was before the Heian Period, when Kyoto was the capital.)

A: *Jaa, Narajidai to Heianjidai to dochira ga _____ .*
(Then, which _____ , the Nara or the Heian Period?)

J: *Heianjidai. Narajidai wa 80 nen gurai dakedo, Heianjidai wa 400 nen gurai tsuzuita kara ne.*
(The Heian Period. The Nara Period lasted about 80 years, but the Heian Period lasted about 400 years.)

A: *Dakara Kyooto ni wa mukashi no tatemono ga takusan aru n da ne.*
(That's why there are so many old buildings in Kyoto, right?)

3 Comparative sentences

In small groups: Each group is given three or four cards with an adjective written on each. Make as many comparison sentences as possible using the adjectives on the cards. The sentences should be based on facts. The group with the most correct sentences is the winner.

Examples of adjectives: *ookii, chiisai, nagai, mijikai, furui, atarashii, yasui, takai, omoshiroi, wakai, shizuka, nigiyaka, isogashii, hima, ooi, sukunai, hiroi, tsuyoi, atsui, samui*

Example: *ookii* → *Akebono wa Takanohana yori ookii.* (Akebono is bigger than Takanohana.)
(big)   *Amerika wa Nihon yori zutto ookii.* (Ameria is much bigger than Japan.)
   Watashi no kaban wa sensei no yori ookii.
   (My bag is bigger than the teacher's.)

shizuka → *Toshokan wa kyooshitsu yori shizuka da.*
(quiet)   (The library is quieter than a classroom.)
   Fuyu wa natsu yori shizuka da. (Winter is quieter than summer.)

4 Comparative questions

In small groups: Change the sentences made in APE 3 into questions. Use the sentence pattern *--- to dochira ga --- desu ka?* The adjectives may be changed to their opposite meanings. (*ookii* → *chiisai*) Group members then ask other groups their questions. Groups get points for correct answers.

Lesson 9   69

Example: 1) A: *Akebono to Takanohana to dochira ga ookii desu ka?*
B: *Akebono desu.* (1 point)/*Takanohana desu.* (0 points)

2) A: *An no kaban to sensei no to dochira ga chiisai desu ka?*
B: *An no kaban desu.* (0 points)/*Sensei no kaban desu.* (1 point)

5 Which do you prefer?

In pairs: Choose three topics from those listed below and make a comparison question for each topic. Partners then ask each other about their preferences or which they like better. Make a different pair for each of the three questions.

Topics: *kudamono* (fruit), *okashi* (sweets), *nomimono* (beverages), *tabemono* (food), *supootsu* (sports), *ongaku* (music), *eiga* (movies), *kamoku* (subjects), *basho* (places)

Example: *kudamono* A: *Momo to nashi to dochira ga suki desu ka?*
(fruit)   (Which do you prefer, peaches or pears?)
                B: *Soo desu ne. Watashi wa momo yori nashi no hoo ga suki desu. A san wa doo desu ka?*
                (Let me see. I prefer pears to peaches. How about you?)
                A: *Boku wa nashi yori momo no hoo ga suki desu.*
                (I like peaches better than pears.)

nomimono   B: *Kokakoora to Pepushikoora to dochira ga suki desu ka?*
(beverages)   (Which do you like, Coke or Pepsi?)
              A: *Boku wa Pepushikoora yori Kokakoora no hoo ga suki desu. B san wa?*
              (I prefer Coke to Pepsi. How about you?)
              B: *Onaji desu. Pepushikoora yori Kokakoora no hoo ga suki desu.*
              (Me, too. I like Coke better than Pepsi.)

6 I would like to ...

In groups of five or six: Each group chooses one person to play the role of a Japanese student who will come to America for a homestay. Others play the roles of American students who will welcome the Japanese student.

① The Japanese students get together to talk about what they would like to do during their stay in America. In their original groups, the American students talk about the places and things they would like to show and do with the Japanese student. Each group makes a list of what they would like to do.

Example: Japanese students:

Kyanpu o shitai. Tozan o shitai. Uma ni noritai. Omiyage o kaitai. Tiishatsu o kaitai. Ryoori o oboetai.
   (I would like to ... go camping, go mountain climbing, go horseback riding, buy souvenirs, buy T-shirts, learn how to cook)

American students:
Yuuenchi, gorufujoo etc. *e annai shitai.* --- *san no uma,* --- *san no noojoo* etc. *o misetai. Suiei, geemu* etc. *o issho ni shitai. Nihongo de hanashitai.*

(We would like to ... take [him/her] to an amusement park, golf course.
                show [him/her] ---'s horse, ---'s farm.
                go swimming, play games, speak Japanese.)

② The Japanese students go back to their original group and talk with the Americans about what they want to do. The Americans comment on what the Japanese student wants to do. Use the expression A *nara*, B (*ga ii*) *desu*. Then they talk about what they would like to show and do with the Japanese student. Use expressions such as --- *wa suki desu ka?*, --- *wa doo desu ka?*, and *-mashoo*.

Example: (J: Japanese student; A, B, C, D: American students)

    A: *--- (place) de nani o shitai desu ka?* (What do you want to do in ---?)

    J: *Iroiro arimasu. Mazu noojoo o kengaku shitai desu ne.*
        (Lots of things. First, I would like to see a farm.)

    A: *Noojoo nara, B san no noojoo ga ii desu ne. Totemo hiroi kara.*
        (Speaking of farms, I recommend B's farm. It's very large.)

    B: *Hai. Zehi mi ni kite kudasai.* (Yes. Please come over and see it.)

    J: *B san no noojoo de wa nani o tsukutte imasu ka?*
        (What are you growing on your farm, B?)

    B: *Jagaimo to toomorokoshi desu.* (Potatoes and corn.)

    J: *Jaa, zehi misete kudasai.* (I would really like to see it.)

    B: *Ee, doozo. Hoka ni nani o shitai desu ka?* (Sure. What else do you want to do?)

    J: *Natsu no supootsu ga shitai desu. Tatoeba, saafin ya suijoo sukii. Mada yatta koto ga nai kara, zehi oshiete moraitai desu.*
        (I want to do some summer sports, like surfing and waterskiing, for example. I have never done them, so I would like you to teach me.)

    C: *Suijoo sukii nara, boku ga oshiemasu yo. ---ko de maitoshi yatte imasu kara ne.*
        (I can teach you how to waterski. I go on Lake --- every year.)

    J: *Arigatoo. Onegai shimasu.* (Thank you. I appreciate it.)

    D: *Hoka wa?* (What else?)

    J: *Iroiro na mise o mitai desu.* (I want to go to various stores.)

    D: *Mise nara, --- mooru ga ii desu yo. Machi de ichiban ookii mooru desu kara, takusan mise ga arimasu.*
        (For shopping, I recommend the --- Mall. It's the biggest mall in town and has lots of shops.)

    J: *Ii desu ne.* (Sounds good.)

    A: *Sorekara, --- yuuenchi ni mo ikimashoo. Jettokoosutaa ga arimasu.*
        (Let's go to [amusement park], too. There's a roller coaster there.)

    J: *Hai.* (OK.)

    B: *Jooba wa suki desu ka?* (Do you like horseback riding?)

    J: *Uma ni notta koto ga nai kara, wakarimasen.*
        (I have never ridden on a horse, so I don't know.)

    B: *Jaa, uchi no uma ni notte mite kudasai. Otonashii uma desu kara, daijoobu desu.*
        (You can try riding our horse. He's calm, so don't worry.)

    J: *Sore wa tanoshimi desu ne.* (I'm looking forward to it.)

7 May I . . . ?

In class: Divide the class into two groups. Each student from the first group gets a big card with a different place written on it. Those students will be the receptionist, clerk, or person with information at that place. The students from the other group will visit the various places. They will ask the receptionists if they can do something there. Use the expression *-te mo ii desu ka?* The receptionists answer with *Hai, ii desu yo,* or *Iie, dame desu*. If the answer is no, the visitors may ask why, and the receptionist should give a specific reason using *--- kara*. After 10 to 15 minutes, switch roles between the two groups.

Example: Place → *Nihon no otera* (a Japanese temple)

    A: *Koko de shashin o totte mo ii desu ka?* (May I take pictures here?)
    B: *Soto wa ii desu ga, naka wa dame desu*.
       (You may outside, but not inside.)
    A: *Dooshite naka wa dame desu ka?* (Why can't I inside?)
    B: *Naka ni totemo taisetsu na e ya butsuzoo ga aru kara desu*.
       (Because there are very precious pictures and statues of the Buddha inside.)
    A: *Soo desu ka. Wakarimashita*. (Really? I understand.)

8 Making suggestions

In small groups: In English or Japanese, each student writes down a problem that they are dealing with right now. They should not write their names on the paper. The teacher collects the papers and randomly passes them back out to the students. In small groups, students discuss how each problem could be solved or settled. Use the expression *-tara* to suggest some ideas. On the back of the paper, write down a few suggestions for each student's problem. The teacher collects the papers again, and the students get their original paper back. They should read their classmates' suggestions and write down what they think of the ideas.

Examples of problems
- *Kyonen yori taijuu ga fueta.* (I have gained weight since last year.)
- *Suugaku no seiseki ga warui.* (I am not doing well in math.)
- *Kurasumeito ga ijimeru.* (Some classmates bully me.)
- *Oya ga amari kozukai o kurenai.* (My parents don't give me much allowance.)

Example: Problem

    A: *Taijuu ga fuete komatte iru no.* (I am troubled by the weight that I have gained.)
    Suggestions
    B: *Daietto shitara.* (I suggest you go on a diet.)
    C: *Mainichi undoo o shitara.* (I suggest you exercise every day.)
    D: *Yaseru kuriimu o tsukattara.* (I suggest you use cream that makes you thinner.)
    Decision
    A gets his/her paper back and writes the following below the classmates' suggestions.
    A: *Daietto wa kurushii shi, kuriimu wa takai shi, undoo ga ichiban ii to omou wa.*
       (Going on a diet is difficult, and the cream is expensive. I think exercise is the best idea.)
       Mainichi undoo o suru. (I will exercise every day.)

9 Verb conjugation: passive voice

In pairs: Using verb cards or a list of verbs, change verbs from the dictionary form into the passive voice.

Example: • *kaku* → *kakareru*; *yomu* → *yomareru* (*-u* → *-areru*)
- *miru* → *mirareru*; *kakeru* → *kakerareru* (*-iru*; *-eru* → *-rareru*)
- *suru* → *sareru* (*suru* → *sareru*)
- *kuru* → *korareru* (*kuru* → *korareru*)

10 Passive voice

In small groups: Following the examples, make original sentences in the passive voice. Use the three verbs shown in the examples. Afterward, each group presents their sentences to the class.

Example: 1) *kaku* → *kakareru*:
- *"Genji monogatari" wa 11 seiki ni Nihon de kakaremashita.*
  (*The Tale of Genji* was written in Japan in the 11th century.)
- *"Genji monogatari" wa Murasaki Shikibu ni yotte kakaremashita.*
  (*The Tale of Genji* was written by Murasaki Shikibu.)

2) *tsukuru* → *tsukurareru*:
- *Nihon no furui ie wa ki de tsukuraremashita.* (Old houses in Japan were made of wood.)
- *Osake wa kome kara tsukuraremasu.* (Sake is made from rice.)

3) *yobu* → *yobareru*
- *Shuwarutsunegaa wa nihonjin ni "Shuwa chan" to yobaremasu.*
  (Schwarzenegger is called "Shuwa chan" by Japanese people.)
- *Watashi wa tomodachi ni "Yotchan" to yobaremasu.*
  (I am called "Yotchan" by my friends.)

11 Have you ever had something stolen?

In class:
① Make five groups. Each group gets one of the following question cards.
  1. *Dare ka ni nani ka o torareta/nusumareta koto ga arimasu ka?*
     (Have you ever had something taken/stolen?)
  2. *Dare ka ni nani ka o kowasareta koto ga arimasu ka?*
     (Have you ever had something broken by someone?)
  3. *Dare ka ni nani ka himitsu na mono o mirareta koto ga arimasu ka?*
     (Have you ever had something secretive seen?)
  4. *Dare ka ni shikarareta koto ga arimasu ka?* (Have you ever been scolded?)
  5. *Dare ka ni ijimerareta koto ga arimasu ka?* (Have you ever been bullied?)

Each group asks the rest of the class their question and records their responses.
Example: A: *B san wa nani ka o nusumareta koto ga arimasu ka?*
    (Have you ever had something stolen, B?)

B: *Hai. Kyonen, jitensha o <u>nusumaremashita</u>.* (Yes. My bike was stolen last year.)
A: *Soo desu ka. Dare ga <u>nusumimashita ka</u>?* (Really? Who stole it?)
B: *Wakarimasen. Hontoo ni hara ga <u>tachimashita</u>.* (I don't know. I was really mad.)
A: *Hidoi desu ne.* (That's terrible.)

② Each group combines their results, and a representative makes a presentation to the class.
Example: *Nusumareta koto ga aru: 8 nin*

Nusumareta koto ga nai: 7 nin

Nusumareta mono: okane - 5 nin; jitensha - hitori; tokei - hitori; kaban - hitori

Watashitachi no guruupu no shitsumon wa "Nani ka nusumareta koto ga arimasu ka?" desu. Nusumareta koto ga aru no wa 8 nin desu. Nusumareta mono wa, okane ga 5 nin, jitensha ga hitori, tokei ga hitori, kaban ga hitori desu. Zannen desu ne. Minasan ki o tsukemashoo.
(The question we asked was "Have you ever had something stolen?" Eight people have had something stolen. Five people had money stolen, one person a bike, one person a watch, and one person a bag. It's a shame. Be careful everybody.)

12 Fast reading practice

Individually: Read the following passage and answer the questions following it. Time how long it takes to finish the entire activity.

　さとみが私に浴衣を貸してくれた。青い花と赤い花の模様のきれいな浴衣だ。浴衣は木綿で作られているので、涼しい。お母さんが浴衣の着方を教えてくれた。帯がちょっと難しかったので、何回も練習した。さとみの家族は浴衣を着た私を見て「良く似合う。」と言ってくれた。さとみは黄色と緑の蝶々の模様の浴衣を着た。

　夕方、さとみと一緒に近所の公園へ夏祭りを見に行った。浴衣を着た人がたくさんいた。女の人の浴衣は色がはなやかだ。男の人の浴衣は色は地味だけど、なかなかかっこいい。子供の浴衣もとてもかわいい。

　屋台がたくさん並んでいた。りんごあめ、わたがし、ポップコーン、焼きとうもろこし、いか焼き、たこ焼き、金魚すくい、ヨーヨーなど、いっぱいあってにぎやかだ。さとみと私はたこ焼きを買った。たこ焼きは小さい丸い食べ物で、小麦粉で作られている。中にたこが入っていて、おいしい。アメリカ人はあまりたこを食べないが、日本人はよくたこを食べているようだ。

　盆踊りが始まった。公園のまん中にステージがあって、その上で男の人が大きなたいこをたたき、スピーカーから日本のみんようが流れてきた。人々が台の回りに集まり、輪になって踊り始めた。さとみが「一緒に踊りましょう。」と言った。私は踊り方がわからないと言ったが、さとみは「私もよくわからないけど、大丈夫。他の人のまねをす

るから。同じ踊りを何回も繰り返すだけだから、だれでも踊れるの。」と言って、私の手を引っぱって、踊りの輪の中へ連れて行った。最初は踊り方がよくわからなかったけれど、徐々にわかってきて楽しかった。盆踊りを見ているとアメリカのフォークダンスを思い出します。

夏祭りで、食べたり、飲んだり、踊ったり、いろいろな人と話したりした。本当に楽しかった。浴衣も気に入った。私は日本の夏祭りが大好きになった。

From Alice's diary:

Satomi ga watashi ni yukata o kashite kureta. Aoi hana to akai hana no moyoo no kirei na yukata da. Yukata wa momen de tsukurarete iru node, suzushii. Okaasan ga yukata no kikata o oshiete kureta. Obi ga chotto muzukashikatta node, nankai mo renshuu shita. Satomi no kazoku wa yukata o kita watashi o mite "yoku niau" to itte kureta. Satomi wa kiiro to midori no choochoo no moyoo no yukata o kita.

Yuugata, Satomi to issho ni kinjo no kooen e natsumatsuri o mi ni itta. Yukata o kita hito ga takusan ita. Onna no hito no yukata wa iro ga hanayaka da. Otoko no hito no yukata wa iro wa jimi dakedo, nakanaka kakkoii. Kodomo no yukata mo totemo kawaii.

Yatai ga takusan narande ita. Ringoame, watagashi, poppukoon, yakitoomorokoshi, ikayaki, takoyaki, kingyosukui, yooyoo nado, ippai atte nigiyaka da. Satomi to watashi wa takoyaki o katta. Takoyaki wa chiisai marui tabemono de, komugiko de tsukurarete iru. Naka ni tako ga haitte ite, oishii. Amerikajin wa amari tako o tabenai ga, nihonjin wa yoku tako o tabete iru yoo da.

Bon'odori ga hajimatta. Kooen no mannaka ni suteeji ga atte, sono ue de otoko no hito ga ooki na taiko o tataki, supiikaa kara Nihon no min'yoo ga nagarete kita. Hitobito ga dai no mawari ni atsumari, wa ni natte odorihajimeta. Satomi ga "Issho ni odorimashoo" to itta. Watashi wa odorikata ga wakaranai to itta ga, Satomi wa "Watashi mo yoku wakaranai kedo, daijoobu. Hoka no hito no mane o suru kara. Onaji odori o nankai mo kurikaesu dake dakara, dare demo odoreru no" to itte, watashi no te o hippatte, odori no wa no naka e tsurete itta. Saisho wa odorikata ga yoku wakaranakatta keredo, jojo ni wakatte kite tanoshikatta. Bon'odori o mite iru to Amerika no fookudansu o omoidashimasu.

Natsumatsuri de, tabetari, nondari, odottari, iroiro na hito to hanashitari shita. Hontoo ni tanoshikatta. Yukata mo ki ni itta. Watashi wa Nihon no natsu matsuri ga daisuki ni natta.

Satomi let me borrow her *yukata*. It was pretty with a pattern of blue and red flowers. *Yukata* are made of cotton, so they are cool. Satomi's mother taught me how to wear a *yukata*. The *obi* was a little difficult to tie, so I practiced it again and again. Satomi's family saw me in the *yukata* and said, "You look good in it." Satomi wore a *yukata* with a yellow and green butterfly pattern.

In the evening, Satomi and I went to a nearby park to see the summer festival. There were many people wearing *yukata*. The colors of the women's *yukata* were brilliant. The men's *yukata* were not as colorful, but they were still nice. The children's *yukata* were really cute.

There were many *yatai* stands lined up. There were candy apples, cotton candy, popcorn, grilled corn, *ikayaki*, *takoyaki*, goldfish catching, yo-yos, and many other things. All of the stands were crowded with people. Satomi and I bought *takoyaki*. *Takoyaki* is a small, round food made from flour with sliced octopus in it. It's very tasty. Americans don't eat octopus a lot, but Japanese people do.

The *bon'odori* began. There was a stage in the middle of the park. The men on the stage began to play the Japanese drums, and Japanese folk music came out of the speakers. People came up to the stage, formed a circle, and started dancing. Satomi said, "Let's dance together." I said that I didn't know how to do the dance. Then Satomi said, "I don't really know it either, so it's OK. We'll just imitate the others. Anyone can do the dance because the same steps and movements are repeated again and again." She took my hand, and we joined everyone dancing in the circle. At first I didn't really know how to do the dance, but I gradually got the hang of it and began to have fun. It reminded me of an American folk dance.

At the summer festival I ate, drank, danced, and talked to many people. I had a really good time. I also liked wearing the *yukata*. I came to really like Japanese summer festivals.

Questions:
Write O if the sentence is true, and write X if it is false.
1. (　) *Onna no hito wa yukata o kiru ga, otoko no hito wa kinai.*
   (Women wear *yukata*, but men don't.)
2. (　) *Yukata wa momen da.* (*Yukata* are made of cotton.)
3. (　) *Yatai wa chiisai mise da.* (A *yatai* is a small shop.)
4. (　) *Nihonjin wa takoyaki ga suki da.* (Japanese people like *takoyaki*.)
5. (　) *Bon'odori wa muzukashii.* (*Bon'odori* is difficult.)
6. (　) *Bon'odori wa minna ga chigau sutairu no odori o odoru.*
   (Everyone has a different style of dancing *bon'odori*.)
7. (　) *Arisu wa bon'odori ga suki ni natta.* (Alice became fond of *bon'odori*.)
Time spent: (　) minutes

13 Summary practice

In small groups: After reading the passage in APE 12, discuss the following questions. A representative from each group makes a presentation to the class.
1. *Yukata wa nani de tsukurarete imasu ka?* (What are *yukata* made of?)
2. *Doko de natsumatsuri ga arimashita ka?* (Where was the summer festival held?)
3. *Onna no hito to otoko no hito no yukata wa doko ga chigaimasu ka?*
   (What is the difference between women's and men's *yukata*.)
4. *Bon'odori wa donna odori desu ka?* (What kind of dance is *bon'odori*?)
5. *Nihon no natsumatsuri no tokushoku o iinasai.*
   (What are the characteristics of a Japanese summer festival?)

14 Demonstration

In groups:
① Demonstrate how to wear a *yukata*.
② Demonstrate how to do *bon'odori* with the appropriate music.
You may ask for help from Japanese students in your school or Japanese people living in your town. You may also use videotapes and pictures.

2. Actualization

1 Practice the following conversation and develop your own dialogue on a similar subject with your partners.

4 nen 2 kumi no seito wa, shuto toshite no Tookyoo no yakuwari o manande imasu.
(The 4th grade, class 2 students are learning about the role of Tokyo as the capital city.)

Nakamura sensei:	*Tookyoo wa Nihon no shuto desu ne. Tookyoo ni wa donna mono ga arimasu ka?*
	(As you know, Tokyo is the capital of Japan. What is in Tokyo?)
Suzuki kun:	*Kuni no kaku shoochoo ga arimasu.* (Government offices.)
Nakamura kun:	*Saikoosaibansho.* (The Supreme Court.)
Hirota san:	*Iroiro na kuni no taishikan mo aru wa.* (The embassies of many countries, too.)
Nakamura sensei:	*Hoka ni wa?* (What else?)
Yamada san:	*Daigaku ga takusan arimasu.* (There are many universities.)
Kobayashi kun:	*Bijutsukan ya hakubutsukan mo aru yo.* (Art museums and other museums.)
Nakamura sensei:	*Dewa, Tookyoo wa donna mondai o kakaete imasu ka?*
	(Well, what kind of problems does Tokyo have?)
Yoshida kun:	*Hito ga oosugite, juutaku ga tarimasen.*
	(There are so many people that there is a shortage of housing.)
Takagi kun:	*Kootsuujuutai ga hidoi desu.* (Traffic jams are very heavy.)

2 Practice the following conversation and develop your own dialogue on a similar subject with your partners.

Getsuyoobi no 2jikanme, shakaika no jugyoo desu. 4 nen 3 kumi no seito wa Nihon no chiri no benkyoo o shite imasu.
(Second period on Monday is social studies. The 4th grade, class 3 students are studying the geography of Japan.)

Suzuki sensei:	*Nihon no ichiban kita ni aru todoofuken wa nani desu ka?*
	(What is Japan's northernmost prefecture?)
Hirota san:	*Hokkaidoo desu.* (Hokkaido.)
Suzuki sensei:	*Kikoo wa doo desu ka?* (How is the climate there?)
Hirota san:	*Fuyu wa totemo samuku, yuki ga takusan furimasu.*
	(Winter is very cold, and it snows a lot.)
Suzuki sensei:	*Dewa, ichiban minami ni aru ken wa?*
	(Then what is the southernmost prefecture?)
Kobayashi kun:	*Okinawa desu.* (Okinawa.)
Suzuki sensei:	*Samui desu ka?* (Is it cold?)
Kobayashi kun:	*Ie, ichinenjuu atatakaku, yuki wa mattaku furimasen.*
	(No, it's warm all year round, and it never snows there.)

3 Social and international problems

① In pairs: First the teacher asks the students to give some examples of social or international problems. Then students ask their partner which problem concerns him/her the most. Use the expression *ki ni naru*.

Examples of social and international problems:

hanzai no zooka (the increase of crime), *gakkoo de no ijime* (bullyings at school), *shitsugyoo* (unemployment), *hoomuress* (homeless), *chiiki funsoo* (regional conflicts), *nanmin* (boat people), *tero* (terrorism), *kankyoo osen* (environmental pollution)

Example: A: *B san, dono mondai ga ichiban ki ni narimasu ka?*
(B, what problem concerns you the most?)
B: *Gakkoo de no ijime no mondai desu. A san wa?*
(I'm most concerned with bullyings at school. How about you?)
A: *Watashi wa hoomuresu no mondai ga ki ni narimasu.*
(I'm most concerned with the homeless.)

② In groups: Discuss a specific problem with which everyone in the group is concerned. Talk about the problem and how you can help solve it. The group representative reports their discussion to the class.

Example: Homeless
A: *Hoomuresu ni tsuite, donna mondai ga arimasu ka?*
(What kind problems are there with the homeless?)
B: *Hoomuresu no hitotachi wa ie ga nai node, kooen ya michi de nete imasu.*
(Homeless people don't have homes, so they sleep on the streets and in parks.)
C: *Fuyu taihen samui toki wa shinu hito mo imasu.* (Some die from the cold in winter.)
D: *Byooki ni naru hito mo ooi soo desu.* (I hear that many become ill, too.)
B: *Dooshitara ii deshoo ka?* (What can we do?)
A: *Hoomuresu no hitotachi ni shigoto no chansu o ageru koto ga daiji desu.*
(It's important to give them a chance to work.)
C: *Byooki no hito o chiryoo shite agenakya naranai to omoimasu.*
(I think that we should take care of sick, homeless people.)

3. Enrichment

1 *Kanji* for Lesson 7

遅い	窓	外	見る	女
人	多い	屋台	沢山	金魚
持つ	忘れる	近い	屋	使い捨て
取る				

2 *Kanji* for Lesson 8

京都	絶対	奈良	大仏	世界
一番	大きい	仏様	位	自由
女神	小さい	出来る	世紀	確
古い	他			

3 Other useful *kanji*

田、川、石、橋、海、泳、入、出、焼、回、少、毎、運、男

4 Strategies

Shape and sequencing of *kanji*:

Generally speaking, the original shapes of *kanji,* as written in Chinese, have experienced many changes and have gradually been transformed into the current shapes. The official style printed in newspapers, magazines, and official documents is called *kaisho*. Following are some rules.

(1) Each *kanji* occupies one square.

(2) Most *kanji* are made with straight horizontal and vertical lines.

(3) Diagonal lines are an exception.

(4) Circles are written as squares.

(5) Curved lines have become straight lines.

(6) When a *kanji* is composed of two components that are aligned vertically, as in 曇, each component is written with horizontal expansion. Therefore, 日 looks like 日. However, when two components are placed horizontally, as in 明, the components are written with vertical extension. 日 becomes 日.

(7) In general, both stroke order and *kanji* component sequencing are written from left to right and top to bottom; however, there are many more detailed rules and exceptions.

5 Exercise

Try to figure out the number of strokes of the *kanji* in **1** *Kanji* for Lesson 7 and indicate whether left to right and top to bottom rules are applicable to them.

Lesson 10: Calling home

I. PERSPECTIVE

1. Objectives

1 Function:

(1) Asking someone to speak in a certain language: *(Nihongo) de hanashite goran.*
(2) Describing an action that is happening presently: *Ima (ame ga fut)te imasu.*
(3) Expressing that two things are opposites: *(Hiru) to (yoru) ga abekobe da ne.*
(4) Indicating time differences:
    Ima (Koobe) wa (yoru 11)ji desu ga, (San Franshisuko) wa (asa 6)ji desu.

2 Language:

(1) *(Nihongo) de (hanashi)te goran.*   (2) *(Boku) wa ima (Tookyoo) ni (i)masu.*
(3) *(Tookyoo) wa (i)i (tokoro) daroo.*   (4) *Ima (ame) ga (fut)te imasu.*
(5) *(Hiru) to (yoru) ga abekobe da ne.*   (6) *Ima ... desu ga, ... wa (6ji) desu.*

3 Culture:

(1) Telephone conversation expressions
(2) Tokyo
(3) Japan's climate

II. PREPARATION

1. Context

旅先からの電話

日本旅行も今日で５日が過ぎた。日本の生活環境にすっかり慣れたが、まだ両親に連絡していない。心配しているだろう。時差を計算して、電話を掛ける。時差は１４時間。今が夜の９時だから、アメリカの自分の家は同じ日の午前７時。日曜日だから、両親は家にいるはず。コレクトコールで電話する。

Five days of Peter's trip to Japan have passed. He has gotten used to the surrounding environment, but he hasn't called his parents yet. They are probably worried about him. He calculates the time difference and calls them. The time change is fourteen hours. It's now nine at night in Japan, so it's 7 a.m. the same day at his house in America. It's Sunday, so his parents should be home. He calls collect.

2. Sample Conversation

P: もしもし、おとうさん。
V: Excuse me. Who is this?
P: おとうさん、ピーターです。
V: ピーター、今どこなんだ。
P: I'm in Tokyo.
V: 日本語で話してごらん。
P: 僕は今東京にいます。

V: 東京はいい所だろう。
P: はい。大都会です。今雨が降っていますが、アメリカは。
V: 天気予報は晴れ。今は午前7時だ。東京は夜だね。
P: はい。今午後9時です。
V: 昼と夜があべこべだね。

P: *Moshi moshi[1], otoosan.*
V: Excuse me. Who is this?
P: *Otoosan, Piitaa desu.*
V: *Piitaa, ima doko na n da[2]?*
P: I'm in Tokyo.
V: *Nihongo de hanashite goran[3].*

P: *Boku wa ima Tookyoo[4] ni imasu.*
V: *Tookyoo wa ii tokoro daroo[5].*
P: *Hai, daitokai desu. Ima ame[6] ga futte imasu ga Amerika wa?*
V: *Tenkiyohoo wa hare. Ima wa gozen shichiji da. Tookyoo wa yoru da ne.*
P: *Hai. Ima gogo kuji desu.*
V: *Hiru to yoru ga abekobe da ne.*

P: Hello? Dad?
V: Excuse me. Who is this?
P: Dad, it's Peter.
V: Peter, where are you now?
P: I'm in Tokyo.
V: Try and speak Japanese./Go ahead and speak Japanese.
P: I'm in Tokyo now.
V: Is Tokyo a nice place?
P: Yes. It's a big city. It's raining now. How is it in America?
V: The weather forecast is clear. Now it's 7 a.m. It's nighttime in Tokyo, right?
P: Yes. It's 9 p.m.
V: Day and night are reversed, right?

P: ピーター スミス   *Piitaa Sumisu*   Peter Smith
V: ビクター スミス（お父さん） *Bikutaa Sumisu (otoosan)* Victor Smith (father)

3. Language & Culture Notes

1 There are a few expressions that people commonly use while speaking on the telephone. When the phone rings, one picks it up and says "*Moshi moshi,*" which is equivalent to "Hello?" To ask a person to wait a moment, one says "*Chotto matte kudasai,*" or the more polite "*Shooshoo omachi kudasai.*" In handing the telephone receiver over to a third person, one may say, "*Kawarimasu.*" It literally means "to change," but there really isn't an English equivalent for this expression. When hanging up, people typically say "*Sayoonara*" or "*Ja, mata ne,*" which mean "Good-bye" and "Well, later," respectively.

2 *Doko na n da?* is roughly equivalent to "So, where are you?" It is common for the expression *n desu* to follow an interrogative word such as *doko* or *dooshite*. It indicates an attempt to prompt a response and/or an explanation from the listener.

Doko na n desu ka? (So, where are you?)
(Indicates that the speaker not only wants to know the location, but also wants to hear about it.)
Dooshite kinoo no shiken ni shippai shita n desu ka? (Why did you fail yesterday's test?)
(The speaker wants to hear an explanation.)

3 *Hanashite goran* means "try and speak" or "go ahead and speak." *Goran* is an expression that comes after a verb and asks someone to do something. It is often used with *nasai*, the imperative form of *nasaru*, a more polite, informal equivalent of *suru*. Since it is an imperative form, *hanashite gorannasai* is more polite than *hanashite goran*; however, neither is as polite as *hanashite kudasai* or *hanashite mite kudasai*.

4 One of the largest cities in the world, Tokyo is the political, industrial, and commercial capital of Japan and one of the world's greatest business centers. It is also a fascinating blend of the traditional and modern: sleek, futuristic skyscrapers can be found right alongside traditional Japanese structures. Tokyo began as a small fishing village but gradually became a major metropolitan center when the government was moved there in the late 17th century. Since that time, the city has been through devastating fires, numerous earthquakes, and the bombings of World War II; however, the city has always managed to rebuild itself and flourish.

In the center of Tokyo is the Imperial Palace, the home of the emperor. The beautiful palace grounds and traditional gardens are open to visitors several times a year. Near the palace grounds are many government buildings, including the Diet building and the offices of various government ministries, such as education, finance, health, and justice. Ginza is an area of Tokyo that is close to the Imperial Palace. It is Tokyo's classy shopping district which includes famous department stores, such as Takashimaya and Mitsukoshi, founded in 1673. Two other districts of Tokyo, Shinjuku and Roppongi, are a myriad of nightclubs, discos, and trendy shops and restaurants that attract both young people who want excitement and businessmen who want to relax after a long workday. Other noteworthy areas of Tokyo include the Asakusa entertainment district, full of traditional and modern theaters, and Ueno Park, known for its art museums, ponds, and a large, well-inhabited zoo. No tour of Tokyo would be complete without a stop at Tokyo Disneyland, which is as impressive and popular as its California counterpart.

5 *Daroo,* in *Ii tokoro daroo,* is an informal *oo* form of *da*. *Da* is the informal non-past tense of *desu*.

6 The climate in Japan's four main islands varies only slightly. Winters are cold throughout most of Japan, and it is always coldest in Hokkaido. Summers are hot, and naturally, it is always hottest in Kyushu. Spring and autumn are mild throughout the country. The Okinawa islands are warm all year round and very hot in the summer. The annual rainy season, *tsuyu,* usually starts between mid and late May in the South and works its way up and across the archipelago, lasting until mid to late July. In other words, *tsuyu* starts and ends earlier in Kyushu than it does in northern Honshu. Hokkaido does not have a rainy season.

III. PARTICIPATION

1. Vocabulary

1 From sample conversation:

abekobe (reversed, opposite)
daitokai (big city, metropolis)
gogo (p.m.)
hanashite (speak)
hiru (afternoon, daytime)
shichiji (7 o'clock)
tokoro (place)
ame (rain)
futte imasu (is raining)
gozen (a.m.)
hare (clear, fine [weather])
kuji (9 o'clock)
tenkiyohoo (weather forecast)
yoru (night, nighttime)

2 Useful for activities:

bunka (culture)
ha o migaku (to brush one's teeth)
kion (temperature)
saitei (lowest, low)
do (degree [temperature])
kaisan shokuhin (seafood)
saikoo (highest, high)
yasuku (cheaply)

2. Activity, Practice, & Exercise

1 Team competition: Gesture game

In two groups: The teacher gives each student card with an action written on it. The action should be written using the target phrase --- *o -te imasu*. The students line up side by side in two horizontal lines so that the two teams are facing each other. The first student in the Team B line steps forward and faces his/her teammates with his/her back to Team A. The first student in the Team A line shows the Team B student the action written on his/her card. The Team B student must then do a gesture for his/her own teammates to convey the action written on the card. The Team A student who showed the Team B student the card will ask Team B what the Team B student is doing. The Team B members must guess the gesture using the target expression. From the time when student B begins to do the gesture, his/her teammates have about 30 to 45 seconds to correctly guess it. Next, the Team A and B students switch roles. Then the next student in each team's line does the same thing. Teams get one point for each correct guess. Follow the example.

Example: A: (Shows B a card and asks Team B) *B san wa nani o shite imasu ka?*
(What is B doing?)

    B: (does a gesture)
    Team B: *B san wa ha o migaite imasu.* (B is brushing his/her teeth.)

2 Where is your aunt?

In pairs: Ask one of your classmates where his/her relatives are.

Example: A: *Obasan wa doko ni imasu ka.* (Where is your aunt?)
    B: *Furorida ni imasu.* (She's in Florida.)

3 Answering machine message

Individually: You are traveling in Japan and tried to call your Japanese friend back in the States. Your friend was not home, so you got his/her answering machine. Leave a message that includes a greeting, the time of your call, where you are, what the weather is like, and some comments about Japan.

4 What would you suggest ... ?

In pairs: Complete the following in Japanese.
What would you suggest when your friend ...
(1) is looking for the English meaning of a Japanese word that he/she does not understand.
(2) is looking for a book about Japanese culture in order to write a paper.
(3) wants to try some Japanese seafood.
(4) wants to travel in the United States very cheaply.

Example: Your friend is talking with a Japanese person in English, but the Japanese person does not understand.
Nihongo de hanashite goran. (Try speaking in Japanese.)

5 Weather report

In pairs: You are a weather reporter. Report the national weather according to a weather map.
Example: *Nyuu Yooku wa hare, saikoo kion wa 55 do desu. Saitei kion wa 40 do desu.*
(New York is clear with a high temperature of 55 degrees and a low temperature of 40 degrees.)

6 What time is it in ... ?

In pairs: You are an international telephone operator. Your customers want to know the time in various world cities. Answer each question according to the following international time zone chart.
(1) *Ima Nihon wa gogo rokuji desu ga, Bosuton wa nanji desu ka?*
(2) *Ima Furansu wa gozen juuji han desu ga, Tookyoo wa nanji desu ka?*
(3) *Ima Rondon wa gogo ichiji desu ga, Honoruru wa nanji desu ka?*
(4) *Nihon to Hawai wa hiru to yoru ga abekobe desu ka?*

7 What would you say ... ?

In pairs: What would you say in an informal style when ...
(1) you ask your friend where he/she is?
(2) you ask someone if Tokyo is a nice place?
(3) you want to state that day and night are reversed?

Lesson 11: A farewell dinner

I. PERSPECTIVE

1. Objectives

1 Function:

(1) Guessing the reason(s) why something happened: *(Tabe)ta node, (futot)ta kamo shiremasen.*
(2) Stating the only thing that could not be done:
   Hitotsu dake (tabe)rarenai mono ga arimashita yo.
(3) Asking why: *Dooshite?*
(4) Expressing reasons: *(Kyoo ga saigo) dakara.*
(5) Confirming information: *(Kono kamera, jidoo shattaa) deshita ne.*

2 Language:

(1) *Moo (Piitaa) ga (kae)ru n desu ne.*   (2) *(Nihonryoori) wa doo deshita ka?*
(3) *(Takusantabe)ta node, (futot)ta kamo shiremasen.*
(4) *(Hitotsu dake tabe)rarenai (mono) ga arimashita yo.*   (5) *(Kyoo) ga (saigo) dakara...*

3 Culture:

(1) Popular Japanese food   (2) Not so popular Japanese food

II. PREPARATION

1. Context

別れの夕食

日本国内旅行が終わって、ピーターはあきらの家へ戻った。この旅行もそろそろ終りに近づいた。あきらの家族とも別れなければならない。あきらの家族は両親におばあさん、そして兄の5人だ。おばあさんはテレビを見るのが大好きだ。よくテレビを見ていた。ピーターは自分のおばあさんのことを思い出した。兄は大学生で、あまり家にいなかった。アルバイトで忙しいらしい。家族と今日は最後の夕食。すき焼きパーティーだ。

Peter went back to Akira's house after traveling around Japan. His trip will soon come to an end. He has to say good-bye to Akira's family. There are five people in Akira's family: his parents, his grandmother, his older brother, and himself. His grandmother loves watching TV and watches it often. She reminded Peter of his own grandmother. Akira's brother is a college student, so he wasn't home a lot. He seems to be busy with his part-time job. Today is Peter's last dinner with the family, so they're having a *sukiyaki* party.

2. Sample Conversation

MF: もうピーターが帰るんですね。
MS: そう言えば、ピーターは好き嫌いがなかったね。
MC: 日本料理はどうでしたか。
P: はい、大好きです。たくさん食べたので、太ったかもしれません。
MA: 一つだけ食べられない物がありましたよ。
MI: 僕、それ覚えていますよ。
MF: 何ですか。
P: するめです。
MS: どうして。
P: あの臭いが。
MC: だめな物もあるんだねえ。
MI: 記念写真をとりませんか。今日が最後だから・・・。
MA: このカメラ、自動シャッターでしたね。

MF: *Moo Piitaa ga kaeru n desu ne.*
MS: *Soo ieba[1], Piitaa wa sukikirai ga nakatta ne.*
MC: *Nihonryoori[2] wa doo deshita ka?*
P: *Hai, daisuki desu. Takusan tabeta node, futotta kamo shiremasen.*
MA: *Hitotsu dake taberarenai mono ga arimashita yo.*
MI: *Boku, sore oboete imasu yo.*
MF: *Nan desu ka?*
P: *Surume[3] desu.*
MS: *Dooshite?*
P: *Ano nioi ga.*
MC: *Dame na mono mo[4] aru n da nee.*
MI: *Kinenshashin o torimasen ka? Kyoo ga saigo dakara ...*
MA: *Kono kamera, jidoo shattaa deshita ne.*

MF: Peter's going home soon, isn't he?
MS: That reminds me, Peter isn't very particular.
MC: How was Japanese food?
P: I liked it very much. I ate so much I probably gained weight.
MA: There is one thing you don't eat.
MI: I remember what it is.
MF: What is it?
P: Dried cuttlefish.
MS: How come?
P: I don't like the smell.
MC: So there is something you don't like.
MI: Since today is his last day, why don't we take a picture?
MA: This camera has an automatic shutter, right?

MS:	もり　しろう（お父さん）	*Mori Shiroo (otoosan)*	Shiro Mori (father)
MF:	もり　ふみこ（お母さん）	*Mori Fumiko (okaasan)*	Fumiko Mori (mother)
MC:	もり　ちよ（おばあさん）	*Mori Chiyo (obaasan)*	Chiyo Mori (grandmother)
P:	ピーター　スミス	*Piitaa Sumisu*	Peter Smith
MA:	もり　あきら	*Mori Akira*	Akira Mori
MI:	もり　いわお（お兄さん）	*Mori Iwao (oniisan)*	Iwao Mori (brother)

3. Language & Culture Notes

1 *Soo ieba*, a discourse function word, means "when reminded" or "when you talk about that."

2 *Sushi* and *sashimi* are probably the two most common types of Japanese food known to foreigners because they are so popular among Japanese people. Other popular and well liked meals are *yakitori*, *sukiyaki*, and *okonomiyaki*. *Yakitori* is bite-sized pieces of sauteed chicken on a stick. *Sukiyaki* is meat and vegetables boiled in a flavored broth, and *okonomiyaki* resembles a pancake. Any combination of shrimp, squid, pork or beef along with some vegetables are combined into a batter and cooked on a grill until it fluffs up like a giant pancake. Many foreigners enjoy these foods as much as Japanese people do.

3 Not all Japanese food is as tasty as *sushi* and *yakitori*. Dishes such as *surume*, *nattoo*, *tsukemono*, and *umeboshi* are known to make many cringe in disgust; however, there are many who do like these interesting items. *Nattoo* is fermented soy beans, which create a sticky, awful smelling meal. *Tsukemono* are pickled radishes, cucumbers, or other vegetables in vinegar. *Umeboshi* are small, very sour plums.

4 *mo*, a function marker, means "even" here.

III. PARTICIPATION

1. Vocabulary

1 **From sample conversation:**

daisuki (like very much)
ieba (be said)
kaeru (to go home)
mono (thing)
nioi (smell, scent)
oniisan (elder brother)
sukikirai (particular, picky)

futotta (gained weight)
jidoo (automatic)
kinenshashin (a souvenir photo)
nihonryoori (Japanese food)
oboete imasu (remember)
saigo (last)
taberarenai (cannot eat)

2 **Useful for activities:**

atari (right, correct)
daitai (about)
densha (train)
hairu (to enter)
hazure (wrong)
iya (unpleasant, disgusting)
kuraku naru (to become dark)
manga (comic book)
moo (already)
sentaku (laundry)
tokehajimeru (to start melting)
yuki (snow)

byooki (sick)
dekakenakereba narimasen (has/have to go out)
dooshite (why)
haku (to wear)
iro (color)
jiinzu (jeans)
kyooshi (teacher)
misoshiru (miso soup)
puro futtobooru (professional football)
shigoto (work, job)
tsuchi (soil)

2. Activity, Practice, & Exercise

1 Sentence completion

In pairs: write a second sentence that gives a reason for the first one.

Example: *Moo kaerimasu. Densha ga kuru jikan desu kara.*
            Moo haru desu ne. Yuki ga tokehajimemashita kara.

1. *Moo dekakenakereba narimasen.* (I have to leave now.) _____ *kara.*
2. [To a child] *Moo ie no naka ni hairinasai.* _____ *kara.*
   (It's time for you to come inside [the house].)
3. *Moo shigoto o hajimemashoo.* (Let's start the work.) _____ *kara.*
4. *Moo natsu desu ne.* (It is already summer.) _____ *kara.*

2 What kind of food ... ?

In pairs: Ask three or four classmates what kinds of food they dislike and why. Keep track of the responses in the task sheet below.

Example: A: *Tabemono no sukikirai ga arimasu ka?*
          (Are there any kinds of food that you particularly dislike?)
       B: *Daitai daijoobu desu ga, misoshiru wa dame desu.*
          (I'm OK with almost everything, but I don't like miso soup.)
       A: *Dooshite desu ka?* (Why not?)
       B: *Misoshiru wa iro ga iya nan desu yo. Tsuchi mitai de.*
          (I don't like the color. It's like soil.)

Example task sheet:

Namae	Aru/Nai	Kirai na mono	Kirai na riyuu
Samu	nai		
Debora	aru	misoshiru	Iro ga tsuchi mitai.

3 Classmate quiz

Individually: Each student gives a quiz to the class about what was learned in APE 2. Follow the example.

Example: A: *Debora san wa hitotsu dake taberarenai mono ga arimasu. Sore wa nan desu ka? Wakatta hito, te o agete kudasai.*
          (There's one kind of food that Deborah doesn't eat. What is it? Raise your hand if you know what it is.)
       B: *Supagettii.* (Spaghetti.)
       A: *Hazure. Hoka ni dare ka?* (Wrong. Anyone else?)
       B: *Misoshiru.* (Miso soup.)
       A: *Atari.* (You guessed it.)

4 What do you know about your classmates?

In pairs: Check to see if you know correct information about your partner's possessions or family. Pair up with at least three different classmates.

Example: A: *B san no kamera, Nihon no kamera <u>deshita ne</u>.* (You have a Japanese camera, right?)

B: *Ee. Soo desu yo.* (Yes, I do.)

A: *B san no otoosan, kookoo no sensei <u>deshita ne</u>.*
(Your father is a high school teacher, isn't he?)

B: *Iie, chigaimasu yo. Shoogakkoo no kyooshi desu.*
(No, he isn't. He's an elementary school teacher.)

5 Why do you ... ?

In pairs: Partners ask each other why they do or like something specific. Ask at least three different people.

Example: 1) A: *B san wa itsumo jiinzu o haite imasu <u>ne</u>. <u>Dooshite desu ka</u>?*
(B, you always wear jeans. Why?)

B: *Jiinzu wa kakkoii shi, sentaku mo kantan dakara desu.*
(Because jeans look cool and are easy to wash.)

2) B: *A san wa yoku manga o yomimasu <u>ne</u>. <u>Dooshite desu ka</u>?*
(A, you often read comic books. Why?)

A: *Omoshiroi kara desu.* (Because they're interesting.)

6 Topic talk

In pairs: Talk about the following topics with each other. Use the expression --- *kamo shiremasen*. Do not change partners.

Example: *Kyoo no gogo no tenki* (Today's afternoon weather)

A: *Sora ga kuraku narimashita ne.* (The sky has become dark.)

B: *Soo desu ne. Ame ga furu <u>kamo shiremasen ne</u>.* (It has. It may rain.)

1. *Asu no tenki* (Tomorrow's weather)
2. *Kotoshi no puro futtobooru* (This year's football season)
3. *Kondo no tesuto* (The next test)

7 Matching situations and reasons

In four groups: Groups A and B each make five situations, and groups C and D each make five reasons. The reasons should use the form --- *dakara*. Then Group A joins with Group C, and Group B joins with Group D to see how many matches can be made among the situations and reasons. After about five minutes, groups A and D and groups B and C join to look for more matches. The groups get one point for each match. The group with the most points (or matches) wins.

Example: Group A: (1) *Kyoo wa gakkoo e ikanai.* (2) *Ie de asobimasu.*
Group B: (1) *Kooen de yakyuu o shimasu.* (2) *Shukudai o shimasu.*
Group C: (1) *Kyoo wa doyoobi dakara.* (2) *Ii tenki dakara.*
Group D: (1) *Ame dakara.* (2) *Watashi wa byooki dakara.*

A(1) matches with C(1) and D(2); A(2) matches with C(1) and D(1) ... **Group A=4 points**
B(1) matches with C(1) and C(2); B(2) has no matches ... **Group B=2 points**
C(1) matches with A(1), B(1) and A(2); C(2) matches with B(1) ... **Group C=4 points**
D(1) matches with A(2); D(2) matches with A(1) ... **Group D=2 points**

8 Substitution

In pairs: Change the underlined word and answer the question. Make at least four new questions and answers.

Q: *Nihon wa doo deshita ka?*
A: *Takusan tomodachi ni aimashita.*

Lesson 12 — Review & Application

IV. PERFORMANCE

1. Application

1 Conversation completion

In small groups: The following is a conversation between an American student (A) who is making a trip to Shinshu and his Japanese friend (J). Guess what the American student would say in the conversation. Choose the most appropriate sentence from below.

A: (   ) (Hello. Kenji?)
J: *Aa, Maiku ka. Genki?* (Oh, Mike. How are you?)
A: (   ) (I'm just fine. Shinshu is a nice place.)
J: *Soo. Ima doko ni iru no?* (Is it? Where are you now?)
A: (   ) (Kurohime Heights.)
J: *Sotchi wa yama no naka dakara suzushii daroo.* (You're in the mountains, so it must be cool.)
A: (   ) (Yeah. It gets hot around noon, but mornings and nights are cool and comfortable.)
J: *Kyoo wa nani o shita no?* (What did you do today?)
A: (   ) (Oh, we cycled around a lake and went boating. We went with a group of university students we got to know at the inn.)
J: *Hee, yokatta ne.* (Good for you.)
A: (   ) (Tomorrow we're going to climb a mountain with the group.)
J: *Jaa, asa hayai n daroo? Hayaku neta hoo ga ii yo.*
   (Well, you'll have to get up early in the morning, won't you? You should go to bed early.)
A: (   ) (I will. I have to go.)
J: *Un. Jaa, tanoshinde koi yo. Oyasumi.* (OK. Have a good time. Good night.)
A: *Oyasumi.* (Good night.)

   1. *Un. Hiru wa atsuku naru kedo, asa to yoru wa suzushikute, kimochi ga ii yo.*
   2. *Asu wa sono daigakusei guruupu to tozan suru yotei nan da.*
   3. *Mizuumi no mawari o saikuringu shitari, booto ni nottari shita n da.*
      Penshon de shiri atta daigakusei no guruupu to issho ni.
   4. *Moshi moshi. Kenji?*
   5. *Un, soo suru yo. Ja, kore de denwa kiru yo.*
   6. *Un, totemo genki da yo. Shinshuu wa ii tokoro da ne.*
   7. *Kurohimekoogen.*

2 Conversation completion

In small groups: The following is a conversation between an American high school student (A) who is staying in Japan and his host mother (M). Guess what they would say in the underlined parts in the conversation. After completing it, each group presents their conversation to the class.

M: *Maiku san, moo sugu kikoku ne.* (Mike, you're going back home soon, aren't you?)

A: *Hai. 2 shuukan wa totemo mijikakatta desu.* (Yes. Two weeks was so short.)

M: *Soo ne. Tokorode, Maiku san wa nan demo yoku tabete kureta wa ne.*
(It was. By the way, you ate rather well.)

A: *Boku wa _____ . Nihon ni iru aida, chotto futotta kamo shiremasen.*
(I _____ . I may have gained weight during my stay in Japan.)

M: *Ara, soo? Demo, nihonshoku ga ki ni itte moraete ureshii wa.*
(Really? Anyway, I am glad you liked Japanese food.)

A: *Demo, hitotsu _____ .* (But there's one _____ .)

M: *Sore, nattoo deshoo.* (It's *nattoo*, right?)

A: *Hai. Nioi ga _____ .* (Yes. Its smell _____ .)

M: *Nihonjin demo nattoo ga kirai na hito ga iru kara, ki ni shinakute mo ii no yo. Nihonshoku no naka de _____ ?*
(Even some Japanese don't like it, so don't worry about it._____ Japanese food _____?)

A: *Chirashizushi desu. _____ ?* (Chirashizushi. _____ ?)

M: *Iie, kantan ni tsukuru koto ga dekiru wa. Tsukurikata o eigo de kakimashoo ka?*
(No, it's easy to make. Shall I write down the recipe in English?)

A: *Hai, onegai shimasu.* (Yes, please.)

3 **About how long is summer vacation?**

① In pairs: Take turns asking and answering questions about the length of school's summer, winter, and spring vacations and examination periods.

Example: A: *B san, gakkoo no natsuyasumi wa dore kurai desu ka?*
(B, about how long is school's summer vacation?)

B: *Nikagetsu han gurai desu. Gakkoo no fuyuyasumi wa dore kurai deshita ka?*
(About two and a half months. About how long was school's winter vacation?)

A: *Nishuukan gurai deshita. Gakkoo no haruyasumi wa dore kurai deshita ka ne?*
(About two weeks. About how long was school's spring vacation?)

B: *1 shuukan gurai deshita. Gakkoo no shikenkikan wa dore kurai deshita ka?*
(About a week. About how long was the examination period?)

A: *Mikka(kan) kurai deshita ne.* (About three days.)

② In pairs: Make a conversation about a specific activity and how long it was done.

Examples of activities: trips, camp, boy/girl scouts, studying for exams, school clubs

Example: A: *Nagai ryokoo o shita koto ga arimasu ka?* (Have you ever taken a long trip?)

B: *Hai. Sannen mae, kazoku to Mekishiko ni ikimashita. Ikkagetsu ryokoo shimashita. A san wa?*
(Yes. I went to Mexico with my family three years ago. We went for a month. How about you?)

A: *Watashi wa kyonen Arasuka e ikimashita. Sanshuukan imashita.*
(I went to Alaska last year. I stayed there for three weeks.)

B: *A san wa yakyuu chiimu ni haitte imashita ne. Dore kurai yatte imasu ka?*
(You belong to a baseball team, don't you? How long have you been playing?)

A: *Shoogakkoo no toki kara yatte imasu kara, <u>gonen gurai desu</u>. B san wa supootsu o yatte imasu ka?*
(I've played since I was in elementary school. It's been about five years. Do you play any sports?)

B: *Hai. Tenisu kurabu ni haitte imasu. <u>Sannen gurai desu</u>.*
(Yes. I belong to the tennis club. I've played for about three years.)

4 Have you already ... ?

① In groups of four: Each group makes seven or eight questions asking if something has already been finished or done.

Example:
- *Orinpikku wa <u>moo owarimashita ka</u>?* (Have the Olympics already ended?)
- *Yasuko san no tanjoo paatii wa <u>moo owarimashita ka</u>?*
  (Is Yasuko san's birthday party already over?)
- *Takao kun wa <u>moo benkyoo shimashita ka</u>?* (Has Takao already finished studying?)

② In class: Each student needs two pieces of paper or cards, each a different color. One color means "already," and the other means "not yet." The teacher asks the questions that the students made in ①. The students answer the questions by holding up the appropriate color paper or card within five seconds. Students who answer correctly may proceed to the next question. Students who remain in the game the longest are the winners.

5 Celebrity talk

In small groups: Each group is given a picture of a celebrity. Ask each other questions about the celebrity, following the example.

Example: Madonna

A: *Kao wa doo desu ka?* (How about her face?)

B: *Kirei desu. / Sekushii desu. / Sugoi keshoo o shite imasu.*
(Beautiful. / Sexy. / She wears a lot of make-up.)

C: *Kami wa doo desu ka?* (How about her hair?)

D: *Nagai desu. / Kinpatsu desu. / Hontoo wa kuroi kami desu ga, ima wa kinpatsu ni somete imasu.*
(Long. / Blond. / Her hair is really black, but now it's dyed blond.)

E: *Fuku wa doo desu ka?* (How about her clothes?)

A: *Kakkoii desu. / Sekushii desu. / Shitagi mitai desu.*
(Cool. / Sexy. / They look like undergarments.)

B: *Shigoto wa?* (How about her occupation?)

C: *Kashu desu. / Joyuu desu.* (A singer. / An actress.)

D: *Seikaku wa?* (How about her personality?)

E: *Amari yasashikunai desu. / Kowai hito desu. / Ii hito desu.*
(Not so nice. / Scary. / Good-natured.)

A: *Madonna ni tsuite hoka ni shitte iru koto ga arimasu ka?*
(Do you know anything else about Madonna?)

B: *Kodomo ga hitori imasu.* (She has a child.)

6 Mystery classmate

In groups of four: First, each student chooses a classmate. Observe his/her physical appearance and take notes. In the group, students describe their chosen classmate, and the other group members try to guess who he/she is. Group members take turns describing and guessing classmates.

Example: A: *Kao ga marui desu. Yasashii kao desu. Kami wa chairo de, mijikai desu.*
(His/Her face is round. His/Her face is kind. His/Her hair is brown and short.)

B: *Tomu desu ka?* (Is it Tom?)

A: *Iie, chigaimasu. Onna no ko desu. Akai burausu o kite imasu.*
(No, it isn't. It's a girl. She's wearing a red blouse.)

C: *Jenii desu ka?* (Is it Jenny?)

A: *Iie. Shootopantsu o haite imasu.* (No. She's wearing shorts.)

D: *Jaa, Kyashii desu ne.* (Then it's Cathy.)

A: *Hai, soo desu.* (Yes, it is.)

7 You like music, don't you?

In class: Students wander around the classroom listening to music. When the teacher stops the music, students pair up with someone near them. Tell your partner things that you know about him/her. Use the expression *deshita ne* to make sure the information is correct. When the music starts again, walk around until the music stops and pair up with someone else. Repeat the activity several times, always choosing a different partner.

Example: A: *B san wa rokku ga suki deshita ne.* (B, you like rock music, don't you?)

B: *Soo desu yo. A san mo rokku ga suki desu ka?*
(Yes, I do. Do you like rock music, too?)

A: *Hai, daisuki desu.* (Yes, I like it very much.)

B: *A san wa yakyuu chiimu no pitchaa deshita ne.*
(A, you're a pitcher on a baseball team, aren't you?)

A: *Hai, soo desu.* (Yes, I am.)

8 Sentence completion

In small groups: Fill in the underlined parts of the following sentences with an appropriate word or phrase.

Example:
- *Hanako san wa ashi ga hosoi desu.* (Hanako has slender legs.)
- *Jimu san wa ashi ga nagai desu.* (Jim has long legs.)
- *Panda wa kao ga kawaii desu.* (Pandas have cute faces.)

1. *Kirin* (giraffe) *wa* _____ *desu.*
2. *Kujira* (whale) *wa* _____ *desu.*
3. _____ *wa koe* (voice) *ga* _____ *desu.*
4. _____ *wa karada* (body) *ga* _____ *desu.*
5. _____ *wa me* (eye) *ga* _____ *desu.*

9 Listening comprehension and/or oral production

Individually: Listen to the following conversations between two people. From the list below, determine the relationship between the pair.

Example: A: *Iroiro osewa ni narimashita. Amari ii gakusei ja nakute sumimasen deshita.*
(Thank you for your kindness. I'm sorry I wasn't a very good student.)
B: *Sonna koto arimasen yo. Zutto basukettobooru no kyaputen toshite ganbatta deshoo. Daigaku de mo ganbareru to omoimasu yo.*
(Not at all. You did a good job as captain of the basketball team. I hope you do your best in university, too.)
Answer: b

1. A: *Yamada san no uchi ni taizai dekite, hontoo ni yokatta desu. Kazoku no minasan wa mina shinsetsu ni shite kudasaimashita. Taihen osewa ni narimashita.*
(Mrs. Yamada, it was really great that I was able to stay at your house. Your family was kind to me. I really appreciate everything you have done for me.)
B: *Biru san ga uchi ni kite kureta node, kono natsuyasumi wa totemo tanoshikatta wa.*
(Bill, we had a good time this summer vacation because you visited us.)
A: *Iroiro arigatoo gozaimashita. Kanarazu tegami o kakimasu.*
(Thank you for everything. I'll definitely write to you.)
B: *Mata zehi Nihon ni kite kudasai ne. Mattemasu yo.*
(Please come to Japan again. We are looking forward to it.)

2. A: *Kono aida wa arigatoo. Hontoo ni tanoshii yoru datta yo.*
(Thank you for the other day. I had a really good night.)
B: *An san mo Tomu san mo kite kureta shi, chichi mo haha mo minna ni aete ureshii tte itteta wa.*
(My mother and father were glad that Tom and Ann could come, too, and that they were able to see everyone.)
A: *Okaasan, ryoori ga joozu da ne.* (Your mother is a good cook.)
B: *Sore o kiite, haha mo yorokobu wa. Mata kite ne.*
(She'll be glad to hear that. Please come again.)

3. A: *Ohisashiburi desu.* (It's been a while.)
B: *Yaa, Jimu. Shibaraku awanai uchi ni, mata se ga takaku natta na. Kookoojidai wa shuumatsu goto ni yoku ganbatta ne.*
(Hi, Jim. You've grown taller since I last saw you. You really worked hard on weekends during high school.)
A: *Kono mise de hataraita keiken ga, zuibun yaku ni tatte imasu yo.*
(The experience that I gained working at the store is helping me a lot now.)
B: *Soo ka. Ureshii ne. Ja, kyoo wa tokubetsu gochisoo suru yo.*
(Is it? I'm glad to hear that. I'll treat you to dinner tonight.)

Answers:
1. (   )   2. (   )   3. (   )

Lesson 12

Choices:
   a. *Kookoojidai no sensei to gakusei* (A student and a teacher from the student's high school days)
   b. *Kookoo no sensei to sotsugyoo suru gakusei*
      (A high school teacher and a graduating student)
   c. *Arubaito saki no sekininsha (keieisha) to arubaito shita gakusei*
      (A student and a former boss from a part-time job)
   d. *Hoomusutei saki no hosutomazaa to hoomusutei shita gakusei*
      (A student and his/her host mother)
   e. *Kankookyaku to annai o shita hito* (A tourist and a tour guide)
   f. *Tomodachi no ie ni shootai sareta hito to shootai shita hito*
      (A person and a friend who was invited to his/her house)

10 Listening comprehension and/or oral production

Individually: Listen to the following conversations between two people. Fill in the underlined parts of the sentence that follows each conversation with appropriate words to describe the situation.

Example: A: *Doa o nokku shite mo, chaimu o oshite mo, dare mo dete konai yo.*
   (Even though I knocked and rang the doorbell, no one answered.)
B: *Rusu no yoo da ne.* (No one seems to be inside.)
Answer: *Ima, ie no naka ni <u>dare mo inai</u> yoo desu.* (It seems like no one is home now.)

1. A: *Aa, mado ga warete iru.* (Oh, the window is broken.)
   B: *Dareka ga booru o nagete, garasu o watta yoo ne.*
      (It looks like someone threw a ball and broke it.)
   A: *Kitto tonari no kodomo da wa.* (It must be the child next door.)
   Answer: _____ ga _____ yoo desu.
      (It seems that the child next door has broken the window)

2. A: *Aa, ki o tsukete.* (Oh. Be careful.)
   B: *Nani?* (What?)
   A: *Shita ni chuuingamu ga ochiteru. Moo chotto de fumisoo datta wa.*
      (There's chewing gum on the ground. I almost stepped on it.)
   B: *Komaru wa ne. Michi ni gamu o suteru nan te.*
      (It's a shame that people throw gum on the street.)
   Answer: _____ o _____ soo ni narimashita.
      (It seemed that she was about to step on chewing gum.)

3. A: *Kono kamibukuro, ippai tabemono ga haitte iru ne.*
      (This paper bag is filled with a lot of food.)
   B: *Yoisho ... Omoi naa.* (Oof! ... It's heavy.)
   A: *Aa, ana ga aite iru. Moo sukoshi de yaburesoo da yo.*
      (Oh, there's a hole in it. It's about to break.)
   B: *Jaa, hoka no fukuro ni irekaeru yo.* (Well, I'm going to put the stuff into another bag.)
   Answer: *Tabemono ga ippai na node* _____ ga _____ soo ni narimashita.
      (Since the bag was filled with a lot of food, it looked like it would break.)

Lesson 12   97

11 Fast reading practice

Individually: Read the following thank you letter and answer the questions following it. Time how long it takes to finish the entire activity.

山田さんへ

　日本のお父さん、お母さん、お姉さん、たかしさん、そして、犬のまるちゃん、皆さんお元気ですか。私は８月２５日にシアトルへ帰りました。シアトルに着いたばかりの時は、時差ボケでした。家で１日ずっと寝ました。今はもう元気です。
　日本ではいろいろお世話になりました。皆さんに会えて本当に良かったと思います。盆踊りや、富士山登山、とても楽しかったです。日本の木のお風呂や浴衣が大好きになりました。お母さんとお姉さんの料理もとてもおいしかったです。たかしさんとはいい友達になりました。３週間、日本でいい経験をしました。どうもありがとうございました。
　私の家族は日本のお土産が大変気に入りました。父と母に浴衣、弟にＴシャツとゲーム、祖母と祖父に日本人形をあげました。次は私の家族が日本へ行きたいと言っています。
　皆さんと一緒にとった写真が出来ましたので、同封します。この写真を見ると日本がなつかしくなります。また皆さんに会いたいです。
　ではまた手紙を書きます。どうかお元気で。

　　　１９９７年９月７日　　　　　　エレン

Yamada san e,

　Nihon no otoosan, okaasan, oneesan, Takashi san, soshite, inu no Maru chan, minasan ogenki desu ka? Watashi wa 8gatsu 25nichi ni Shiatoru e kaerimashita. Shiatoru ni tsuita bakari no toki wa, jisaboke deshita. Ie de 1nichi zutto nemashita. Ima wa moo genki desu.
　Nihon de wa iroiro osewa ni narimashita. Minasan ni aete hontoo ni yokatta to omoimasu. Bon'odori ya, Fujisan tozan, totemo tanoshikatta desu. Nihon no ki no ofuro ya yukata ga daisuki ni narimashita. Okaasan to oneesan no ryoori mo totemo oishikatta desu. Takashi san to wa ii tomodachi ni narimashita. 3shuukan, Nihon de ii keiken o shimashita. Doomo arigatoo gozaimashita.
　Watashi no kazoku wa Nihon no omiyage ga taihen ki ni irimashita. Chichi to haha ni yukata, otooto ni tiishatsu to geemu, sobo to sofu ni nihonningyoo o agemashita. Tsugi wa watashi no kazoku ga Nihon e ikitai to itte imasu.
　Minasan to issho ni totta shashin ga dekimashita node, doofuu shimasu. Kono shashin o miru to Nihon ga natsukashiku narimasu. Mata minasan ni aitai desu.
　Dewa mata tegami o kakimasu. Dooka ogenki de.

　　　1997nen 9gatsu 7nichi　　　　　Eren

Dear Mr. Yamada,

How are my Japanese father, mother, sister, Takashi and the dog Maru? I came back to Seattle on August 25. I got jet lag shortly after arriving. I slept all day. Now I am fine.

Thank you for your kindness while I was in Japan. It was really great meeting you. I really enjoyed dancing *bon'odori* and climbing Mt. Fuji. I became very fond of Japanese wooden bathtubs and *yukata*. Mother and sister's cooking was so delicious. Takashi and I became good friends. I had a good three-week experience in Japan. Thank you so much.

My family liked the Japanese souvenirs very much. I gave *yukata* to my mother and father, a T-shirt and a game to my brother, and a Japanese doll to my grandmother and grandfather. My family said that they would like to go to Japan some day.

I am enclosing the pictures that I took with you. These pictures make me miss Japan. I would like to see you again.

I will write to you again. Take care.

September 7, 1997   Ellen

Questions:

A. Write an appropriate word in the underlined parts to complete the sentence.

1. *Yamada san no kazoku wa ___ nin desu.*

   (There are _____ people in Mr. Yamada's family.)

2. *Eren wa _____ ni natta node, 1 nichijuu zutto nemashita.*

   (Ellen slept all day because she had _____ .)

3. *Eren wa Nihon de _____ ya _____ o shimashita.*

   (Ellen [did] _____ and _____ in Japan.)

4. *Eren wa Nihon no_____ ya _____ ga totemo ki ni irimashita.*

   (Ellen became fond of Japanese _____ and _____ .)

5. *Eren wa Yamada san ni _____ o okurimasu.*

   (Ellen is going to send _____ to Mr. Yamada.)

B. Circle the most appropriate word(s).

1. *Eren wa Nihon ni [10ka / 20ka / 30nichi] gurai imashita.*

   (Ellen was in Japan for about [10 days / 20 days / 30 days])

2. *Eren wa [chichi to haha / otooto / sofu to sobo] ni geemu o agemashita.*

   (Ellen gave a game to her [mother and father / brother / grandmother and grandfather])

3. *Shashin ni wa [Yamada san no kazoku / Eren no kazoku] ga utsutte imasu.*

   ([Mr. Yamada's family / Ellen's family] are in the pictures.)

Time spent: (   ) minutes

12 Summary practice

In groups of three: After reading the letter in Application 11, discuss the following in groups. A representative from each group presents the summary to the class.

1. *Eren wa itsu Nihon e ikimashita ka?* (When did Ellen go to Japan?)
2. *Eren wa Nihon taizai o dono yoo ni tanoshimimashita ka?*

   (How did Ellen enjoy her stay in Japan?)
3. *Eren wa Yamada san no kazoku o doo omotte imasu ka?*

   (What did Ellen think of Mr. Yamada's family?)
4. *Eren wa mata Nihon e iku to omoimasu ka?* (Do you think Ellen will go to Japan again?)

13 Research and discussion

In six groups: Each group chooses one of the following topics: *bon'odori*, Mt. Fuji, Japanese baths, *yukata*, Japanese dolls, Japanese games. After researching the topic, a representative from each group gives a presentation to the class.

2. Actualization

1 Practice the following conversation and develop your own dialogue on a similar subject with your partners.

Kayoobi no 5jikanme, bijutsu no jikan desu. 4 nen 6 kumi no seito wa hanga o hotte imasu.
(Fifth period on Tuesday is art. The 4th grade, class 6 students are making *hanga*, or woodblock prints.)

Tanaka kun:	*Aa, machigaete, koko hotchatta.* (Oh, I carved in the wrong place.)
Hayashi sensei:	*Daijoobu. Sono kurai ki ni shinai de.* (No problem. Don't worry about it.)
Hirota san:	*Sensei, ita ga katakute umaku horemasen.*
	(Sensei, the board is too hard to carve.)
Hayashi sensei:	*Yubisaki ni motto chikara o irete.* (Use more force in your fingertips.)
Kobayashi kun:	*Chookokutoo no tsukaikata tte muzukashii yo.*
	(It's difficult to use a carving knife.)
Yamada san:	*Itai.* (Ouch!)
Hirota san:	*Daijoobu? Taihen da wa. Yubi kara chi ga deteru wa. Sensei!*
	(Are you OK? Oh, your finger is bleeding. Mrs. Hayashi!)
Hayashi sensei:	*Minasan, Yamada san o hokenshitsu ni tsurete iku node, sono aida, shizuka ni tsuzukete kudasai.*
	(Everyone, continue working quietly while I take Yamada to the nurse's office.)
Zen'in:	*Hai.* (OK)

2 Practice the following conversation and develop your own dialogue on a similar subject with your partners.

4 nen 5 kumi no seito wa gakkoo no chikaku no kooen de shasei o shite imasu.
(The 4th grade, class 5 students are making sketches in a park near the school.)

Yoshida san: *Sensei, happa no iro ga kitanaku natte shimaimashita.*
(Mrs. Takahashi, the color of the leaves has become dirty.)
Takahashi sensei: *Fude o yoku aratta?* (Did you wash your brush well?)
Yoshida san: *Hai.* (Yes.)
Takahashi sensei: *Ara, omizu ga konna ni yogoreteru wa. Torikaenai to.*
(Oh, the water is so dirty. You should change it.)
Yoshida san: *Hai.* (I see.)
[*Shibaraku shite*] [After a while]
Takahashi sensei: *Doo kashira?* (How is it?)
Yoshida san: *Kondo wa kirei na iro ni narimashita.* (I've got a beautiful color this time.)
Takahashi sensei: *Soo ne. Yokatta wa ne.* (Yes, you do. Good for you.)

3 Choose a topic from the following and discuss it both in English and Japanese.
suibokuga, byoobuga, ukiyoe

3. Enrichment

1 *Kanji* for Lesson 10

語　　話す　　東京　　所　　都会
雨　　降る　　天気　　予報　　晴れ
午前　　夜　　午後　　昼

2 *Kanji* for Lesson 11

帰る　　好き嫌い　　料理　　食べる　　太る
物　　覚える　　臭い　　記念　　最後
自動

3 Other useful *kanji*

残、案、消、解、歌、作、長、短、卒業、勉強、学校、銀行、駅、結婚

4 Strategies

Kanji classifiers - introduction:
Kanji characters are frequently arranged according to classifiers, some of which carry meaning/ concept, some indicate the kind, and some suggest classification/grouping. Most dictionaries list more than 200 classifiers, which are called *bushu* (部首). The following listed classifiers, many of which have been listed in previous lessons, may be helpful clues for identifying and understanding *kanji*. Some classifiers are original *kanji* and others are derived from an original *kanji*.

1. 亻 (human [derived from 人]): 人、使、体、休、仏、今、位、他
2. 氵 (water [derived from 水]): 浴、治、沢
3. 言 (speech): 言、話、語、記
4. 口 (mouth): 口、同、味、古、由
5. 日 (sun): 日、昼、時、明
6. 目 (eyes): 目、着、眼
7. 田 (field): 田、界、番、男、町
8. 糸 (thread): 糸、終、紙、絶、紀
9. 木 (tree): 木、林、森、本、机、楽
10. 門 (gate): 門、聞、問、開
11. 女 (woman): 女、姉、妹、好、嫌
12. 心 (heart): 心、思、忘、念
13. 大 (big): 大、夫、奈、天、太、奮
14. 貝 (shell → money): 買

5 Exercise

Study the *kanji* listed in 1, 2, and 3. Determine the classifiers and then try to figure out the meanings of the *kanji*. Write them down.

Lesson 13: At Narita Airport

I. PERSPECTIVE

1. Objectives

1 Function:

(1) Asking someone to convey a message to others: *(Kazoku) ni mo soo tsutaete kudasai.*
(2) Expressing that one enjoyed something: *(Piitaa) ga (ki)te kurete tanoshikatta desu.*
(3) Expressing that something happened really fast: *Atto iu ma (no ryokoo deshita).*
(4) Asking if someone did something: *Nani ka (kai)masen deshita ka?*
(5) Suggesting it would be good if one did something: --- *(sagas)e ba ii desu yo.*
(6) Expressing consent or agreeing to do something: *Soo shimasu.*

2 Language:

(1) *(Gokazoku no minasan) ni mo (soo tsutae)te kudasai.*
(2) *(Piitaa) ga (ki)te kurete (tanoshi)katta desu.*
(3) *(Obaasan) ni (nihonningyoo), (otoosan) ni (omamori).*
(4) *Nani ka (kai)masen deshita ka?*   (5) *(Menzeiten) de (sagas)eba ii desu yo.*
(6) *(Boku) mo.*   (7) *Kondo kara wa (---) desu yo.*

3 Culture:

(1) Significant gifts   (2) *Omamori*

II. PREPARATION

1. Context

成田空港で

あらゆる荷物を抱えて成田空港へ。鞄が一つ増えてしまった。あきらは増えた荷物の中身を聞いた。何のお土産を買ったのだろう。おばあさんに日本人形、お父さんに交通安全のお守り、お母さんには扇子。そして、自分と弟のためにファミコンソフトを買った。あきらは持っていた荷物を渡した。ゲートに入るには時間があったが、ピーターはまだ買い忘れた物があると言う。姉へのお土産だった。免税店で探すことになった。2人は再会を約束して別れた。

Peter went to Narita airport with all of his luggage. He needed an extra bag for all of his souvenirs. Akira asked him what was in the extra bag, wondering what souvenirs he bought. Peter bought a Japanese doll for his grandmother, a traffic safety charm for his father, a fan for his mother, and video games for his brother and himself. Akira handed Peter the luggage he had been carrying for him. Peter had time to get to his gate, but he realized that he forgot to buy a present for his sister. He decided to look for something in the duty-free shop. The two friends parted, promising to see each other again.

2. Sample Conversation

P: お世話になりました。家族にもそう伝えてください。
MA: ピーターが来てくれて楽しかったです。
P: あっと言う間の旅行でした。
MA: お土産たくさん買ったんですね。
P: おばあさんに日本人形、お父さんにお守り、お母さんに扇子。
MA: 秋葉原で何か買いませんでしたか。
P: 知ってたんですね。ファミコンソフトです。僕と弟に。
MA: お姉さんには何か買いませんでしたか。
P: あ、忘れていました。
MA: 免税店で探せばいいですよ。
P: そうします。
MA: また手紙を書きます。
P: 僕も。今度からは日本語半分と英語半分ですよ。

P: *Osewa ni narimashita[1]. Kazoku ni mo[2] soo tsutaete kudasai.*
MA: *Piitaa ga kite kurete tanoshikatta desu.*
P: *Atto iu ma[3] no ryokoo deshita.*
MA: *Omiyage[4] takusan katta n desu ne.*
P: *Obaasan ni nihonningyoo, otoosan ni omamori[5], okaasan ni sensu.*
MA: *Akihabara[6] de nani ka kaimasen deshita ka?*
P: *Shitteta n desu ne. Famikonsofuto desu. Boku to otooto ni.*
MA: *Oneesan ni wa nani ka kaimasen deshita ka?*
P: *A, wasurete imashita.*
MA: *Menzeiten[7] de sagaseba ii desu yo.*

P: *Soo shimasu.*
MA: *Mata tegami o kakimasu.*
P: *Boku mo. Kondo kara wa[8] nihongo hanbun to eigo hanbun desu yo.*

P: Thank you for taking care of me. Please tell your family as well.
MA: I'm glad that you could come.
P: It was over just like that.
MA: You sure bought a lot of gifts.
P: A Japanese doll for my grandmother, a charm for my father, and a fan for my mother.
MA: Didn't you buy something in Akihabara?
P: You knew that, didn't you? I bought video games for my [younger] brother and me.
MA: Didn't you buy anything for your [older] sister?
P: Oh! I forgot.
MA: You can look for something in the duty-free shop.
P: I'll do that.
MA: I'll write you again.
P: Me too. From now on, they will be half Japanese and half English.

P: ピーター　スミス　　　*Piitaa Sumisu*　　　Peter Smith
MA: もり　あきら　　　　*Mori Akira*　　　　Akira Mori

3. Language & Culture Notes

1 *Osewa ni narimashita* is an expression of gratitude or indebtedness for someone's kindness or assistance. *Sewa suru* means "to take care of" or "to look after." It is typical of Japanese manners to humbly express appreciation for another's kindness or good deeds.

2 *Kazoku ni mo* means "to your family also." Many functional markers can be used in combination. *Mo* and *no* always come last in multiple formation.

    Tomodachi <u>kara no</u> tegami desu. (It's a letter from my friend.)
    Kyoto <u>e no</u> michi desu ka? (Is this the road to Kyoto?)
    Gakkoo <u>de mo</u> uchi <u>de mo</u> manga o yomimasu. (I read comics both at school and at home.)
    Watashi <u>ni mo</u> kudasai. (Please give it to me, too.)

3 *Atto iu ma* literally means, "the time it takes to say 'Oh!'" The expression may correspond to "in an instant," "just like that," "before you can say ---," and other such expressions.

4 There are various types of gifts that can be bought in Japan. Some of the more significant ones are *omamori*, *nihonningyoo*, and *sensu*. An *omamori* is a charm or ornament bought at a temple or shrine. Some are general good luck charms, which students often like to attach to their backpacks. Others are for traffic safety and are hung in cars to protect people while they are driving. A *nihonningyoo* is a Japanese doll. A traditional *nihonningyoo* is handmade and dressed in a *kimono* and placed on a lacquer base. *Sensu*, as mentioned in Lesson 2, are hand-painted folding fans made of rice paper.

5 An *omamori*, which literally means "a guard," is a religious charm or amulet. *Omamori* contain a blessing or prayer written on a small piece of wood or paper that is enclosed in a cloth pouch. People carry different *omamori* for different types of protection. For example, a student wishing to

do well on exams might get an *omamori* at a shrine or temple where the god of learning is worshipped. For protection in traffic a driver may buy an *omamori* from a shrine where a deity of traffic safety is worshipped. A pregnant woman may carry an *omamori* from the shrine of the guardian deity of children.

6 Akihabara is the famous district in Tokyo where there are literally hundreds of electronics shops. The area is therefore called "Electric Town." Because of the vast variety of merchandise and the low advertized prices, this area attracts shoppers from all over Japan. Many stores offer electronics and small appliances made to run on foreign voltage; therefore, Akihabara attracts foreign tourists as well. The district's shops carry everything from washing machines and rice cookers to stereo systems, word processors, computer software, and, of course, cameras. In fact, aside from restaurants, it is difficult to find any other kind of store in this area.

7 Japanese people do a lot of their *omiyage* shopping at duty-free shops (*menzeiten*) at airports or in tourist cities. It is a very convenient way of shopping since, when Japanese go away, they buy something for almost everyone they know. It is not unusual to see Japanese people in a duty-free shop buying ten of the same boxes of chocolate, bottles of liquor, or cartons of cigarettes.

8 --- *kara wa* --- is another example of multiple function words. *Wa* comes last in multiple formation. *Kara,* in this case, refers to sequential action and means "since" or "after."

III. PARTICIPATION
1. Vocabulary

1 **From sample conversation:**

atto iu ma (in an instant)
kaimasen (does/did not buy)
kite (could come/came)
menzeiten (duty-free shop)
nihonningyoo (Japanese doll)
oneesan (elder sister)
sagaseba (if [one] looks for)
wasurete imashita (forgot)

hanbun (half)
katta (bought)
kondo (this time)
nani ka (anything)
omamori (charm)
ryokoo (trip, travel)
shitteta (knew)

2 **Useful for activities:**

aete (meet, met)
hontoo ni (really)
jishin (earthquake)
kowai (scary, fearful)
ningyoo (doll)
obaasan (grandmother)
ototoshi (the year before last)
sukaafu (scarf)
tsutaeru (to tell, to inform)

hannin (criminal)
jibun no (one's own)
koibito (lover)
Mekishiko (Mexico)
nyuusu (news)
obake (ghost)
soshite (then)
tsukamaru (be caught)
zannen (too bad, a shame)

Lesson 13

2. Activity, Practice, & Exercise

1 Conveying messages

In groups of three: We are often in a situation where we need to tell a friend something, but we do not know where our friend is. Therefore, we give the message to a mutual friend and ask him/her to convey the information. Write your own scenario in Japanese, following the example.

Example: (formal)

    A → B: *C san ni "Kyoo no yoru 8ji goro denwa shimasu" <u>to tsutaete kudasai</u>.*

    B → C: *A san ga kyoo no yoru 8ji goro denwa suru <u>to itte imashita yo</u>.*

    (informal)

    A → B: *C san ni "Kyoo no yoru 8 ji goro denwa suru" <u>tte tsutaete</u>.*

    B → C: *A san ga kyoo no yoru 8 ji goro denwa suru <u>tte itteta</u> yo/wa yo.*

2 Current events

In pairs: Bring up a topic of conversation by asking a person if he/she did a certain action, using the expression *---masen deshita ka?* or *---nakatta?* Discuss a current event that you learned through the TV, the newspaper, a friend, or elsewhere. Follow the example.

Example: 1) (formal)

    A: *B san, kinoo terebi no nyuusu o <u>mimasen deshita ka</u>?*
       (B, didn't you watch the news on TV yesterday?)

    B: *Mimashita yo.* (Yes, I did.)

    A: *Koobe de ooki na jishin ga atta soo desu ne?*
       (I heard there was a big earthquake in Kobe.)

    B: *Ee, jishin wa hontoo ni kowai desu ne.* (Yeah. Earthquakes are really scary.)
    (informal)

    A: *B san, kinoo terebi no nyuusu, <u>minakatta</u>?*

    B: *Mita yo/wa yo.*

    A: *Koobe de ooki na jishin ga atta soo da ne/ne?*

    B: *Un, jishin tte hontoo ni kowai ne/wa ne.*

    2) (formal)

    A: *B san, kinoo terebi no nyuusu o <u>mimasen deshita ka</u>?*
       (B, didn't you watch the news on TV yesterday?)

    B: *Ee, kinoo wa mimasen deshita.* (No, I didn't.)

    A: *Koobe de ooki na jishin ga atta soo desu yo.*
       (I heard there was a big earthquake in Kobe.)

    B: *Ee, soo desu ka? Shirimasen deshita.* (Really? I didn't know.)
    (informal)

    A: *B san, kinoo terebi no nyuusu, <u>minakatta</u>?*

    B: *Un, kinoo wa minakatta naa/wa.*

    A: *Koobe de ooki na jishin ga atta soo da yo/yo.*

    B: *Ee, shiranakatta.*

3 Trips and souvenirs

① In pairs: Ask your partner about trips that he/she has taken. Find out where he/she has gone, what souvenirs he/she bought, and for whom he/she bought them.

Example: A: *Ima made ni <u>ryokoo shita tokoro</u> wa doko desu ka?* (Where have you traveled?)

B: *Ototoshi, Dizuniirando e ikimashita. Sorekara, kyonen Mekishiko e ikimashita.*
(I went to Disneyland the year before last, and I went to Mexico last year.)

A: *Ryokoo no toki, dare ka ni <u>omiyage o kaimashita ka</u>?*
(Did you buy any souvenirs for people?)

B: *Hai. Dizuniirando e itta toki, tomodachi no Ruushii ni ningyoo o kaimashita. Mekishiko e itta toki, obaasan ni sukaafu o kaimashita.*
(Yes. I bought a doll for my friend Lucy in Disneyland, and I bought a scarf for my grandmother in Mexico.)

Example task sheet

B san:

<u>Ryokoo shita tokoro</u>	<u>Itsu</u>	<u>Katta omiyage</u>	<u>Omiyage o ageta aite</u>
Dizuniirando	*ototoshi*	*ningyoo*	*tomodachi no Ruushii*
Mekishiko	*kyonen*	*sukaafu*	*obaasan*

② Make another pair and tell your new partner what you learned in ①.

Example: *B san wa ototoshi Dizuniirando e ikimashita. Soshite tomodachi no Ruushii san ni ningyoo o kaimashita. Sorekara, B san wa kyonen Mekishiko e ikimashita. Soshite, obaasan ni sukaafu o kaimashita.*
(B went to Disneyland the year before last. She bought a doll for her friend Lucy. She went to Mexico last year and bought a scarf for her grandmother.)

4 Sentence completion

In pairs or individually: Complete each sentence, following the example.

Example: *Watashi wa penparu ni aete, ureshikatta.* (I was glad to meet my pen pal.)
Watashi wa penparu ni aenakute zannen deshita.
(It's too bad that I was unable to meet my pen pal.)

1. _____ *te, ureshikatta.*
2. _____ *te, kanashikatta.*
3. _____ *te, shiawase datta.*
4. _____ *te, zannen datta.*

5 What would you say ... ?

In pairs: Complete the following.

What would you say when

(1) you want to thank someone who has helped or hosted you?

(2) you want to ask someone to send your regards to his/her family?

(3) you feel that time passed by very quickly during your trip?

(4) you realize that you have forgotten to do something?

6 Matching phrases

In groups of six: The teacher makes a set of cards for each group of students. Each group should have six Group A cards and six Group B cards. (See the lists below.) The cards should be in random order. Each group member needs one Group A and one Group B card. One person starts the game by reading his/her own A card. The other members must look at their B card to determine if it matches with his/her Group A phrase and makes a complete sentence. Those students who think their B card matches should read their phrase aloud. More than one student may respond at the same time. In this case, the A phrase is read again and each student who responded with a B phrase takes turns reading their phrase out loud. The other group members ask "*Dooshite?*" and the students must explain in Japanese why they think their B phrase completes the sentence. If the others think that the explanation is reasonable and that the phrase completes the sentence, those A and B phrases may be discarded. However, if no one can come up with an acceptable reason, then the players must keep their cards until they have another chance to get rid of them. The game continues around the circle with each person taking turns reading their A phrase until all of the cards have been used. The first person to get rid of both of their cards is the winner.

Group A

1. *Ame ga futte kurete ...*
2. *Otoosan ga pasokon o katte kurete ...*
3. *Tenki ga yoku natte kurete ...*
4. *Kare ga kite kurenakute ...*
5. *Hannin ga tsukamatte kurete ...*
6. *Oneesan ga chooshoku o tsukutte kurete ...*

Group B

yokatta desu.
zannen desu.
tasukatta yo.
kanashii desu.
gakkari desu.
anshin desu.

7 Making suggestions

In pairs: The teacher makes cards with a situation on each and gives 4 to each pair of students. Students take turns giving each other a situation and responding with a suggestion. Use --- *sureba ii desu yo* in giving advice. The students then agree or disagree with their partner's advice. Change roles and do the activity again with the same partner. Then change partners. Students should use a different card each time they change partners. Follow the example.

Example: A: *Nihon e ikitai desu.* (I want to go to Japan.)
      B: *Natsuyasumi ni <u>ikeba ii desu yo</u>.* (It would be good if you go during summer vacation.)
      A: *Soo shimasu.* OR *Soo shitakunai desu.*
         (I'll do that./I'll go then. OR I don't want to do that./I don't want to go then.)

Examples of situations:
1. *Jibun no kuruma ga hoshii.*
2. *Chuugoku e ikitai.*
3. *Toofu o kaitai.*
4. *Bahama ni ikitai.*
5. *Kaimono ni ikitai.*
6. *Konpyuutaa ga hoshii.*
7. *Bideo geemu o shitai.*
8. *Aibii Riigu* (Ivy League) *daigaku ni hairitai.*
9. *Okane ga hoshii.*
10. *Koibito ga hoshii.*

8 Sentence word order

In pairs: Put the words in the appropriate order to make a correct sentence.

(1) Please tell your mother, too.
   (*tsutaete, mo, ni, okaasan, kudasai, soo*)

(2) Starting today, let's speak in Japanese.
   (*nihongo, wa, kyoo, kara, hanashimashoo, de*)

(3) (I will) go to the library, too.
   (*toshokan, ikimasu, mo, e*)

(4) (We) talked about Japanese ghosts, too.
   (*hanashimashita, mo, Nihon, ni tsuite, no, obake*)

9 I'll do that.

In pairs: Students ask their partners a question, and partners should respond with *Soo shimasu.*

Lesson 14: Videotapes of Peter's trip

I. PERSPECTIVE

1. Objectives

1 **Function:**

(1) Stating resemblance: *(Gaikokujin) rashii (hito)* and *(Kaimono) ni (kiteru) mitai.*
(2) Indicating strong agreement or rejection: *Soryaa,*

2 **Language:**

(1) *(Gaikokujin) rashii (hito).* (2) *(Kaimono) ni (kite)ru mitai.*
(3) *Soryaa, (seinoo) no (i)i (mono) ga (hoshii) yo.* (4) *Zuibun (yasu)i mitai da yo.*

3 **Culture:**

(1) Japanese technology

II. PREPARATION

1. Context

旅行のビデオテープ

ピーターの家に２本のビデオテープが届いた。日本のあきらからだ。２本のうち１本は、あきらと一緒に秋葉原へ行った時に撮ったもの。もう１本は日本のテレビ番組で人気のあるクイズ番組を録画したもの。ピーターは早速ビデオを見たいと思った。日本語クラブの友達を家に誘った。みんなで見た方がおもしろいと思ったからだ。

Two videotapes arrived at Peter's home. They were from Akira. One was taken when they went to Akihabara together. The other is a copy of a popular Japanese TV quiz show. Peter wanted to watch the videos right away. He invited his Japanese language club friends to his house because he thought it would be more fun if they watched the tapes together.

2. Sample Conversation

P: ここは秋葉原。
D: 外国人らしい人が、たくさんいるね。
P: みんな買い物に来てるみたい。
D: 電気製品がたくさん。あ、カメラやビデオもある。
P: ジェシー、新しいカメラが欲しくなった。
J: そりゃあ、性能のいい物が欲しいよ。
P: ずいぶん安いみたいだよ。
J: 何か買ったのかい。
P: 僕はファミコンソフトだけ。
J: ファミコンマニアだな。
P: ラジカセ、ＣＤプレーヤー、ウォークマン、買いたい物がいっぱいあったよ。

P: *Koko wa Akihabara.*
D: *Gaikokujin rashii[1] hito ga takusan iru ne.*
P: *Minna kaimono ni kiteru mitai[2].*
D: *Denkiseihin ga takusan. A! kamera ya bideo mo aru.*
P: *Jeshii, atarashii kamera ga hoshiku natta[3]?*
J: *Soryaa[4], seinoo no ii mono ga hoshii yo.*
P: *Zuibun yasui mitai da yo.*
J: *Nani ka katta no kai[5]?*
P: *Boku wa famikonsofuto dake[6].*
J: *Famikon mania da na.*
P: *Rajikase, shiidiipureeyaa, uookuman, kaitai mono ga ippai atta yo[7].*

P: This is Akihabara.
D: There are many people who look like foreigners.
P: It seems like everybody comes to go shopping.
D: There are many electrical appliances. Oh, there are cameras and VCRs, too.
P: Jesse, you've wanted a new camera, right?
J: Yeah. I want a good performance one.
P: The prices seem very low.
J: Did you buy anything?
P: I only bought video games.
J: You're a video game fanatic.
P: There were radio/cassette players, CD players, walkmans, and so many other things I wanted to buy.

P: ピーター　スミス	*Piitaa Sumisu*	Peter Smith
D: デニス　ゴードン	*Denisu Goodon*	Dennis Gordon
J: ジェシー　ジョーンズ	*Jeshii Joonzu*	Jesse Jones

3. Language & Culture Notes

1 *rashii* indicates the speaker's subjective guess.

2 *mitai* after a noun, a dictionary form verb, or an adjective means "be like" or "look like." After a verb in the *-te* form, it means "would like to try."
   Ryokoo shite mitai.

3 *natta*, the past tense form of the informal verb *naru*, means "has become" after the *-ku* form of an adjective.
   Samuku natta. (became cold.)

4 *Soryaa* is the contraction of *sore wa*.

5 *kai* is the more informal and intimate equivalent of *ka*.

6 *dake* means "only," "just," or "no more than," and indicates limitation.

7 Japan has introduced high technology mainly from the U.S. since the end of World War II. Today Japan is known for high technology especially in the field of electronics.

III. PARTICIPATION

1. Vocabulary

1 From sample conversation:

denkiseihin (electrical appliances)
hoshii (want)
kaimono (shopping)
kiteru (come, has come)
soryaa (of course)

gaikokujin (foreigner)
hoshiku natta (wanted, has wanted)
kaitai (want to buy)
seinoo (performance)

2 Useful for activities:

bideokamera (camcorder)
chigau (different)
gaikokuryokoo (travel abroad)
ichiban ii (the best)
kanarazu (certainly, surely)
kenka suru (to fight)
kirei na ji de kaku (write neat characters, write neatly)
kono aida (the other day)
kyoo wa zutto (all day long)
mane (imitation)
mikake (one's appearance)
okuresoo (seem to be late)
otoko rashii (manly, macho)
ryuugakusei (foreign student)
seetaa (sweater)
shinamono (merchandise)
sugoi (amazing, great)
sutairu (style, one's figure)
tanomu (to ask a favor)
todokeru (to deliver)
tsuyoi (strong)
unten suru (to drive)
yamakaji (forest fire)
yatsura (guys)
zehi (certainly)

burausu (blouse)
fasshon (fashion)
hareru (become clear [weather])
iyaringu (earring)
karui (light [weight])

kyanpu (camping)
machi de (on the street)
masshiro (pure white)
nekkuresu (necklace)
onna rashii (typical of a woman)
rashii (I heard that ...)
saafin (surfing)
senchi (centimeter)
shokuji (meal, food)
sukaato (skirt)
takkyuubin (a package delivery service)
tanoshimi (pleasure, delight, be looking forward to)
totemo --- dekinai (could never do)
umi (sea)
uookuman (walkman)
yasashii (soft, kind)
yattsukeru (to beat)
zenzen --- nai (not ... at all)

2. Activity, Practice & Exercise

1 Giving suggestions

In pairs: Ask at least three classmates one by one what kind of electric appliances they want. Give them suggestions on good brands and stores where they can buy the appliances. Use the expression --- *nara*, --- *ga ii*.

Example: A: *B san, ima hoshii denkiseihin wa arimasu ka?*
(B, are there any electric appliances that you want?)

B: *Hai, arimasu. Uookuman to bideokamera ga hoshii desu.*
(Yes, there are. I want a walkman and a camcorder.)

A: *Uookuman <u>nara</u>, Sonii <u>ga ii</u> desu ne. Bideokamera mo Sonii ga ichiban ii to omoimasu.*
(Sony is known for making good walkmans. I think that Sony makes the best camcorder, too.)

B: *Soryaa soo desu yo.* (Of course, that's right.)

A: *--- ten ni iku to ii desu yo. Yasui shi, shinamono mo ooi kara.*
(I suggest you go to --- [store]. The prices are reasonable, and they have a lot of merchandise.)

2 I heard that ...

In pairs: Tell your partner something that you have heard or judged using the expression --- *rashii*. Before starting, the teacher should give some examples using current topics.

Example: 1) A: *Kinoo Kariforunia de yamakaji ga <u>atta rashii</u> ne/wa ne.*
(I heard that there was a forest fire in California yesterday.)
B: *Un, boku/watashi mo sono nyuusu o kiita yo/wa. Kowai ne/wa ne.*
(Yeah, I heard the news, too. It's scary, isn't it?)

2) A: *Kondo Nihon kara atarashii ryuugakusei ga <u>kuru rashii</u> ne/wa ne.*
(I heard that a new foreign student will be coming from Japan.)
B: *Hee, donna gakusei ga kuru ka, tanoshimi da ne/ne.*
(Really? I'm looking forward to meeting him/her.)

3 It looks like ...

In pairs: Observe the objects and people around you, such as your classmates or the scenery outside. Tell your partner what you have noticed or judged using the expression --- *mitai da*. Add a reason for your comment.

Example: 1) Looking at the sky → *Kyoo wa zutto <u>hareru mitai da</u> ne. Kumo ga zenzen nai kara.*
(It looks like we'll have sunny weather all day. There are no clouds at all.)

2) Looking at Jenny → *Jenii san no seetaa wa <u>atarashii mitai da</u> ne. Masshiro dakara.*
(Jenny's sweater seems to be brand new. It's pure white.)

4 Listening comprehension and/or oral production

Individually: Listen to the following conversations between two people who are talking about someone else. If they are talking about a man, write M, and if a woman, write W. Pay attention to the words *otoko/onna rashii* and *otoko/onna mitai*. The former means "typical of a man/woman" and the latter means "like a man/woman." Note: Some students might think that the conversations in this activity are stereotypical. Make sure that they understand that Japanese people often use these kinds of expressions very naturally. In Japan, the people in these conversations would not be thought of as stereotyping, quite contrary to the American point of view.

1. A: *Yamamoto san tte, koe ga takakute, yasashii kao o shite iru ne.*
(Yamamoto has a high voice and a soft face.)
B: *Chotto, onna no hito mitai ne.* (He looks a little like a woman.)

A: *Ee. Demo Yamamoto san wa karate o yatte iru n datte.* (Yes. But he practices karate.)
B: *Hee, soo. Mikake to chigatte, otoko rashii supootsu ga suki na no ne.*
   (Really? Contrary to his appearance, he likes masculine sports.)

2. A: *Nakamura san, se ga 180 senchi mo aru n datte.* (Nakamura is 180 cm tall.)
   B: *Hee, boku yori 5 senchi mo takai n da ne.* (She is five centimeters taller than me.)
   A: *Nakamura san ga sukaato haiteru no, mita koto nai naa.* (I have never seen her wear a skirt.)
   B: *Hanashikata mo otoko mitai dashi.* (And she talks like a man, too.)

3. A: *Minami san, itsumo, burausu to sukaato ne.* (Minami always wears blouses and skirts.)
   B: *Nekkuresu to iyaringu mo kanarazu tsuketeru wa.*
      (She always wears necklaces and earrings, too.)
   A: *Onna rashii fasshon ga suki nan desu tte.* (I heard she is conscious of women's fashion.)
   B: *Soo. Minami san ni wa soo iu sutairu ga niatteru wa ne.* (Really? That style suits her.)

4. A: *Itoo san tte, otoko rashii yo na.* (Ito is manly/macho.)
   B: *Dooshite?* (Why?)
   A: *Kono aida, machi de warui yatsura to kenka shita n da. Aite ga 3 nin mo ita no ni, Itoo san wa hitori de 3 nin o yattsuketa n da. Tsuyoi yo na.*
      (He fought against some bad guys on the street the other day. There were three of them, and he beat them all by himself.)
   B: *Hee, sugoi ne. Totemo mane dekinai na.* (Really? That's amazing. I could never do that.)

Answers:
   1. (   ) 2. (   ) 3. (   ) 4. (   )

Lesson 14   117

5 Review of expressions

In three groups: Following is a list of nine expressions that were learned in lessons 1 through 14. Each group writes two sentences for each expression. This may take about 15-20 minutes. Groups will then present their sentences to the class. Group A will present one sentence for each of the first three expressions; Group B, expressions 4-6; and Group C, expressions 7-9. Afterward, the teacher will collect all of the sentences and make a compiled list of the two or three best sentences for each expression. The students may use the list as a study guide.

List of expressions:

1. *Yappari*
2. *Tootoo*
3. *Pittari*
4. *Tonikaku*
5. *Demo*
6. *Ara*
7. *Soo ne*
8. *Atto iu ma*
9. *Soryaa*

6 What would you say ...?

In pairs: Answer the following questions in Japanese.
What would you say when

(1) asking someone what he/she was doing?
(2) realizing that you have made a mistake?
(3) asking someone what is the matter?

7 Giving advice

In pairs: The teacher writes seven situations on the blackboard. One student gives his/her partner each of the situations one at a time. The partner responds by giving advice or a suggestion using the form *-tara*. Then exchange partners with another pair, but take a different role. Each person asks one time and answers one time only.

Example: A: *Onaka ga itai n desu.* (My stomach hurts.)
B: *Kusuri o nondara.* (Why don't you take some medicine?)

Examples of situations:

1. *Ashita no suugaku no tesuto ga shinpai desu.*
2. *Karui shokuji ga ii desu.*
3. *Kantan na shokuji ga ii to omoimasu.*
4. *Kirei na ji de kaite kureru hito ga ii na.*
5. *5ji no yakusoku ni okuresoo.*
6. *Hayaku todoketai no.*
7. *Soto wa taihen samui desu.*

8 Interview

In three groups:

① Each group deals with one of the following themes:

1. What would you like to do during vacation?
2. What would you like to do next year?
3. What would you like to do when you become an adult?

First group members interview each other and then interview the rest of the class. Decide who will interview whom to avoid interviewing people twice.

Example: A: *Natsuyasumi ni <u>zehi shitai koto wa nan desu ka</u>?*
(What would you really like to do during summer vacation?)
B: *Natsuyasumi desu ka? Zehi umi ni itte, saafin ga <u>shitai desu</u> ne.*
(Summer vacation? I would like to go surfing.)

② After the interviews are finished, each group presents the results to the class.

Example: *Watashitachi wa "natsuyasumi ni zehi shitai koto" o kikimashita. Kyanpu o shitai hito ga 6 nin, umi e ikitai hito ga 5 nin, gaikokuryokoo o shitai hito ga 3 nin, unten no renshuu o shitai hito ga hitori, benkyoo shitai hito ga hitori imashita.*
(We interviewed people about what they would like to do during summer vacation. Six people want to go camping; five want to go to the beach; three want to travel abroad; one wants to practice driving; and one wants to study.)

Lesson 15 — Review & Application

IV. PERFORMANCE

1. Application

1 Conversation completion

In small groups: The following is a conversation between an American student (A) who is planning to go to a shop to buy souvenirs and one of his Japanese friends (J). Guess what the American student would say in the conversation. Choose the most appropriate sentence from below.

A: (   ) (There are so many electronics stores that it's difficult to decide where to go.)

J: *Soo da ne. Koko wa denkiseihin ga yasui kara.* (Yeah. Electric appliances are cheap in this area.)

A: (   ) (There are many people who look like foreigners.)

J: *Kebin, kimi wa nani ga hoshii no?* (Kevin, what do you want?)

A: (   ) (Computer games.)

J: *Sore nara, geemusofuto ten ga ii yo.* (I suggest we go to a computer software store.)

A: (   ) (I also want an electronic Japanese-English dictionary.)

J: *Jaa, denki no depaato e ikoo. Asoko nara, iroiro sorotte iru kara.*
   (Then let's go to an electronics store. They carry a lot of different things.)

A: (   ) (Hideki, is there anything you want to buy?)

J: *Boku wa shiidii wookuman ga hoshii na.* (I want a CD walkman.)

A: (   ) (You already have a walkman, don't you?)

J: *Are wa kasettoteepu yoo da yo. Shiidii yoo mo hoshii n da.*
   (That one is for cassette tapes. I want one for CDs, too.)

A: (   ) (What a luxury! It's a waste of money.)

J: *Soo kana. Demo, arubaito o shite tameta okane ga aru kara daijoobu. Jaa, ikoo.*
   (Oh well. But I have the money that I saved from my part-time job. So, let's go.)

1. *Hontoo ni denkiseihin no mise ga ippai de, dono mise o mitara ii ka, mayotchau ne.*
2. *Wookuman nara, moo motteru ja nai ka?*
3. *Gaikokujin rashii hito ga takusan iru ne.*
4. *Sorekara, Nihongo, Eigo no denshijisho mo hoshii n da.*
5. *Zeitaku da naa. Okane ga mottainai yo.*
6. *Famikonsofuto.*
7. *Hideki, kimi mo kaitai mono aru no?*

2 Conversation completion

In small groups: The following is a conversation between an American high school student (A) who is about to leave Japan and his host mother (M). Guess what the American student would say in the underlined parts in the conversation. Each group presents their conversation to the class.

M: *Kebin san, ashita wa moo owakare desu ne.* (Kevin, you're leaving tomorrow, aren't you?)

A: *Hai.* _____ . (Yes. _____ .)

M: *Tokubetsu na koto nani mo shite agerarenakute, gomennasai ne.*
(I'm sorry that we didn't do anything special for you.)

A: _____ .

M: *Soo itte moraeru to ureshii wa. Watashitachi mo Kebin san to issho ni sugoshita 2shuukan wa hontoo ni tanoshikatta wa.*
(I'm glad you say so. We really enjoyed spending these two weeks with you.)

A: _____ .

M: *Soo ne. 2shuukan wa hontoo ni mijikakatta wa ne.*
(I agree. These two weeks were really short.)

A: _____ .

M: *Nihongo de kaite kureru?* (Could you write it in Japanese?)

A: *Nihongo hanbun to eigo hanbun de.* (Half Japanese and half English.)

M: *Ee, watashitachi mo nihongo hanbun to eigo hanbun de kaku wa.*
(OK. We'll write in half Japanese and half English, too.)

3 Family members

In pairs: In class, review the way of addressing one's own and others' family members: father, mother, elder brother, elder sister, younger brother, younger sister, grandmother, grandfather, aunt, uncle, husband, and wife. Then practice with a partner, following the example.

Example: A: *Watashi no chichi* → B: *A san no otoosan*
A: *B san no okaasan* → B: *Watashi no haha*

4 Getting to know each other's family

① In class: Split the class in half and make two circles, one inside the other. With the students in the two circles facing each other, the inner circle begins to rotate clockwise and the outer circle counterclockwise when the teacher starts the music. When the music stops, students stop walking. Students pair up with the person who they are facing and ask each other questions about their family members.

Example: A: *B san wa oniisan, oneesan ga imasu ka?*
(Kate, do you have any older brothers or sisters?)

B: *Hai, ani ga imasu. Namae wa Biru desu. Biru wa daigakusei de, ima Nyuuyooku ni imasu.*
(Yes, I have an older brother. His name is Bill. He is a university student and is now in New York.)

A: *Oniisan wa donna hito desu ka?* (What kind of person is he?)

B: *Se ga takakute, megane o kakete imasu. Totemo yasashii hito desu.*
(He is tall and wears glasses. He's very kind.)

A: *Oniisan no shumi wa nan desu ka?* (What's his hobby?)

B: *Gitaa o hiku koto desu. Tokidoki uta mo utaimasu. Totemo joozu desu yo.*
(He plays the guitar. He sometimes sings. He's very good.)

A: *Soo desu ka? Ii desu ne.* (Is he? Sounds good.)
B: *A san wa oniisan, oneesan ga imasu ka?*
(Mary, do you have any older brothers or sisters?)
A: *Iie, imasen. Demo, imooto ga imasu. Namae wa Roozu de, ima shoogakusei desu.*
(No, I don't. But I have a younger sister. Her name is Rose. She's an elementary school student.)
B: *Imootosan wa nansai desu ka?* (How old is she?)
A: *10 sai desu.* (Ten years old.)
B: *Imootosan wa donna onna no ko desu ka?* (What is she like?)
A: *Kawaii desu ga, chotto urusai desu. Imooto wa tomodachi ga ooi desu.*
(She's cute, but a little noisy. She has a lot of friends.)
B: *Imootosan no shumi wa nan desu ka?* (What's her hobby?)
A: *Geemu o suru koto desu. Uno ya daiamondo geemu ga suki desu.*
(Playing games. She likes UNO, Chinese checkers, and so on.)

② The teacher starts the music again. When it stops, students tell their new partner about what they learned in ①. Use the expression --- *soo desu*.

Example: A: *Watashi wa Keito no oniisan ni tsuite kikimashita. Oniisan wa daigakusei de, Nyuuyooku ni <u>sunde iru soo desu</u>. Se ga takakute, megane o kakete ite, totemo <u>yasashii soo desu</u>. Gitaa to uta ga totemo <u>joozu da soo desu</u>.*
(I asked Kate about her older brother. I heard he's a university student and lives in New York. He's tall, wears glasses, and is very kind. He's good at playing the guitar and singing.)

B: *Boku wa Bobu no ojisan ni tsuite kikimashita. Ojisan wa <u>keisatsukan da soo desu</u>. Chikara ga tsuyokute, omoshiroi <u>hito da soo desu</u>. Ojisan no shumi wa tsuri to <u>karate da soo desu</u>.*
(I asked Bob about his uncle. I heard he is a policeman. He is strong and interesting. His hobbies are fishing and karate.)

5 Stating opinions

In small groups: Group members tell each other whether or not they agree with the following statements and give reasons for their opinions. Use either the expression --- *shita hoo ga ii* or --- *shinai hoo ga ii*. A representative from each group reports the discussion to the class.

Example: *Nihon e iku toki, jibun no kuni no tabemono o motte iku.*
(When going to Japan, bring food from one's own country.)

A: *Sukoshi <u>motte itta hoo ga ii</u> to omoimasu. Kuni no tabemono ga tabetaku naru kamo shiremasen kara.*
(I think it is better to bring some because you may miss food from your country.)

B: *Boku wa <u>motte ikanai hoo ga ii</u> to omoimasu. Kaban ga omoku naru kara desu. Nihon ni wa iroiro na tabemono ga aru kara daijoobu desu.*
(I think it is better not to bring any because your bag will get heavy. There is a variety of food in Japan, so you'll be OK.)

1. *Yasetai toki, kusuri o nomu.* (Take medicine when you want to lose weight.)
2. *Michi de hyaku doru o mitsuketa toki, keisatsu e motte iku.*
   (Take a hundred dollar bill that one has found to the police.)
3. *Tomodachi to kenka o shita toki, oya ni hanasu.*
   (Tell your parents when you have had a fight with your friend.)

6 Tour schedule

In small groups: Each group is given a group tour schedule. Discuss what has been decided for each day. Use the expression --- *koto ni narimashita*.

Example: Schedule

    July 1 - 1 p.m.: Leave Seattle (airplane)
           3 p.m.: Arrive at Narita
                 Stay overnight at a hotel in Tokyo

    July 2 - 9 a.m.: Leave the hotel → Sightseeing in Tokyo (bus)
           5 p.m.: Return to the hotel

    July 3 - 8 a.m.: Leave the hotel → Tokyo Disneyland

A: *7gatsu tsuitachi ni Shiatoru o shuppatsu suru <u>koto ni narimashita</u>.*
   (It has been decided that we leave Seattle on July 1st.)
B: *7gatsu tsuitachi ni Tookyoo ni iku <u>koto ni narimashita</u>.*
   (It has been decided that we go to Tokyo on July 1st.)
C: *7gatsu tsuitachi ni Tookyoo no hoteru de tomaru <u>koto ni narimashita</u>.*
   (It has been decided that we stay at hotel in Tokyo on July 1st.)
D: *7gatsu futsuka ni Tookyoo o kenbutsu suru <u>koto ni narimashita</u>.*
   (It has been decided that we go sightseeing around Tokyo on July 2nd.)

Lesson 15

7 Making conversations

In pairs: Think about the relationship between the people in the following situations and what kind of conversation they might have. Several pairs act out the conversations in class.

1. An American student who has stayed with a family in Japan and his host mother (at the family's house).
2. A Japanese student who will go back to Japan and his American friends (at the airport).
3. A student who will leave America for a one-month trip abroad and his friends (at the airport).

8 Listening comprehension and/or oral production

Individually: Listen to the following conversations between two people. Complete the sentences at the end of the conversations, stating where the person went or will go.

Example: A: *Kerii, suteki na fuku ne. Doko e iku no?*
(Kelly, you're wearing a nice outfit. Where are you going?)
B: *Rikku to yakusoku ga aru no.* (I'm meeting Rick.)
A: *Deeto deshoo?* (Are you going on a date with him?)
B: *Maa ne. Myuujikaru o miru no yo.* (Well, yes. We're going to see a musical.)
A: *Hee, doko de miru no?* (Really? Where are you going to see it?)
B: *Shitiihooru. "Rokkii Horaa Shoo" o miru no.*
(At the city auditorium. We're seeing the Rocky Horror Picture Show.)
A: *Ii wa ne. Jaa, tanoshinde kite ne.* (That's nice. Have a good time.)
Answer:
→ *Kerii wa Shitiihooru e myuujikaru o mi ni ikimasu.*
(Kelly is going to see a musical at the city auditorium.)

1. A: *Jimu, kono mae no renkyuu, nani shiteta?* (Jim, what did you do over the holidays?)
   B: *Renkyuu wa inaka no ojiichan no ie e itteta n da.*
   (I went to my grandfather's house in the country.)
   A: *Soo. Tanoshikatta?* (I see. Did you have a good time?)
   B: *Asobi ni itta n ja nakute, ojiichan no noojoo o tetsudatta n da yo. Choodo noojoo ga isogashii toki datta n da. Demo, okozukai o moratta kara, arubaito mitai na mono da ne.*
   (I didn't go there for fun but to help him with his work on the farm because it was the busy time. I got some money, so it was like a part-time job.)
   → (Jim went to his grandfather's house to help him with his farm work.)

2. A: *An, kinoo toshokan de anata o mikaketa wa.* (Ann, I saw you in the library yesterday.)
   B: *Ee, dooshite koe o kakete kurenakatta no?* (Did you? Why didn't you come up to me?)
   A: *Datte, totemo isshookenmei benkyoo shite ita deshoo. Jama shitara warui to omotte.*
   (You were studying very hard, so I didn't want to disturb you.)
   B: *Benkyoo ja nai no yo. Natsu ni Nihon e iku yotei dakara, Nihon ni tsuite iroiro shirabeteta no yo.*
   (I wasn't studying. I'm going to Japan this summer, so I was checking out some things about Japan.)
   → (Ann went to the library to check out things about Japan.)

3. A: *Raigetsu, Nihon no penparu no Yasuo ga kuru n da.*
   (My Japanese pen pal, Yasuo, is coming next month.)
   B: *Hee, natsuyasumi no amerikaryokoo ka?*
   (Really? He's traveling in America during summer vacation?)
   A: *Ryokoo ja nai yo. Kono machi ni zutto taizai suru n dakara.*
   (It's not a trip. He's going to stay in this town for a while.)
   B: *Kono machi dake ja, omoshirokunai kamo shirenai yo.*
   (It may not be interesting for him to stay only in this town.)
   A: *Ii n da yo. Amerikajin no seikatsu o taiken suru tame ni kuru n dakara.*
   (That's OK. He's coming to experience the American way of life.)
   B: *Soo ka.* (I see.)
   → (Yasuo is coming to America to experience the American way of life.)

4. A: *Eren no oniisan wa maiban jazukurabu e iku no yo.*
   (Ellen's brother goes to a jazz club every night.)
   B: *Hee, jazu ga suki na no ne.* (Really? He must be fond of jazz.)
   A: *Soo. Demo jazu o kiku tame ni iku n ja nai wa.* (Yes, but he doesn't go there to listen to jazz.)
   B: *Ja, dooshite?* (Then why?)
   A: *Jazukurabu de piano o hiku no yo.* (He plays the piano at the club.)
   B: *Waa, suteki.* (Wow! That's cool.)
   → (Ellen's brother goes to a jazz club every night to play the piano.)

Answers:
1. *Jimu wa* _____ *e* _____ *ni ikimashita.*
2. *An wa* _____ *e* _____ *ni ikimashita.*
3. *Yasuo wa* _____ *e* _____ *ni kimasu.*
4. *Eren no oniisan wa* _____ *e* _____ *ni ikimasu.*

2. Actualization

1 Practice the following conversation and develop your own dialogue on a similar subject with your partners.

4 nen 2 kumi no seito wa rika no jugyoo de, jikken o shite imasu. Suisoo ni iroiro na mono o ire, uku ka, shizumu ka, shirabete imasu.
(The 4th grade, class 2 students are doing an experiment in science class. They are putting items in a tank of water to check which items float and which sink.)

Suzuki sensei: *Dewa, jikken yame. Tanaka kun, nani ga ukimashita ka?*
(It's time to stop. Tanaka, which items floated?)
Tanaka kun: *Happoosuchirooru to ki to roosoku ga ukimashita.*
(Styrofoam, wood, and the candle.)
Suzuki sensei: *Dewa, shizunda mono wa? Yamada san.* (Then which items sank? Yamada.)

Yamada san:	*Hai. Hasami to kugi to hari ga shizumimashita.* (Scissors, nails, and needles.)
Suzuki sensei:	*Dewa, uku mono to shizumu mono no chigai wa nan deshoo?* (What is the difference between those that floated and those that sank?)
Nakamura kun:	*Omoi mono ga shizunde, karui mono ga uku to omoimasu.* (I think that heavy things sink, and light things float.)
Yoshida san:	*Ara, demo roosoku wa, hari yori omoi noni uita wa yo.* (Oh, but the candle floated even though it is heavier than the needles.)
Hirota san:	*Fushigi ne.* (It's strange.)

2 Practice the following conversation and develop your own dialogue on a similar subject with your partners.

Suiyoobi no 2jikanme, rika no jugyoo desu. 4 nen 1 kumi no seito wa mizu no seishitsu ni tsuite benkyoo shite imasu.
(Second period on Wednesday is science. The 4th grade, class 1 students are learning about the nature of water.)

Yamada sensei:	*Mizu wa nando ni naru to futtoo shimasu ka?* (At what temperature Celsius does water boil?)
Tanaka kun:	*100 do desu.* (At 100 degrees.)
Yamada sensei:	*Dewa, 0 do ni naru to, mizu wa doo narimasu ka?* (Then what happens to water at 0 degrees?)
Suzuki kun:	*Koorimasu.* (It freezes.)
Yamada sensei:	*Soo desu ne. Dewa, kootta jootai o nan to yobimasu ka?* (Right. What do you call water in its frozen state?)
Yoshida san:	*Kotai desu.* (A solid.)
Yamada sensei:	*Hai. Soredewa, kitai to wa, mizu no dooitta jootai no koto desu ka?* (Right. Then what is water in its gaseous state?)
Kobayashi kun:	*Suijooki ni natta jootai desu.* (It's steam.)
Yamada sensei:	*Hai. Yoku dekimashita.* (Right. Very good.)

3 Try to answer the following questions in Japanese.
1. Objects in water get rising power from the water. What is this power called?
2. Is it correct to say the reason why buoyancy works is that the pressure on the bottom of the object is greater than the pressure on the top of the object?
3. Do clothes dry faster in the sun or in the shade?
4. Does water in a glass decrease faster in the sun or in the shade?
5. As water in a glass decreases, it turns into _____ .

4 Answer the following questions in English.
1. *Sentaku mono ga hayaku kawaku no wa, hinata to hikage no dochira desu ka?*
2. *Koppu no mizu ga hayaku heru no wa hinata to hikage no dochira desu ka?*
3. *Koppu ni ireta mizu ga hetta no wa, koppu no naka no mizu ni nani ka henka ga atta no desu ka?*

3. Enrichment

1 *Kanji* for Lesson 13

お世話　　家族　　伝える　　旅行　　お土産
人形　　お守り　　扇子　　秋葉原　　弟
免税店　　探す　　半分

2 *Kanji* for Lesson 14

外国人　　電気　　製品　　新しい　　欲しい
性能　　安い

3 Other useful *kanji*

夫、主、奥、趣味、働、遊、売、洗濯、郵便局、住、笑、発、泣、到

4 Strategies

Kanji classifiers – analysis:

As introduced in Lesson 12, some classifiers carry meaning, some indicate a kind or category, and some suggest grouping. This section introduces *kanji* based on classifiers.

(1) 亻 (derived symbol for person)

    a) 休　*yasumu* (rest)

        people resting under a tree

    b) 仙　*sen* (a hermit)

        hermits stay in the mountain

    c) 信　*shinjiru* (to place confidence in)

        言 means "speech," when people tell the truth, there is confidence.

(2) 氵 (derived symbol for water)

    a) 泳　*oyogu* (to swim) *ei*

        永 means "long time" and is pronounced /*ei*/

    b) 浅　*asai* (shallow) *sen*

        戋 is also pronounced /*sen*/

    c) 濃　*koi* (thick) *noo*

        農 is also pronounced /*noo*/

    d) 汽　*ki* (steam)

        気 is also pronounced /*ki*/

    e) 洗　*arau* (to wash) *sen*

        先 is also pronounced /*sen*/

(3) 艹 (derived symbol for grass)

    a) 草　*kusa* (grass)　　b) 葉　*ha* (leaves)　　c) 芽　*me* (bud)

    d) 苗　*nae* (seedling)　　e) 芝　*shiba* (lawn)　　f) 茶　*cha* (tea)

(4) 口 (mouth)
- a) 呼 *yobu* (to call)
- b) 叫 *sakebu* (to shout)
- c) 告 *tsugeru* (to announce)
- d) 吐 *haku* (to vomit)
- e) 舌 *shita* (tongue)
- f) 品 *shina* (materials)

(5) 木 (tree)
- a) 林 *hayashi* (woods)
- b) 森 *mori* (forest)
- c) 株 *kabu* (stump)
- d) 樹 *ju* (tree)
- e) 松 *matsu* (pine tree)
- f) 桜 *sakura* (cherry tree)
- g) 柳 *yanagi* (willow tree)
- h) 桑 *kuwa* (mulberry tree)
- i) 机 *tsukue* (desk)

(6) 日 (sun)
- a) 明 *akarui* (bright)
- b) 暗 *kurai* (dark)
- c) 星 *hoshi* (star)
- d) 早 *hayai* (early)
- e) 春 *haru* (spring)
- f) 昇 *noboru* (to rise)
- g) 昔 *mukashi* (old times)
- h) 昼 *hiru* (daytime, noon)

(7) 目 (eyes)
- a) 眼 *me* (eyes)
- b) 眠 *nemuru* (to sleep)

(8) 田 (field)
- a) 畑 *hatake* (field)
- b) 町 *machi* (town)
- c) 男 *otoko* (man)
- d) 里 *sato* (village)

(9) 門 (gate)
- a) 問 *tou* (to ask)
- b) 開 *hiraku* (to open)
- c) 閉 *shimeru* (to close)
- d) 閑 *kan* (quiet)
- e) 聞 *kiku* (to listen)

(10) 雨 (rain)
- a) 霜 *shimo* (frost)
- b) 雲 *kumo* (cloud)
- c) 雷 *kaminari* (thunder)
- d) 霧 *kiri* (fog)
- e) 電 *den* (electric)

(11) 扌 (hand [derived symbol]): 指 (finger); 打 (to hit); 持 (to hold, to have)

(12) 大 (big): 天 (heaven); 太 (fat, big); 奇 (strange, curious)

(13) 魚 (fish): 鯉(carp); 鯨(whale)

(14) 礻 (altar [derived symbol]): 神 (god); 祈 (to pray); 福 (luck)

(15) 忄 (heart [derived from 心]): 性 (gender); 情 (emotion, circumstance); 忙 (busy)

(16) 囗 (enclosure): 国 (country); 囚 (prisoner)

(17) 广 (roof): 店 (shop, store); 庫 (warehouse)

(18) 厂 (cliff): 原 (original); 厚 (thick); 厄 (suffering)

5 Exercise

Most *kanji* have two readings: *on*, from the Chinese pronunciation, and *kun,* the Japanese pronunciation and meaning of the *kanji*. Try to figure out the pronunciation or meaning of the *kanji* listed in 3 **Other useful *kanji*** in the Enrichment sections of review lessons 3, 6, 9, 12, and 15.

6 Indicate the pronunciation of the following *kanji* on the right and match each with the appropriate pronunciation of the *kanji* from the column on the left.

1. 青　せい
2. 生　せい
3. 寺　じ
4. 官　かん
5. 反　はん
6. 吾　ご
7. 同　どう
8. 交　こう

a. 棺
b. 時
c. 牲
d. 清
e. 梧
f. 胴
g. 飯
h. 姓
i. 持
j. 館
k. 校

Lesson 16: New Year's cards

I. PERSPECTIVE

1. Objectives

1 Function:

(1) Confirming information: *Kore wa (Nihon no nengajoo) desu ne.*
(2) Greetings for a New Year's card: *Kingashinnen*
(3) Summarizing or stating simply: *Kantan ni ieba*
(4) Discovering with surprise: *Oya,*
(5) Expressing that something has been done completely or happened unexpectedly: *(Wasure)te shimaimashita.*
(6) Giving something to someone: *...(kashi)te agemasu*
(7) Suggesting/Ordering someone to do something: *(Shirabe)te minasai/gorannasai.*

2 Language:

(1) *(Kore) wa (Nihon) no (nengajoo) desu ne.*
(2) *Kantan ni ieba, "---" desu.*
(3) *... to iu imi desu ne.*
(4) *(Wasure)te shimaimashita.*
(5) *(Shirabe)te minasai/gorannasai.*

3 Culture:

(1) *Nengajoo*
(2) *Oshoogatsu* events
(3) Chinese calendar

II. PREPARATION

1. Context

年賀状

あきらからふた通りの年賀状が届いた。漢字で書かれた葉書と、英語で書かれたカードの２種類だった。ピーターは漢字の辞書を持っていなかった。あきらの漢字は難しそうである。今度の日本語の授業の時、はやし先生に質問することにした。そして、どんな辞書を買ったらいいか相談してみることにした。

Two kinds of New Year's cards arrived from Akira. One was written in *kanji* and the other was written in English. Peter did not have a *kanji* dictionary. Akira's *kanji* looked very difficult, so Peter decided to ask Hayashi *sensei* about it in the next Japanese class. He also decided to consult with her on what kind of dictionary to buy.

2. Sample Conversation

K: あら、これは日本の年賀状ですね。
P: ペンパルからお正月にもらいました。
K: 謹賀新年。
P: この漢字は難しいです。
K: 簡単に言えば、「明けましておめでとう。」です。
P: Happy New Year と言う意味ですね。
K: そうです。おや、この猿はかわいらしい顔ですね。
P: どうして猿なんですか。
K: 今年は猿年だからですよ。十二支って覚えてますか。
P: すみません。忘れてしまいました。
K: この辞書を貸してあげます。調べてみなさい。
P: ありがとうございます。

K: *Ara, kore wa Nihon no nengajoo[1] desu ne.*
P: *Penparu kara oshoogatsu[2] ni moraimashita[3].*
K: *"Kingashinnen."*
P: *Kono kanji wa muzukashii desu.*
K: *Kantan ni ieba, "Akemashite omedetoo" desu.*
P: Happy New Year *to iu imi desu ne.*
K: *Soo desu. Oya[4], kono saru wa kawai rashii kao desu ne.*
P: *Dooshite saru na n desu ka?*
K: *Kotoshi wa sarudoshi dakara[5] desu yo. Juunishi[6] tte oboete imasu ka?*
P: *Sumimasen. Wasurete shimaimashita[7].*
K: *Kono jisho o kashite agemasu[8]. Shirabete minasai[9].*
P: *Arigatoo gozaimasu.*

K: Oh, this is a Japanese New Year's card.
P: I got it from my pen pal.
K: "Happy New Year."
P: These *kanji* are difficult.
K: In short it means "*Akemashite omedetoo.*"
P: It means "Happy New Year," right?
K: That's right. Oh, this monkey has such a cute face.
P: Why is there a monkey on the card?
K: Because it is the year of the monkey. Do you remember the Chinese way of designating an animal to each year of the twelve-year cycle?
P: I'm sorry. I forgot.
K: I'll lend you this dictionary so you can check it.
P: Thank you very much.

K: はやし かおり先生　　*Hayashi Kaori sensei*　　Kaori Hayashi (teacher)
P: ピーター　スミス　　*Piitaa Sumisu*　　Peter Smith

3. Language & Culture Notes

1 The Japanese New Year (*oshoogatsu*) is the most important and most cultural holiday of the year. Similar to Americans sending family and friends Christmas and holiday greetings, Japanese send *nengajoo*, New Year's cards or postcards. Postcards are much more common than regular cards. Some people buy pre-printed postcards and others write their own messages of health and happiness for the new year. *Nengajoo* should be mailed by December 20. Like the Christmas season in the United States, post offices in Japan handle large volumes of mail for the Japanese New Year. In the U.S. it is customary to send Christmas cards any time during the two weeks before Christmas; however, *nengajoo* should not be received prior to January 1. Writing "*nenga*" on the front of the card ensures that the post office will deliver it on New Year's Day. Most postcards have "*Akemashite omedetoo gozaimasu*" written on them. This literally means "Congratulations on the opening of the new year."

2 Since *oshoogatsu* is such an important event, relatives who had moved away return home to celebrate the holidays with their family. During the few days preceding the New Year, the women of the household usually thoroughly clean the house and make enough food for New Year's Day and the few days following it. On January 1, 2, and 3, families spend time together visiting shrines and temples as well as friends. It is the one time of year that the entire family can relax and spend quality time together.

3 *Moraimasu* means "receive something from someone." The person from whom one is receiving is followed by *kara*. *Morau* is the dictionary form of the verb.

4 *Oya* shows the speaker's surprise in discovering something.

5 *Dakara* points out the reason(s) for something.

6 The Japanese have borrowed many things from the Chinese. The calendar is an example. Both the Chinese and Japanese use the twelve month lunar calendar; however, it is unique in that it consists of a cycle of twelve years in which each year is represented by a different animal. For example, 1996 was the year of the mouse, or rat, 1997 the cow, 1998 the tiger, 1999 the rabbit, and 2000 the year of the dragon. *Nengajoo* with a picture of the new year's animal on it are popular. (See page 182 of <u>Japanese for Young English Speakers Volume I</u>)

1936	1948	1960	1972	1984	1996	2008	mouse/rat (*nezumi*)
1937	1949	1961	1973	1985	1997	2009	cow/bull (*ushi*)
1938	1950	1962	1974	1986	1998	2010	tiger (*tora*)
1939	1951	1963	1975	1987	1999	2011	rabbit (*usagi*)
1940	1952	1964	1976	1988	2000	2012	dragon (*tatsu*)
1941	1953	1965	1977	1989	2001	2013	snake (*hebi*)
1942	1954	1966	1978	1990	2002	2014	horse (*uma*)
1943	1955	1967	1979	1991	2003	2015	sheep (*hitsuji*)
1944	1956	1968	1980	1992	2004	2016	monkey (*saru*)
1945	1957	1969	1981	1993	2005	2017	hen/rooster (*tori*)
1946	1958	1970	1982	1994	2006	2018	dog (*inu*)
1947	1959	1971	1983	1995	2007	2019	wild boar (*inoshishi*)

7 When the *-te* form of a verb is followed by *shimaimashita*, the sentence means that an action has ended up in an unexpected situation, or that something has been done completely.

8 When the *-te* form of a verb is followed by *agemasu*, the sentence means that an action will be conducted for the listener.

9 When the *-te* form of a verb is followed by *minasai*, it means "try to do." However, this expression is not as polite as a verb in the *te* form followed by *mite kudasai*.

III. PARTICIPATION

1. Vocabulary

1 From sample conversation:

akemashite ([literally] open) *iu/yuu* (to say, to mean)
juunishi (twelve animals of the Chinese twelve-year cycle)
kantan (simple, in short) *kashite* (lend)
Kingashinnen. (Happy New Year.) *kotoshi* (this year)
muzukashii (difficult) *nengajoo* (New Year's card)
saru (monkey) *sarudoshi* (the year of the monkey)
shirabete (check)

2 Useful for activities:

dezaato (dessert) *fuku* (clothes)
gomi (trash, dirt) *hako* (box)
hen (strange) *heta* (poor, be bad at)
hone (bone) *hon'yaku* (translation)
ji (characters, letters) *kaesu* (to return)
komaru (be troubled, be in trouble) *kontakuto renzu* (contact lens)
kowareru (to break) *morau* (to receive)
nakanaka (hardly) *naku* (to cry)
nigiru (to grasp) *noseru* (to give a ride, to give a lift)
oishii (taste good, delicious) *otosu* (to drop)
pedaru (pedal) *saikuringu* (cycling)
sakki (a while ago) *sentaku suru* (to do laundry)
shinbun kiji (newspaper article) *sooji suru* (to clean)
sugu (immediately) *tana* (shelf)
tasukaru (be helpful) *todoku* (to reach)
unten menkyoshoo (driver's license)

2. Activity, Practice, & Exercise

1 Have you ever . . . ?

In pairs: Students ask their partners if they have ever done something specific. If they haven't, ask them to try to do it. Use the expression --- *te mite kudasai*. Practice the activity with at least three different classmates.

Example: 1)   A: *B san, Yoshimoto Banana no "Kitchin" o yonda koto ga arimasu ka?*
          (B, have you ever read <u>Kitchen</u> by Banana Yoshimoto?)

      B: *Iie.* (No.)

      A: *Omoshiroi desu yo. Eigo no hon'yaku mo arimasu kara, zehi <u>yonde mite kudasai</u>.*
         (It's interesting. There's an English translation, so you should try to read it.)

      B: *Soo desu ka. Jaa yonde mimasu.* (Really? I will.)

    2)   A: *B san, tenpura tabeta koto aru?* (B, have you ever eaten tenpura?)

      B: *Uun, mada tabeta koto nai n da/wa.* (No, not yet.)

      A: *"Resutoran Hanako" no tenpura wa yasukute oishii yo/wa yo. Zehi <u>tabete mitara</u>.*
         (The tenpura at Hanako Restaurant is cheap and delicious. You should try it.)

      B: *Soo. Jaa, kondo tabete miru yo/wa.* (Really? I'll try it.)

2 Word quiz

In pairs: Person A is given a list of words written in English (E), and Person B is given a list of the same words in Japanese (J). Pairs quiz each other on the meaning of the words in the other language. Follow the example.

Example word list:

List E	1. rain	2. animal	3. flower	4. hot
	5. delicious	6. expensive	7. to buy	8. to study
List J	1. *ame*	2. *doobutsu*	3. *hana*	4. *atsui*
	5. *oishii*	6. *takai*	7. *kau*	8. *benkyoo suru*

Example: A: (Looking at List E) *"Rain" wa "ame" to iu imi desu.* ("Rain" means "*ame*.")

        B: (Checking List J) *Soo desu ne.* (That's right.)

           (Looking at List J) *"Doobutsu" wa "school" to iu imi desu.*
                ("*Doobutsu*" means "school.")

        A: (Checking the List E) *Iie, chigaimasu yo. "Doobutsu" wa "animal" to iu imi desu.*
          (No, it doesn't. "*Doobutsu*" means "animal.")

3 New Year's cards

Individually: Write a *nengajoo* (New Year's card). Use the chart in Language & Culture Note 7 to determine what year it is.

4 I belong to the year of the . . .

In small groups: Referring to the chart in Language & Culture Note 7, group members tell each other to which year of the Chinese twelve-year cycle they and their family members belong.

Example: A: *Watashi wa sarudoshi desu. Chichi wa hitsujidoshi de, haha wa toridoshi desu. Imooto wa inoshishidoshi desu. B san no kazoku wa?*
(I belong to the year of the monkey. My father belongs to the year of the sheep, my mother, the hen, and my sister, the boar. How about your family, B?)

B: *Watashi mo sarudoshi desu. Chichi wa toradoshi de, haha wa usagidoshi de, ani wa tatsudoshi desu. C san no kazoku wa?*
(I belong to the year of the monkey, too. My father, the tiger, my mother, the rabbit, and my brother, the dragon. How about your family, C?)

C: *Watashi mo sarudoshi desu. Chichi to otooto wa nezumidoshi de, haha wa inudoshi desu. Watashi no inu wa toridoshi desu. Inu nanoni hen desu ne.*
(I belong to the year of the monkey as well. My father and my brother are the mouse, and my mother, the dog. My dog belongs to the year of the hen. It sounds strange to mention a dog, doesn't it?)

5 Sentence completion

In pairs or small groups: Complete each sentence expressing dissatisfaction using the expression ---*shimaimashita*.

Example: *Kono bideo wa senshuu katta bakari nanoni, <u>moo kowarete shimaimashita</u>.*
(Although I bought this video just last week, it has already broken.)

1. *Kinoo benkyoo shita bakari nanoni* (Although I learned it just yesterday), _____ .
2. *Senshuu okane o moratta bakari nanoni* (Although I got money just last week), _____ .
3. *Asa sooji shita bakari nanoni* (Although I cleaned just this morning), _____ .
4. *Sakki sentaku o shita bakari nanoni* (Although I did the laundry just a while ago), _____ .
5. *Kono fuku wa katta bakari nanoni* (Although I have just bought these clothes), _____ .

6 My mother tells me to . . .

In pairs: Tell your partner about what your parents, brothers and sisters, or teachers usually ask you to do. Use the expression -*nasai*. Follow the example.

Example: A: *Haha wa watashi ni "Kirei na ji o <u>kakinasai</u>" to iimasu.*
(My mother says to me, "Write neatly.")

B: *Sensei wa watashitachi ni "Isshookenmei <u>benkyoo shinasai</u>," to iimasu.*
(The teacher says to us, "Study hard.")

7 Team competition: Gesture game

In three teams: Each team writes four different sentences using the expression *-nasai*. Write each sentence on a separate piece of paper and give two to each of the other two teams. Each team member will get one of the new sentences but should not show it to their teammates. There may not be enough sentences for everyone on the team. Team members take turns conveying the new sentences to each other through gestures within 90 seconds. Teams get one point for each gesture that is correctly guessed within the time limit.

8 Memorizing, practicing, and presenting dialogues

In pairs: The following dialogues are situations in which the form *-te agemasu* is used. The conversations are both practical and useful. In pairs, memorize the dialogues and practice them in skits. Each pair should present one or two dialogues to the class, depending on time. Note: The gender of the speakers in the dialogues have been marked as male, female, or either.

Dialogue 1
A: male
B: either

A: *Anoo, dochira made ikaremasu ka?*
B: *Chotto yuubinkyoku made.*
A: *Nosete agemasu yo.*
B: *A, soo desu ka? Sumimasen.*

Dialogue 2
A: male
B: female

A: *Sakana no hone, joozu ni toremasu ka?*
B: *Watashi heta na no.*
A: *Jaa, boku ga totte agemasu yo.*
B: *Arigatoo.*

Dialogue 3
A: either
B: male

A: *Tegami o kakitai n desu ga. Te ga itakute pen ga nigirenai n desu. Kaite kuremasen ka?*
B: *Ii desu yo. Boku ga kaite agemasu.*
A: *Sumimasen. Onegai shimasu.*

Dialogue 4
A: male
B: either

A: *A, shimatta. Unten menkyoshoo o wasurete kita yo. Komatta na.*
B: *Watashi ga unten shite agemasu.*
A: *Onegai dekiru? Arigatoo.*

Dialogue 5
A: either
B: female

A: *Doo shimashita ka?*
B: *Kontakuto renzu o otoshita n desu. Kurakute yoku mienai n desu.*
A: *Raito o tsukete ageru yo.*
B: *Doomo sumimasen. Atta wa. Arigatoo.*

Dialogue 6	A: *Obaachan, kono shinbun kiji omoshiroi wa yo.*
A: female	B: *Soo. Ara, megane doko ni oita kashira. Megane ga nai to yomenai no yo ne.*
B: female	A: *Jaa, watashi ga yonde ageru.*
	B: *Soo. Tasukaru wa. Arigatoo.*

Dialogue 7	A: *Nani o shiteru n desu ka, Okaasan?*
A: male	B: *Tana no ue no hako o toroo to omotte. Nakanaka te ga todokanai no yo.*
B: female	A: *Boku ga totte ageru yo.*
	B: *Arigatoo.*

Dialogue 8	A: *Mariko san, naitari shite. Dooshita no?*
A: female	B: *Chigau no. Me ni gomi ga haitta mitai na no.*
B: female	A: *Soo na no. Watashi ga mite ageru. Chotto misete.*
	B: *Mite kureru? Arigatoo.*

Dialogue 9	A: *Moshi moshi, --- dakedo.*
A: male	B: *A, --- kun, dooshita?*
B: male	A: *Iya ne. Ashita saikuringu tsuaa ga aru n dakedo, boku no wa pedaru ga kowarechatte, norenai n da yo.*
	B: *Soo ka. Jaa, boku no o kashite ageru yo.*
	A: *Kashite kureru? Tasukatta.*

Dialogue 10	A: *Ara, ame ga futte kita wa.*
A: female	B: *Kasa motte kita?*
B: female	A: *Motte konakatta wa.*
	B: *Jaa, watashi no kashite ageru.*
	A: *Ii no?*
	B: *2 hon aru kara ii wa yo.*
	A: *Arigatoo. Sugu kaesu kara.*

9 Making sentences

In pairs: Student A asks B a question about something that he/she doesn't know or doesn't understand. B answers using the expression *Kantan ni ieba* to explain it to A. Try to write two or three short dialogues. Follow the example.

Example: 1) A: *Shoogi wa nan desu ka?*

B: <u>*Kantan ni ieba*</u> *chesu no yoo na mono desu.*

2) A: *Bon'odori wa nan desu ka?*

B: <u>*Kantan ni ieba*</u> *fooku dansu no yoo na mono desu.*

Lesson 17: Photographs of Japan

I. PERSPECTIVE

1. Objective

1 Function:

(1) Wishing/Hoping for something to happen: *(Yoi ichinen) ni naru yoo ni.*
(2) Stating the purpose for doing something: *(Nagusame)ru tame,*
(3) Seeking permission to do something: *(Shitsumon shi)te ii desu ka?*
(4) Encouraging one to do something without hesitation: *Enryo naku doozo.*
(5) Wanting to confirm something: *Kakunin shitai no desu.*
(6) Asking if both are OK: *Dochira (e itte) mo ii desu ka?*
(7) Indicating that it is all right to do something: *Ee, kamaimasen.*

2 Language:

(1) *(Atarashii toshi) ga (yo)i (ichinen) ni naru yoo ni, (inori)masu.*
(2) *(Rei) o (nagusame)ru tame, (inori)masu.*   (3) *(Shitsumon shi)te ii desu ka?*
(4) *(Enryo naku) doozo.*   (5) *(Omairi) no (basho) o (kakunin) shitai no desu.*
(6) *Dochira (e itte) mo ii (desu ka?)*   (7) *Kamaimasen.*
(8) *(Jinja) e mo (tera) e mo (jiyuu ni ike)masu yo.*

3 Culture:

(1) Shrine & temple visits   (2) Importance of ancestors

II. PREPARATION

1. Context

日本の写真

日本語の授業に、はやし先生がお客を連れて来た。その人はカメラマンで名前はわかいふじお。先日、ニューヨークで個展を開いたという。人間の様々な日常生活をテーマに写真を撮っている。彼が持って来た写真はすべて、日本人を写したものだった。お正月の神社でのお参りの様子とか、お盆の墓参りの様子とか。みんなは興味を持ってその写真を見、説明を聞いた。

Hayashi *sensei* brought a guest to Japanese class. Her friend's name is Fujio Wakai. He is a photographer and recently held an exhibition of his work in New York City. He took pictures of various aspects of daily life in Japan. The pictures that he brought to our class were all of Japanese people. There were scenes at a shrine on New Year's Day and a visit to a grave during the Bon Festival, for example. Everybody looked at the pictures and listened to Mr. Wakai's explanations with great interest.

2. Sample Conversation

F: 右の写真は、日本のお正月の風景です。新しい年がよい一年になるように、祈ります。左の写真はお墓参りの風景です。祖先の霊を慰めるため、祈ります。
P: すみません。質問していいですか。
F: 遠慮無くどうぞ。
P: お参りの場所を確認したいのです。
F: お正月はたいてい神社です。お墓参りは寺ですね。
P: どちらへ行ってもいいですか。
F: ええ、かまいません。神社へも寺へも自由に行けますよ。
P: 何か不思議です。
F: そうですね。でも、日本人には自然なことです。

F: *Migi no shashin wa, Nihon no oshoogatsu no fuukei desu. Atarashii toshi ga yoi ichinen ni naru yoo[1] ni, inorimasu. Hidari no shashin wa ohakamairi[2] no fuukei desu. Sosen no rei o nagusameru tame[3], inorimasu.*
P: *Sumimasen. Shitsumon shite ii desu ka?*
F: *Enryo naku doozo.*
P: *Omairi no basho o kakunin shitai no desu.*
F: *Oshoogatsu wa taitei jinja desu. Ohakamairi wa tera desu ne[4].*
P: *Dochira e itte mo ii desu ka?*
F: *Ee, kamaimasen. Jinja e mo tera e mo jiyuu ni ikemasu yo.*
P: *Nani ka fushigi desu.*
F: *Soo desu ne. Demo, nihonjin ni wa shizen na koto desu.*

F: The picture on the right is a scene of New Year's Day in Japan. We pray that the New Year will be a good year. The picture on the left is a visit to a grave. They are praying to appease the spirits of their ancestors.
P: Excuse me. May I ask a question?
F: Please don't hesitate to ask.
P: I want to confirm the place where people go to pray.
F: People usually go to shrines on New Year's Day and go to temples to visit ancestors' graves.
P: Can you go to both places?
F: Yes, you can. You can go to both shrines and temples if you want to.
P: It's strange.
F: Yes, it is, but it's natural for Japanese.

F: わかい ふじお (ゲストスピーカー) — *Wakai Fujio (Gesuto supiikaa)* — Fujio Wakai (Guest speaker)
P: ピーター スミス — *Piitaa Sumisu* — Peter Smith

3. Language & Culture Notes

1 *Yoo,* when followed by *da*, means "appears to be," or "it seems that." When followed by *na*, it means "such as," "like," "as," or "such." When *yoo* is followed by *ni*, it means "like," "as," or "as --- as." *Yoo* alone refers to a mode, manner, kind, or appearance. It usually signifies outward appearance.

2 During the New Year's holiday, it is customary for families to visit temples and shrines together, as well as the grave sites of their ancestors. Temples are for praying to Buddha and one's ancestors; shrines are for praying to god. The summer Bon Festival is the time when people call to the souls of their ancestors; therefore, people visit only temples during this holiday. During the Bon Festival, priests may come to a family's home and pray with them. Some Japanese continue to visit temples and shrines throughout the year; however, most only go during the holidays.

3 The word *tame* follows the dictionary form of verbs and means "in order to" or "for the purpose of."

Ii ten o toru tame isshookenmei benkyoo shimasu. (I study hard in order to get good grades.)

4 Japanese people strongly believe in the spirits of their ancestors and often pray to them in hopes of happiness and good fortune for the present and future generations of the family. Japanese strive to do good deeds in the present for the benefit of family members to come. It is believed that if one commits wrongdoings, it will directly affect future family members. Also, if a family member suddenly becomes seriously ill, it may be concluded that it is a result of something negative that an ancestor did while alive. This way of thinking has existed in Japan for as long as its history; however, it is becoming less influential as new generations no longer wish to follow the ways of their parents and ancestors.

III. PARTICIPATION

1. Vocabulary

1 From sample conversation:

basho (place)
fushigi (strange, mysterious)
hidari no (on the left)
ikemasu (can go)
jinja (shrine)
kakunin shitai (want to confirm)
migi no (on the right)
ohakamairi (a visit to a grave)
oshoogatsu (New Year's Day)
shizen (natural)
tame ni (for the purpose of, in order to)
toshi (year)

enryo naku (without reserve, hesitation)
fuukei (scene)
ichinen (a year, one year)
inorimasu (pray)
jiyuu ni (freely)
kamaimasen (OK, no problem)
nagusameru (to appease)
omairi (a visit to a temple or shrine to pray)
rei (spirit)
sosen (ancestor)
tera (temple)

2 Useful for activities:

aite iru (be open)	*dochira* (which)
geki (a play)	*hakubutsukan* (museum)
hitotsu zutsu (one of each)	*inoru* (to pray)
isshookenmei (with all one's might)	*jikokuhyoo* (schedule [bus, train])
junban ni (in turns)	*kin'enseki* (no smoking seat)
kitsuenseki (smoking seat)	*kochira* (this way)
koochoo sensei (principal)	*kookuubin* (air mail)
kookuugaisha (airline)	*koonaa* (corner)
madoguchi (ticket window, counter)	*minzoku* (race)
narande susumu (to proceed in a line)	*nedoko no yooi* (making a bed)
Osuwari kudasai. (Please have a seat.)	*Oyasumi kudasai.* (Sleep well.)
rekishi (history)	*shoorai* (future)
shuppatsu (suru) (departure [to depart])	*sukunaku tomo* (at least)
toochaku (suru) (arrival [to arrive])	*yokozuna* (sumo grand champion)
--- *yoo ni.* (May... be ...!; I wish ...)	*yoyaku* (reservation)

2. Activity, Practice & Exercise

1 Stating one's wishes

Individually: Write down your wishes using the expression -*masu yoo ni*.

Examples: *Kazoku ga shiawase ni naremasu yoo ni.* (May my family become happy!)

   Asu haremasu yoo ni. (May tomorrow be sunny!)

   Tesuto de ii ten o toremasu yoo ni. (May I get a good grade on the test!)

2 I wished for ...

In pairs: Students tell their partner what they wished or prayed for in APE 1.

Example: *Watashi wa kazoku ga shiawase ni nareru yoo ni inorimashita.*
   (I wished for the happiness of my family.)

   Watashi wa rainen Nihon ni ikeru yoo ni inorimashita.
   (I wished that I will be able to go to Japan next year.)

3 May I ... ?

In groups of five: Group members take turns asking each other if they may do something specific. Students should use the expression *Enryo naku doozo* to give permission or *Sumimasen. Sore wa chotto ...* to deny the request. Students should continue asking questions and giving or denying permission until everyone feels comfortable using the new expressions.

Example: 1) A: *Chotto shitsumon shite (mo) ii desu ka?* (May I ask you a question?)
   B: *Ee, enryo naku doozo.* (Yes, feel free to do so.)

   2) A: *Koko de tabete (mo) ii desu ka?* (May I eat here?)
   B: *Sumimasen. Sore wa chotto ...* (I'm sorry, but ...)

4 I will go to ... to ...

Groups of four: Each group needs a score card and at least 12 cards with the name of a place written on each. Place all the cards face down. Members take turns drawing a card and making a sentence. Students should state that they will go to the place on the card and include why they will go there. The time limit for making a sentence is 30 seconds. If a student makes a correct sentence within the time limit, mark an O on the score card for that person. If time runs out, or if the sentence is incorrect, mark an X on the score card. The winner of each group is the one with the most O's.

Examples of places: *toshokan, taiikukan, tomodachi no ie, resutoran, kooen, depaato, eki.*
Tokyo (Ginza, Akihabara, Ueno Kooen, Roppongi), any other country or city.
Example: *toshokan* → *Hon o yomu <u>tame ni</u>, toshokan <u>e ikimasu</u>.*
(library → I will go to the library to read a book.)

5 Completing sentences

Groups of four: Each student makes a sentence in the target form, --- *suru tame -masu* or *-te imasu*. Students then divide their sentence after *tame* and write each half on a separate card. The teacher then collects all of the cards and mixes them together. The teacher randomly gives eight cards to each group. Students take turns drawing cards and reading them aloud to the group. Group members work together to write either the first or second half of each sentence to complete the phrases. Examples of sentences:

1. *Kuruma o kau tame...*	*Kuruma o <u>kau tame</u> arubaito o shite imasu.*
2. *... isshookenmei benkyoo shimasu.*	*Tesuto o <u>ukeru tame</u> isshookenmei benkyoo shimasu.*
3. *Genki ni naru tame ...*	*Genki ni <u>naru tame</u> shikkari tabemasu.*

6 Making confirmations

Four groups: The teacher writes the following four situations on the blackboard. Each group chooses a different situation and writes a dialogue in which someone wants to confirm something. Use the expression *kakunin shitai no desu*. The following list of words may be helpful in writing the conversations. Afterward, each group presents a different situation to the class.

Situations:

1. Bus company: confirm bus times
2. Airline/travel agent: confirm flight schedule
3. Restaurant: confirm reservations
4. Theater: confirm movie or show times

Word list:

1. *yoyaku*
2. *jikokuhyoo*
3. *kookuugaisha*
4. *kin'enseki*
5. *kitsuenseki*
6. *eiga*
7. *geki*
8. *shuppatsu (suru)*
9. *toochaku (suru)*

7 Asking permission

In class: In this activity, the teacher makes announcements saying that everyone has permission to do something. Using *dochira*, *doko*, or *dore*, students take turns asking the teacher a question about the rules or the situation. Follow the example below. The activity should continue until each student has had a chance to ask the teacher a question.

Example:

   Sensei: *Minasan, kochira ni nihonryoori to chuugokuryoori ga arimasu. Doozo, tabete kudasai.*

           (There is Japanese and Chinese food. Please help yourselves.)

   Seito: <u>*Dochira*</u> *o tabete* <u>*mo ii desu ka*</u>? (May we have both?)

   Sensei: *Ee, kamaimasen.* (Yes. Go ahead.)

Announcements:

1. *Minasan, 2 ban to 3 ban no madoguchi ga aite imasu. Doozo, junban ni narande susunde kudasai.*
2. *Minasan, koochoo sensei kara purezento desu. Hitotsu zutsu totte kudasai.*
3. *Minasan, nedoko no yooi ga dekimashita. Oyasumi kudasai.*
4. *Minasan, isu no yooi ga dekimashita. Osuwari kudasai.*
5. *Minasan, mondai ga futatsu arimasu. Hitotsu dake yatte kudasai.*
6. *Minasan, kono hakubutsukan ni wa rekishi koonaa to minzoku koonaa ga arimasu. Futatsu to mo mite kudasai.*
7. *Minasan, kore ga Nihon no kareeraisu desu. Supuun ka fooku de tabete kudasai.*
8. *Kore wa Hayashi san kara no purezento desu. Futatsu arimasu ga hitotsu totte kudasai.*
9. *Kore wa Nihon no bideo desu. 3 bon arimasu. Sukunaku tomo 1 pon wa mite kudasai.*

8 Word replacement

In pairs: Replace the underlined word with the following verbs. Change the other words in the sentence accordingly so that the sentence makes sense. Make sure that the form of the verb indicates that one can or that it is possible to do the action.

Example: *Jiyuu ni <u>ikemasu</u> yo.*

kau, yomu, kaku, taberu, utau, nomu

Lesson 18 — Review & Application

IV. PERFORMANCE

1. Application

1 **Conversation completion**

In small groups: The following is a conversation between an American student (S) and a Japanese teacher (T). They are talking about Japanese New Year's cards. Guess what the American student would say in the conversation. Choose the most appropriate sentence from the list below.

T: *Ara, Kimu san, kore wa Nihon no nengajoo desu ne.*
   (Oh, Kim. This is a Japanese New Year's card, isn't it?)
S: (   ) (Yes. It's from the family I stayed with last summer.)
T: *Nan to kakarete imasu ka? Yonde kudasai.* (What does it say? Please read it aloud.)
S: (   ) ("*Akemashite omedetoo gozaimasu.*")
T: *Doo iu imi ka wakarimasu ka?* (Do you know what it means?)
S: (   ) (It means "Happy New Year!")
T: *Sono toori. Maa, kono nezumi, kawaii desu ne. Mikkii Mausu mitai.*
   (That's right. This mouse is so cute. It looks like Mickey Mouse.)
S: (   ) (But why is there a picture of a mouse?)
T: *Kotoshi wa nezumidoshi dakara desu yo. Juunishi tte oboete imasu ka?*
   (Because this year is the year of the mouse. Do you remember the Chinese twelve-year cycle?)
S: (   ) (I'm sorry. I forgot.)
T: *12 shurui no doobutsu de toshi o arawasu n desu yo. Nezumi toka, ushi toka, tora toka, ...*
   (Each year in the twelve-year cycle is represented by a different animal, such as a mouse, cow, tiger, ...)
S: (   ) (Oh, I remember now. I was born in the year of the hen.)

1. Happy New Year *to iu imi desu.*
2. *Hai. Kyonen no natsu hoomusutei shita kazoku kara desu.*
3. *Aa, ima omoidashimashita. Watashi wa toridoshi datta n desu.*
4. *Demo, dooshite nezumi no e nan ka kaite aru n deshoo?*
5. "*Akemashite omedetoo gozaimasu.*"
6. *Sumisasen. Wasurete shimaimashita.*

2 **Conversation completion**

In small groups: The following is a conversation between an American high school student (A) and a Japanese student (J) who is studying in America. They are looking at a picture of a shrine on New Year's Day. Guess what the American student would say in the underlined parts of the conversation. Each group reports its conversation to the class.

J: *Kore, mite. Nihon no oshoogatsu no shashin na no.*
(Look at this. This is a picture of a Japanese New Year's celebration.)

A: *Hee.* _____ . (Really?)

J: *Koko wa jinja. Nihon no kamisama ga iru basho yo.*
(This is a shrine. This is where the Japanese god is.)

A: _____ .

J: *Inoru no yo. Tatoeba "Ii 1 nen ni narimasu yoo ni," toka "Seiseki ga yoku narimasu yoo ni," toka.*
(People pray. They say, for example, "May we have a good new year!" or "May my grades at school get better!")

A: _____ .

J: *Sore wa saisen bako. Okane o ireru hako na no. Kamisama ni inoru toki wa, minna saisenbako ni okane o ireru no yo.*
(It's an offertory box. You put money in it. Everybody puts money in it when they pray to god.)

A: _____ .

J: *10 en ireru hito mo iru shi, 100 en ireru hito mo iru shi, tokidoki 10,000 en ireru hito mo iru wa. Watashi wa itsumo daitai 50 en gurai kana.*
(Some put in 10 yen, some 100 yen, and some people even put in 10,000 yen. In my case, I usually put in about 50 yen.)

A: *Hee, demo saisenbako tte soto ni aru n daro.* _____ .
(Oh. The offertory box is usually placed outside, isn't it?)

J: *Amari kiita koto wa nai wa. Kamisama no mono o nusumu to, bachi ga ataru kara kamo ne.*
(I've never heard that. Maybe it's because god is punishing someone for stealing something from him.)

3 Passive voice

In pairs: Each pair needs a book of paintings or other art, comic books, poems, or a novel created by a well-known artist or author. Partners tell each other who wrote the novel, painted the pictures, or drew the comic books. Use the verb *kaku* in either its active or passive voice, and the partner will change the sentence into the other voice. Pairs exchange books and repeat the process several times.

Example: A: *Kore wa Poo ga kaita shoosetsu desu.* (This is a novel that Poe wrote.)
B: *Kore wa Poo ni yotte kakareta shoosetsu desu.* (This is a novel written by Poe.)
A: *Kore wa Pikaso ga kaita e desu.* (This is a picture that Picaso painted.)
B: *Kore wa Pikaso ni yotte kakareta e desu.* (This is a picture painted by Picaso.)
A: *Kore wa Shurutsu ga kaita manga desu.* (This is a comic book that Schulz drew.)
B: *Kore wa Shurutsu ni yotte kakareta manga desu.* (This is a comic drawn by Schulz.)

4 Made in Japan

① In small groups: Choose an item in the classroom that is foreign made. Say where it was made using one of the following expressions: --- *de tsukuraremashita;* --- *de tsukurareta* ---; *-sei desu;* or *-sei no* ---. Include the brand name using --- *no*. Follow the example.

Example: • *Kono tokei wa <u>nihonsei</u> desu / Kono tokei wa Nihon <u>de tsukuraremashita</u>. Seikoo <u>no</u> tokei desu.*
(This is a Japanese watch. / This watch was made in Japan. It's a Seiko.)
• *Kono shatsu wa <u>chuugokusei desu</u>. / Kore wa Chuugoku <u>de tsukurareta</u> shatsu desu. Karuban Kurain <u>no</u> shatsu desu.*
(This is a Chinese shirt. / This is a shirt made in China. It's a Calvin Klein.)

② Choose something in your home that is foreign made. Write a sentence about it using the same pattern as in ①.

Example: • *Uchi ni <u>nihonsei no</u> terebi ga arimasu. Hitachi <u>no</u> terebi desu.*
(We have a Japanese TV at home. It's a Hitachi.)
• *Uchi ni Doitsu <u>no</u> kuruma ga arimasu. Sore wa BMW desu.*
(We have a German car. It's a BMW.)

5 Contrasting cultures

In groups of four: Discuss the following topic in Japanese. Afterward, a representative from each group presents its responses to the class. Use the expression --- *no wa --- ni wa futsuu no koto desu* and --- *ni wa mezurashii koto desu*.

Discussion topic: Name some customs that are common for Japanese people but not common for Americans. Also name customs that are common in America but not in Japan.

Example: 1) *Ie ni hairu toki kutsu o nugu <u>no wa</u> nihonjin <u>ni wa futsuu no koto desu</u> ga, amerikajin <u>ni wa mezurashii koto desu</u>.*
(It is common for Japanese people to take off their shoes when they enter the house, but it is not common for Americans.)

2) *Kazoku ga kisu o suru <u>no wa</u> amerikajin <u>ni wa futsuu no koto desu</u> ga, nihonjin <u>ni wa mezurashii koto desu</u>.*
(It is common for Americans to kiss their family members, but it is unusual for Japanese people to do so.)

6 What made you and your friends happy?

① In class: Split the class in half and make two circles, one inside the other. With students in the two circles facing each other, the inner circle begins to rotate clockwise and the outer circle counterclockwise when the teacher starts the music. Students stop walking when the music stops. Students pair up with the person they are facing and talk about something that made them feel happy or good.

Example: A: *Watashi wa natsuyasumi ni Nihon e itte, totemo ii tomodachi ga dekimashita. Sore ga sugoku <u>ureshikatta</u> desu.*
(I went to Japan during summer vacation and made a very good friend. It made me really happy.)

B: *Yokatta desu ne. Boku wa sakkaa kurabu ni haitte imasu. Sengetsu, tonari no machi no kookoo to shiai o shite, kachimashita. Taihen <u>ureshikatta</u> desu.*
(Good for you. I belong to a soccer club. Last month we won a game against the high school in the neighboring town. I was very excited.)

② When the teacher restarts the music, students begin walking again. When the music stops, students tell their new partner about their first one. Use the expression --- *to iu koto desu.*

Example: A: *B san wa sakkaa kurabu ni haitte iru to iu koto desu. Sengetsu, tonari no machi no kookoo to shiai o shite, katta toki, taihen <u>ureshikatta</u> to iu koto desu.*

(I heard that B belongs to a soccer club. I heard he was very glad when he won a game against the high school in the neighboring town.)

C: *D san wa ...* (D ...)

7 Verb conjugation: potential (capable/can) form

In pairs: Using verb cards or a list of verbs, change verbs from the dictionary form into the potential or capable/can form.

Example:
- *kaku → kakeru, yomu → yomeru (-u → -eru)*
- *miru → mirareru, okiru → okirareru (-ru → -rareru)*
- *setsumei suru → setsumei dekiru (suru → dekiru)*
- *kuru → korareru (kuru → korareru)*

8 Your goal

In pairs: Tell your partner about a goal that you would like to try hard to achieve. Use the potential form of a verb plus *yoo ni* to express your goal.

Example: A: *Kuruma ga unten <u>dekiru yoo ni</u>, isshookenmei renshuu shimasu.*

(I will practice hard so that I can drive.)

B: *Nihongo ga joozu ni <u>hanaseru yoo ni</u>, ganbarimasu.*

(I will try hard so that I can speak Japanese well.)

9 New Year's greetings

In class: Suppose you are now celebrating the New Year in Japan. Walk around the classroom and exchange greetings with your teacher and friends. Try to bow when you greet them. If the teacher or a student has some Japanese New Year music, it would help to set the atmosphere and make the activity more enjoyable.

Example: A: *B san, akemashite omedetoo. Kyonen wa iroiro arigatoo. Kotoshi mo doozo yoroshiku.*

(B, Happy New Year! Thank you for your kindness last year. I hope we will be good friends this year, too.)

B: *Akemashite omedetoo. Kochira koso doozo yoroshiku.*

(Happy New Year! I hope for the same thing.)

A: *Sensei, akemashite omedetoo gozaimasu. Kyonen wa iroiro osewa ni narimashita. Kotoshi mo doozo yoroshiku onegaishimasu.*

(Mr./Ms. ---, Happy New Year! Thank you for taking good care of me. I hope you will help me this year, too.)

T: *A san, akemashite omedetoo. Kochira koso doozo yoroshiku.*

(A, Happy New Year! I feel the same way.)

10 **What are your plans ... ?**

In pairs: Partners ask each other what they plan to do during a specific time: summer vacation or next weekend, for example. Students should use the expression --- *koto ni shimashita* to say what they have decided to do. They should do the activity with at least three different partners and keep track of classmates' responses as in the example task sheet.

Example: 1) A: *Kotoshi no natsu, doko ka e ikimasu ka?* (Do you plan to go anywhere this summer?)
   B: *Kotoshi no natsu wa Mekishiko ni iku <u>koto ni shimashita</u>.*
      (I've decided to go to Mexico.)
   A: *Waa, ii desu ne.* (That's great.)

2) A: *Kondo no shuumatsu, nani o suru yotei na no?* (What are your plans for this weekend?)
   B: <u>*Mada kimete nai*</u> *n da/no.* (I haven't decided yet.)

Example task sheet

<u>Kiita aite</u>	<u>Itsu</u>	<u>Yotei</u>
An	*natsu*	*Mekishiko ni iku*
Jon	*shuumatsu*	*mada kimete nai*

2. Actualization

1 Practice the following conversation and develop your own dialogue on a similar subject with your partners.

Getsuyoobi no 2jikanme, 4 nen 2 kumi no seito wa warizan no benkyoo o shite imasu.
(In second period on Monday, the 4th grade, class 2 students are working on division exercises.)

Takeda sensei: *1 kara 20 made no seisuu no uchi, 4 de warikireru kazu o itte kudasai.*
   (Name the numbers from 1 to 20 that can be evenly divided by 4.)
Suzuki kun: *4, 8, 12, 16, 20 desu.* (4, 8, 12, 16, and 20.)
Takeda sensei: *Soo desu ne. Dewa, 6 de warikireru kazu wa?*
   (Right. Then how about the numbers that are evenly divisible by 6?)
Tanaka kun: *6, 12, 18 desu.* (6, 12, and 18.)
Takeda sensei: *Hai. Soredewa, 4 demo 6 demo warikireru kazu wa wakarimasu ka?*
   (Right. Do you know what number can be evenly divided by both 4 and 6?)
Yamada san: *12 desu.* (12.)
Takeda sensei: *Hai. Yoku dekimashita.* (Right. Well done.)

2 Practice the following conversation and develop your own dialogue on a similar subject with your partners.

Sansuu no jugyoo desu. Kinoo no shukudai no kotaeawase o shite imasu.
(In math class, the students are checking the answers to yesterday's homework assignment.)

   1) $245 \div 35 =$ 2) $336 \div 12 =$ 3) $4354 \div 58 =$

Yoshida sensei: *Soredewa, saisho ni, shukudai no kotaeawase o shimashoo. Ichiban o Suzuki kun.*
   (First, let's check the answers to your homework. Suzuki, number 1, please.)

Suzuki kun:	*Hai. 7 desu.* (It's 7.)
Yoshida sensei:	*Soo desu ne. Dewa, 2 ban o Yamamoto san.* (Right. number 2, Yamamoto.)
Yamamoto san:	*Hai. 28 da to omoimasu.* (I think it's 28.)
Yoshida sensei:	*Hai. Sono toori desu. Saigo no mondai o Kobayashi kun.* (Yes. That's right. The last question, Kobayashi.)
Kobayashi kun:	*Sumimasen. Muzukashikute wakarimasen deshita.* (I'm sorry. It was too difficult for me to understand.)
Yoshida sensei:	*Jaa, Hirota san.* (OK Hirota.)
Hirota san:	*Hai. 75 amari 4 desu.* (75 with a remainder of 4.)
Yoshida sensei:	*Hai. Yoku dekimashita.* (Right. Good job.)

3 Practice the following conversation and develop your own dialogue on a similar subject with your partners.

Kayoobi no 3jikan me, sansuu no jugyoo desu. 4 nen 2 kumi no seito wa, iroiro na shikakkei no tokuchoo o benkyoo shite imasu.
(Third period on Tuesday is math. The 4th grade, class 2 students are learning about the characteristics of four-sided figures.)

Yamada sensei:	*Seihookei wa donna shikakkei desu ka?* (What kind of a four-sided figure is a square?)
Suzuki kun:	*4 tsu no hen no nagasa ga onaji desu.* (All four sides are the same length.)
Yamada sensei:	*Soo desu ne. Demo, hishigata mo 4 tsu no hen ga onaji nagasa desu ne.* (That's right. But the four sides of a diamond are also equal in length.)
Yoshida san:	*Seihookei wa 4 tsu no kaku ga zenbu chokkaku desu.* (All four corners of a square are right angles.)
Yamada sensei:	*Hai. Yoku dekimashita. Hoka ni 4 tsu no kaku ga chokkaku na shikakkei wa arimasu ka?* (Right. Well done. Are there any other four-sided figures with four right angles?)
Kobayashi kun:	*Choohookei.* (A rectangle.)
Yamada sensei:	*Soredewa, seihookei to no chigai wa?* (So, how is it different from a square?)
Tanaka kun:	*Choohookei wa tate to yoko no hen no nagasa ga chigaimasu.* (The length of rectangle's horizontal sides can be different from its vertical sides.)
Yamada sensei:	*Hai. Soo desu ne.* (Yes, that's right.)

4 Individually: Solve the problems below by making calculations in Japanese. Then compare answers with a partner. Questions should be answered in complete sentences.
Example: *Yamada san wa suupaa de, 200 en no pan to 150 en no miruku to 100 en no aisukuriimu o kaimashita. Kyoo wa tokubetsu saabisu no hi na node, kono suupaa de wa nan demo 10 paasento yasuku narimasu. Tanaka san wa ikura haraimashita ka?*
(At the supermarket, Mr. Yamada bought bread for 200 yen, milk for 150 yen, and ice cream for 100 yen. Today the store had a special 10% discount on everything. How much did he pay?)

200 + 150 + 100 = 450 (*Nihyaku tasu hyakugojuu tasu hyaku wa yonhyakugojuu.*)
450 x 0.1 = 45 (*Yonhyakugojuu kakeru rei ten ichi wa yonjuugo.*)
450 - 45 = 405 (*Yonhyakugojuu hiku yonjuugo wa yonhaykugo*)
Yamada san wa 405 en haraimashita. (Yamada paid 405 yen.)

1. *Tanaka san wa Akihabara no denkiten de, 67,800 en no bideo to 15,800 en no wookuman o kaimashita. Tanaka san wa, menbaa kaado o motteiru node, nan demo 5 paasento biki de kau koto ga dekimasu. Tanaka san wa ikura haraimashita ka?*
   (At an electronics store in Akihabara, Mr. Tanaka bought a VCR for 67,800 yen and a walkman for 15,800 yen. Mr. Tanaka has a membership card, so he receives a 5% discount on anything he buys. How much did he pay for them?)

2. *Kenji kun wa bunbooguya de, 1 pon 90 en no boorupen o 5 hon to, 1 satsu 98 en no nooto o 3 satsu to, 70 en no keshigomu o hitotsu kaimashita. Kenji kun wa 1,000 en dashimashita. Otsuri wa ikura deshoo?*
   (At a stationery store, Kenji bought 5 ball-point pens at 90 yen each, 3 notebooks at 98 yen each, and one eraser that cost 70 yen. Kenji handed over 1,000 yen. How much change did he get back?)

3. *Nashi o 12 ko hako ni iretara, 3,500 guramu ni narimashita. Hako no omosa wa 380 guramu desu. Nashi wa hitotsu nan guramu deshoo?*
   (There are 12 Japanese pears in a box. The box alone weighs 380 grams. The box with 12 pears weighs 3,500 grams. How many grams does each pear weigh?)

5 Translate the following problems into Japanese.
   a) Name the numbers from 1 to 30 that can be evenly divided by 3 and by 5.
   b) Name the numbers from 25 to 50 that can be evenly divided by both 3 and 5.
   c) Name the numbers from 1 to 30 that can be evenly divided by 2, 7, and both 2 and 7.

6 Answer the following problems in Japanese.
   a) 288 ÷ 36 =   b) 900 ÷ 75 =
   c) 377 ÷ 13 =   d) 363 ÷ 11 =
   e) 1200 ÷ 30 =   f) 7652 ÷ 63 =

7 Name the following figures in both English and Japanese.
   a) *Yottsu no kaku ga chokkaku de yottsu no hen no nagasa ga onaji.*
      (It has four right angles, and its four sides are equal in length.)
   b) *Yottsu no kaku ga chokkaku de mukaiatta hen no nagasa ga onaji.*
      (It has four right angles, and each pair of opposite sides is equal in length.)
   c) *Yottsu no hen no nagasa ga onaji de chokkaku o motanai.*
      (Its four sides are equal length, and it does not have any right angles.)

3. Enrichment

1 *Kanji* for Lesson 16

年賀状	お正月	謹賀新年	漢字	難しい
簡単	明ける	猿	顔	今年
十二支	辞書	貸す	調べる	

2 *Kanji* for Lesson 17

右	風景	祈る	左	お墓参り
祖先	霊	慰める	質問	遠慮
無く	お参り	場所	確認	神社
寺	不思議	自然		

3 Other useful *kanji*

正、横、並、落、習、忙、酒、変

4 Strategies

As discussed in Review Lesson 3, **shapes of visual objects** is the first of the six main strategies that can be applied toward *kanji* formation. This strategy is useful for *kanji* that were drawn based on how objects are visualized.

- Environment and nature: sun, mountain, river, names of animals
- Parts of the human body: eye, ear, hand
- Daily necessities and activities: rice, gate, sword, ax, clothing, book

Some *kanji* can easily be traced back to their original forms, and others are nearly impossible. Historic authenticity does not need to be faithfully pursued. Trying to establish a relationship between a *kanji* and the object or concept that it represents can be helpful in the *kanji* learning process. Each person may develop *kanji* object/concept relationships based on their own reasoning. Consider the following examples.

- 人 (person) a walking person
- 手 (hand) the combination of fingers and an arm
- 竹 (bamboo) two bamboo trees with leaves
- 虫 (insect) a head, a body, and a tail
- 象 (elephant) a head, a long nose, four legs, and a tail

5 Exercise

Using the basic rules of *kanji* formation and your own imagination, try to create several *kanji* that represent objects in nature, parts of the body, and daily necessities. Afterward, check with your teacher or consult a dictionary to see how close your *kanji* are to the real *kanji*.

Lesson 19: Geography class

I. PERSPECTIVE

1. Objectives

1 Function:

(1) Stating a theme: *(Ajia) to ieba, (kome) desu.*   (2) Listing things: *(Nihonsei) toka (kankokusei).*
(3) Asking if there is anything else: *Hoka ni nani ka arimasen ka?*
(4) Stating a general theme and something specific which belongs to it:
     (Shuukyoo) dattara, (bukkyoo) desu.
(5) Changing the focus within a topic: *Soo ieba,*   (6) A pause or hesitation in speaking: *Eeto,*
(7) Stating something without definite certainty: *Deshoo ne.*
(8) Expressing uncertainty: *Saa,*

2 Language:

(1) *(Ajia) to ieba, (kome) desu.*   (2) *(Nihonsei) toka (kankokusei).*
(3) *Hoka ni nani ka (ari)masen ka?*   (4) *(Shuukyoo) dattara, (bukkyoo) desu.*
(5) *Soo ieba, (Ajia) ni wa donna (kuni) ga (ari)masu ka?*
(6) *(Minami Asean) no (menbaa) deshoo?*

3 Culture:

(1) Japan as an Asian country

II. PREPARATION

1. Context

地理の時間

世界地図を広げて、世界の諸地域について想像するのは楽しい。地理の先生は旅行が好きで、色々な写真を見せてくれる。今日からアジア地域について学習する。最初に話し合うことは、自分の持っているアジアのイメージだ。資料を見る前と後で、どれだけ考えが変わるか。クラスでは、自由に意見が出された。しかし、次第に話がそれて、アジアにある国をどれだけ知っているか、ということになった。

It is very interesting to open up a map of the world and think about different places. Peter's geography teacher enjoys traveling and often shows the class many pictures. Today the class started to learn about Asia. Peter wonders how much the original impressions of his classmates will change after they have studied the material. At first the class talked about their images of Asia, and many students gave their opinions. However, the conversation gradually turned into a discussion about the different Asian countries that they knew.

2. Sample Conversation

P: アジアと言えば、米です。
C: 私は箸。日本料理や中国料理に使う箸。
G: 僕は自動車です。日本せいとか韓国せい。
W: 他に何かありませんか。
P: 宗教だったら、仏教です。
G: そう言えば、アジアにはどんな国がありますか。
C: 南アジアにはインドとか、パキスタンがありますね。
P: インドネシアとか、マレーとか。フィリピンは東南アジアにありますね。
N: 日本とか中国、それから韓国は東アジアです。
W: ええと、タイとかベトナムとか、カンボジアはどこにありますか。
C: 東南アジアでしょうね。みんなアセアンのメンバーでしょう。
G: バングラデシュは。それから香港や台湾は。
C: さあ・・・。

P: *Ajia to ieba, kome desu.*
C: *Watashi wa hashi. Nihonryoori ya chuugokuryoori ni tsukau hashi¹.*
G: *Boku wa jidoosha desu. Nihonsei toka² kankokusei.*
W: *Hoka ni nani ka arimasen ka?*
P: *Shuukyoo dattara³, bukkyoo desu.*
G: *Soo ieba⁴, Ajia ni wa donna kuni ga arimasu ka?*
C: *Minami Ajia ni wa Indo toka, Pakisutan ga arimasu ne.*
P: *Indoneshia toka, Maree toka, Firipin wa Toonan Ajia ni arimasu ne.*
N: *Nihon toka Chuugoku, sorekara Kankoku wa Higashi Ajia desu.*
W: *Eeto, Tai toka Betonamu toka, Kanbojia wa doko ni arimasu ka?*
C: *Toonan Ajia deshoo ne. Minna Asean no menbaa deshoo?*
G: *Banguradeshu wa? Sore kara Honkon ya Taiwan wa?*
C: *Saa . . .*

P: When one says Asia, I think of rice.
C: Asia reminds me of chopsticks. They are used to eat Japanese and Chinese food.
G: I think of automobiles made in Japan and Korea.
W: Is there anything else?
P: For religion, there's Buddhism.
G: By the way, what countries are in Asia?
C: India and Pakistan are in southern Asia.
P: Indonesia, Malaysia, and the Philippines are in Southeast Asia.
N: Japan, China, and Korea are in East Asia.
W: Well, where are Thailand, Vietnam, and Cambodia located?
C: They are in Southeast Asia. All of them are ASEAN members, right?
G: What about Bangladesh? And Hong Kong and Taiwan?
C: Well ...

P: ピーター　スミス　　　　　*Piitaa Sumisu*　　　　　Peter Smith
C: キャシー　ベーカー　　　　*Kyashii Beekaa*　　　　Cathy Baker
G: ジョージ　カーター　　　　*Jooji Kaataa*　　　　　George Carter
W: ウィンストン　ブラウン（先生）　*Winsuton Buraun* (*sensei*)　Winston Brown (teacher)
N: きのした　のぶお　　　　　*Kinoshita Nobuo*　　　　Nobuo Kinoshita

Lesson 19　153

3. Language & Culture Notes

1 The archipelago of Japan lies in the Pacific Ocean at the eastern end of the Asian continent. Japan's geographic region has been referred to as East Asia, the Far East, and the Orient. Although Japan is isolated by water from the rest of Asia, it is very much a part of the world's largest continent. Japan has much in common with its closest neighbors China and Korea. These three nations share some culture, as many of Japan's customs came from China and Korea. For example, the primary eating utensil in this region is *hashi* or chopsticks. The people of Japan, China, and Korea also share physical characteristics: hair, eye, and skin color and the shape of their eyes. The three countries also follow the teachings of Mahayana Buddhism and Confucianism, ways of life that emphasize harmony with nature.

2 *toka* is used to make a random list of examples.
Atoranta toka Bosuton toka iroiro na toshi ga arimasu.
(There are cities like Atlanta, Boston, and others.)
Sushi toka tenpura toka sukiyaki toka iroiro na nihonryoori ga arimasu.
(There are Japanese foods such as sushi, tempura, sukiyaki, and others.)

3 *dattara* is the *-tara* form of *da*.

4 *Soo ieba*, a discourse function expression, means "By the way..."

III. PARTICIPATION

1. Vocabulary

1 **From sample conversation:**

Ajia (Asia)
Chuugoku (China)
eeto ... (well ...)
higashi (east)
Honkon (Hong Kong)
Kankoku (Korea)
kome (rice [uncooked])
minami (south)
shuukyoo (religion)
toonan (southeast)

bukkyoo (Buddhism)
chuugokuryoori (Chinese food)
hashi (chopsticks)
hoka ni (anything else)
jidoosha (automobile)
kankokusei (made in Korea)
kuni (country)
nihonsei (made in Japan)
Taiwan (Taiwan)

2 **Useful for activities:**

aisu tii (iced tea)
chuurippu (tulip)
ebi (shrimp)
gyuunyuu (milk)
itariaryoori (Italian food)
joozu ni nattara (if ... become good at ...)
kaubooi (cowboy)
Koka Koora (Coca Cola)

chikoku (late)
depaato (department store)
Girisha (Greece)
Irasshaimase. (Please come in./May I help you?)
jookyuusei (upperclassman)
kateika (home economics)
kibishii (strict)
konogoro (these days, recently)

konpyuutaa ruumu (computer room)
Meishiizu (Macy's)
mukashi (old times, long time ago)
nokoru (to remain)
pitchaa (pitcher [baseball])
saikoo (excellent, best)
shiken (examination)
sumire (violet)
Supuraito (Sprite)
terebi bangumi (TV program)
tsukurikata (way of making)
Yooroppa (Europe)

Makudonarudo (McDonald's)
minami no (southern)
myuujishan (musician)
orenji juusu (orange juice)
saikin (recently)
sakura (cherry blossom)
shinema (cinema, movie theater)
Supein (Spain)
tanpopo (dandelion)
tokushuu (special edition)
yasai (vegetables)

2. Activity, Practice, & Exercise

1 Cities, countries, and their claims to fame

In groups of five: Each group makes about 15 to 20 cards with a country or city written on each one. Each person draws a card and tells the group something famous or well known about that place. Begin with the expression --- *to ieba*.

Example: *Pari* → *Pari to ieba, fasshon desu yo. Mukashi kara fasshon no machi deshita kara.*
(Speaking of Paris, I think of fashion. It has been a city of fashion for many years.)

Kyooto → *Kyooto to ieba, furui tera desu yo. Iroiro na furui tera ga takusan nokotte imasu kara.*
(Speaking of Kyoto, I think of old temples. Many old temples remain there.)

2 Sports, subjects, and classmates

In groups of five: Each group makes 15 to 20 cards with a sport or subject on them and then continues in the same manner as APE 1. Sports or subjects may remind students of their classmates.

Example: *Konpyuutaa* → *Konpyuutaa to ieba, Kairu desu yo. Mainichi konpyuutaa ruumu ni imasu kara ne.*
(Computer) (Speaking of computers, I think of Kyle. He's in the computer room every day.)

Yakyuu → *Yakyuu to ieba, Tomu yo/da yo. Sugoi pitchaa nan dakara.*
(Baseball) (Speaking of baseball, I think of Tom. He's a great pitcher.)

3 Listing examples

In pairs: Students ask their partner about something that they know or like. The partners respond by naming some things that pertain to it. Use the expression --- *toka*, --- *toka*.

Example: 1) A: *Kono machi ni ii resutoran aru?* (Are there any good restaurants in this town?)
B: *Eeto, chuugokuryoori no "Chaina" toka, nihonryoori no "Sakura" toka, itariaryoori no "Mirano" toka, suteeki no "Kauboi" toka, iroiro aru yo/wa.*
(Well, there are many, such as "China" for Chinese food, "Sakura" for Japanese food, "Milano" for Italian food, and "Cowboy" for steak.)

2) A: *Yooroppa no donna kuni ga suki?* (Which countries in Europe do you like?)

B: *Supein toka, Itaria toka, Girisha toka, minami no kuni ga ii ne/wa.*
(I like southern countries such as Spain, Italy, and Greece.)

4 Giving examples

In groups: Give examples about the following items using the expression --- *deshoo*. --- *deshoo*.

Example: *Haru no hana* → *Sakura deshoo. Sumire deshoo. Tanpopo deshoo. Sorekara chuurippu.*
(Flowers in spring → Those such as cherry blossoms, violets, dandelions, and tulips.)

1. *Omoshiroi terebi bangumi* (Interesting TV programs) →
2. *Kookoosei ni ninki no aru myuuzishan* (Popular musicians among high school students) →
3. *Ajia no kuni* (Asian countries) →
4. *Nihon no tabemono* (Japanese food) →

5 Listening comprehension and/or oral production

Individually: Listen to the conversations between two people. Each one has two topics; the second one comes after the expression --- *soo ieba*. Write down both topics.

Example: A: *"Resutoran Sakura" no tenpura wa oishii ne. Ebi no tenpura mo yasai no tenpura mo saikoo da yo.*
(Tempura at the "Restaurant Sakura" is delicious. Both shrimp and vegetable tempura are excellent.)

B: *Soo ieba, kondo no kateika no jugyoo de, tenpura no tsukurikata o narau no yo.*
(Come to think of it, I am going to learn how to cook tempura in the next home economics class.)

A: *Hee, soo na no. Ja, kondo boku no tame ni tenpura o tsukutte kureru?*
(Are you? Well, could you cook some tempura for me?)

B: *Ee, joozu ni nattara ne.* (Sure, if I become good at it.)

Answers:

Topic 1: *"Resutoran Sakura" no tenpura wa oishii.*

Topic 2: *Kateika no jugyoo de, tenpura no tsukurikata o narau.*

1. A: *Konogoro, Kimu san, oshare ni natta wa ne. Mae wa itsumo T shatsu to jiinzu datta noni, saikin wa burausu to sukaato yo. Okeshoo mo shiteru shi.*
(Kim has been dressing up recently. She used to wear T-shirts and jeans all the time, but recently she has been wearing blouses and skirts. She even wears make-up.)

B: *Soo ieba, Kimu san, booifurendo ga dekita tte kiita wa.*
(Come to think of it, I heard she has a boyfriend.)

A: *Maa soo na no. Booifurendo tte dare?* (Oh, is that so? Who is he?)

B: *Basukettobu no jookyuusei rashii wa.* (I heard he is an upperclassman in the basketball club.)

Topic 1: _____ .

Topic 2: _____ .

2. A: *Joonzu sensei, kibishii yo na. 5 fun chikoku shita dake de, kyooshitsu ni hairuna tte iu n da.*
    (Mr. Jones is so strict. He told me not to enter the classroom, even though I was only 5 minutes late.)
    B: <u>*Soo ieba*</u>, *raishuu, Joonzu sensei no kurasu, shiken atta wa yo.*
    (Come to think of it, we're having an exam in his class next week.)
    A: *Aa soo datta. Benkyoo shinakya.* (Oh, yeah. I have to study.)
    Topic 1: _____ .
    Topic 2: _____ .

3. A: *Ashita kara 1 shuukan "Shinema 1" de nihon'eiga tokushuu o yaru n datte. Doyoobi ni issho ni mi ni ikanai?*
    (Beginning tomorrow, "Cinema 1" is going to show a special edition of Japanese movies for one week. Can you come see them with me on Saturday?)
    B: *Ii wa yo. Aa,* <u>*soo ieba*</u>, *raigetsu, Nihon kara ryuugakusei ga kuru n datte ne.*
    (Sure. Oh, come to think of it, a new foreign student is coming from Japan next month.)
    A: *Soo ka. Sore wa tanoshimi da ne.* (Oh, yeah. That should be fun.)
    Topic 1: _____ .
    Topic 2: _____ .

6 Substitution

In pairs: Make as many new sentences as possible by replacing the underlined words in the following sentence. The new sentences should be meaningful and accurate.
<u>*Shuukyoo*</u> *dattara* <u>*bukkyoo*</u> *desu.*
Example: *Depaato dattara Meishiizu desu.*

7 At a restaurant

In groups of three: Students make conversations between two people that take place in a restaurant of their choice. One person in the conversation is eating at the restaurant and the other is a server there. The person dining asks what kind of drinks, sandwiches, ice cream, appetizers, and so on are served at the restaurant, and the server lists a few items. The person dining then asks if there is anything else by saying *Hoka ni nani ka arimasen ka?* The server then lists some more items, and the person decides what to order. Follow the form in the example.
Example: At Seiyooken
   A: *Irasshaimase!* (May I help you?)
   B: *Donna nomimono ga arimasu ka?* (What kind of drinks do you have?)
   A: *Koka Koora to Supuraito to aisu tii ga arimasu.* (Coke, Sprite, and iced tea.)
   B: <u>*Hoka ni nani ka arimasen ka?*</u> (Do you have anything else?)
   A: *Gyunyuu to orenji juusu mo arimasu.* (Milk and orange juice.)
   B: *Ja, orenji juusu kudasai.* (Well, I'll have orange juice, please.)

8 Using functional expressions

In pairs: Try to write as many sentences as possible using the following expressions.
   Eeto, --- deshoo ne, saa

Lesson 20: Valentine's Day chocolate

I. PERSPECTIVE

1. Objectives

1 Function:

(1) Stating how something or someone seems: *Nani ka (nemu)soo ne.*
(2) Expressing surprise or doubt: *Masaka,*
(3) Asking something doubtfully: *(Piitaa kara) ja nai deshoo ne.*
(4) Expressing negation (female): *Soo ja nai wa yo.*
(5) Asking curiously what someone did: *Nani o sonna ni (nesshin) ni (hanashi)ta no.*
(6) Expressing interest in what someone is saying: *De?*
(7) Conveying what someone has said: *(Nijukko) datte.*
(8) Expressing surprise: *Ee! Nani?*
(9) Asking what someone said, or asking someone to repeat what has been said: *Ee?*
(10) Starting to answer or respond to someone's question: *Ja,*

2 Language:

(1) *Nani ka (nemu)soo ne.* (2) *Masaka, (Piitaa kara) ja nai deshoo ne.*
(3) *(Nijukko) datte.* (4) *(Kuwashi)ku (oshie)te ageru.*

3 Culture:

(1) Valentine's Day in the United States and Japan (2) *Girimono*

II. PREPARATION

1. Context

バレンタインのチョコレート

夜中に電話がかかってきた。日本からの国際電話。よしこの幼なじみからだった。話題はバレンタインに贈ったチョコレートについて。翌日眠そうにしていたよしこに、キャシーが話しかけてきた。よしこは睡眠不足の理由をキャシーに説明した。そして、日本のバレンタインデーのことも。キャシーは驚くやら、面白がるやら。

Yoshiko received an international call from Japan in the middle of the night. It was from her childhood friend. They talked about the chocolate that her friend sent for Valentine's Day. The next day, Cathy asked Yoshiko why she looked sleepy. Yoshiko explained the reason for her lack of sleep and told Cathy about Valentine's Day in Japan. Cathy was both surprised and amused.

2. Sample Conversation

C: 何か眠そうね。どうしたの。
Y: うん、夜中に電話があって、あまり寝ていないの。
C: まさか、ピーターからじゃないでしょうね。
Y: そうじゃないわよ。日本の友達からよ。
C: 何をそんなに熱心に話したの。
Y: バレンタインデーに送ったチョコの数。
C: で、いくつなの。
Y: ２０個だって。
C: ええ。何。そんなに多いの。
Y: 義理チョコがあるからね。
C: ええ。義理チョコって。
Y: じゃ、これから詳しく教えてあげる。

C: *Nani ka nemusoo[1] ne. Dooshita no?*
Y: *Un[2], yonaka ni denwa ga atte, amari nete inai no.*
C: *Masaka, Piitaa kara ja nai deshoo ne.*
Y: *Soo ja nai wa yo. Nihon no tomodachi kara yo.*
C: *Nani o sonna ni nesshin ni hanashita no?*
Y: *Barentaindee[3] ni okutta choko no kazu.*

C: *De, ikutsu na no?*
Y: *Nijukko datte[4].*
C: *Ee? Nani? Sonna ni ooi no?*
Y: *Girichoko[5] ga aru kara ne.*
C: *Ee? Girichoko tte?*
Y: *Ja, korekara kuwashiku oshiete ageru.*

C: You look sleepy. What happened?
Y: Yeah. I got a phone call in the middle of the night and didn't get enough sleep.
C: Don't tell me the call was from Peter.
Y: No, it was from my friend in Japan.
C: What did you talk about so attentively?
Y: We talked about the number of boxes of chocolate she sent for Valentine's day.
C: How many did she send?
Y: Twenty boxes.
C: Really? That many?
Y: We have *girichoco*.
C: What's *girichoco*?
Y: Well, I'll explain it in detail.

C: キャシー　ベーカー　　*Kyashii Beekaa*　　Cathy Baker
Y: やまだ　よしこ　　　　*Yamada Yoshiko*　　Yoshiko Yamada

3. Language & Culture Notes

1 *---soo* means "to seem," "to look," or "to appear." For example, *nemusoo* means "to look sleepy." Although it resembles *---rashii*, *soo* following the dictionary form or *-ta* form of a verb implies the speaker's opinion or judgment based on what someone else has said. *---rashii* is also used after the dictionary form or *-ta* form of a verb; however, it refers to the speaker's subjective judgment.

2 *Un* is an informal, colloquial equivalent of *hai*. However, *un* should not be used in formal situations or when speaking to one's superiors, especially if one is not well acquainted with them.

3 The Valentine's Day custom in Japan is different from the American style, even though it is celebrated on February 14 in both countries. In the United States, people give gifts and cards to anyone from their spouse or significant other to their relatives and friends. However, on Valentine's Day in Japan, women give presents, usually chocolate, to men: their husband or boyfriend and male coworkers. If women work with other women, they may give them chocolate as well. In return for giving men chocolate, women receive their treat on White Day, March 14. On this occasion, men give candy to their wife or girlfriend and female coworkers. As times have changed, so have the ways of celebrating Valentine's Day.

4 *Datte* comes at the end of a sentence and signifies that the preceeding phrase has been said by someone else.

5 In Japan, there is a concept known as *girimono*; that is, buying, giving, or sending gifts because of one's sense of obligation. For example, a woman may not particularly like her boss, but she will give him chocolate on Valentine's Day or bring him back *omiyage* from a business trip because of *giri*, or duty. In other words, it is the right thing to do. Japanese strongly believe in the saying "It's the thought that counts." It all adds up to doing things for the benefit of human relations.

III. PARTICIPATION

1. Vocabulary

1 **From sample conversation:**

barentaindee (Valentine's Day)
giri ([social] duty, obligation)
kazu (number)
Nani? (What? Really?)
nesshin ni (attentively)
nijukko (twenty [boxes])
oshiete (explain, tell)
yonaka (middle of the night)

choko (chocolate)
hanashita (talked, spoke)
kuwashiku (in detail)
nemusoo (look sleepy)
nete inai (did not sleep)
okutta (sent)
Soo ja nai. (That's not right; No, it isn't.)

2 **Useful for activities:**

achira (over there)
biiru (beer)

aite (companion)
chuusha (shot, injection)

doobutsuen (zoo)
ikaiyoo (stomach ulcer)
kareshi (boyfriend, he)
kookan suru (to exchange)
mite morau (to have [someone] see, to have [something] seen)
motte iku (to bring)
oisha san (doctor)
osara (plates, dishes)
pikunikku (picnic)
saifu (wallet)
shimaru (be closed)
tetsuya ([stay up] all night)
uchi no (my, our)
zenbu (all)

igan (stomach cancer)
kanojo (girlfriend, she)
karichatte (*kariru*) (borrow)

naoru (to get well)
ojiisan/ojiichan (grandfather)
otoshichatta (*otosu*) (dropped)
raishuu (next week)
saraishuu (the week after next)
shutchoo (business trip)
tonari (next, next door)
udon (Japanese noodles)

2. Activity, Practice, & Exercise

1 Expressing feelings through gestures

In groups of four: Each group needs several cards each with an adjective or phrase that describes feelings or physical conditions, such as *nemui* (sleepy), *ureshii* (happy), *atama/te/ashi ga itai* (head/hand/leg hurts) written on it. Students draw cards and take turns gesturing the adjective or phrase on the card. The rest of the group describes the gesture with the expression *Nani ka ---soo ne/da ne*. The person doing the gesture should then explain why they look that way. Follow the example.

Example: A: <u>*Nani ka nemusoo ne*</u>. *Dooshita no?* (You look sleepy. What's the matter?)
B: *Un. Jitsu wa, asa no 3ji goro made bideo o mite ita n da/no.*
(Yeah. As a matter of fact, I was watching a video until 3 a.m.)

2 That much/many?

In pairs: Each student gives his/her partner information about the degree, situation, or quantity of something. The statement should be about something surprising or unusual. Partners respond by using the expression *Ee, sonna ni*. Follow the example.

Example: A: *Kyoo no Nyuu Yooku no kion wa sesshi 37 do datte.*
(I heard that the temperature in New York is 37 degrees Celsius today.)
B: *Ee, Nyuu Yooku wa <u>sonna ni</u> atsui no?* (Huh? It's that hot in New York?)

3 Making conversations

In pairs: The teacher makes a set of seven cards for each pair of students. On one side of each card is the first sentence of a dialogue, and on the other side is the last sentence of the dialogue. The pairs sit facing each other. One person picks up a card and holds it in between them. The person who sees the first sentence should initiate the dialogue. The other person will eventually read the last sentence. The second line will always be *Soo ja nai wa yo*. The pairs work together to make up the third line of the dialogue. Students should take turns starting the conversations. Follow the example as a guide.

A: *Denwa no aite wa kareshi ja nai deshoo ne?* [given]
   (The call was from your boyfriend, right?)
B: <u>*Soo ja nai wa yo*</u>. [standard] (No, it wasn't!)
A: *Jaa, dare na no?* [students] (Well, then who?)
B: *Watashi no otoosan yo.* [given] (It was my father.)

<u>First</u>

1. *Denwa no aite wa kanojo ja nai daroo ne?*
2. *Sore wa koohii ja nai deshoo ne?*
3. *Ojiisan wa igan* (stomach cancer) *ja nai deshoo ne?*.
4. *Raishuu tesuto ja nai deshoo ne?*
5. *Asu kara shutchoo ja nai deshoo ne?*
6. *Pikunikku wa tonari no kooen ja nai deshoo ne?*
7. *Sore wa boku no ja nai deshoo ne?*.

<u>Last</u>

Uchi no okaasan.
Koocha yo.
Ikaiyoo da yo. (stomach ulcer)
Saraishuu da yo.
Raishuu kara da yo.
Doobutsuen da yo.
Achira no.

4 Matching phrases

In groups of three: Each group needs a set of cards in random order. Each of the following ten phrases should be on a different card. Students must correctly match the phrases to make the two parts of person A in a dialogue. B's part will always be *De*, to show interest in what A is saying. After matching all of the phrases, two of the three in the group practice the dialogue while the third member helps them. Switch roles for each of the five dialogues.

Example: *Kinoo depaato de katta osara ga kowarete ita no ...*

   Depaato e motte ikeba, kookan shite kureru tte.

   A: *Kinoo depaato de katta osara ga kowarete ita no ...*
      (The plates that I bought yesterday at the department store are broken.)
   B: <u>*De*</u>? (And?)
   A: *Depaato e motte ikeba, kookan shite kureru tte.*
      (They said I could bring them back to the store and exchange them.)

1. *Chuusha o shite morattara naotta wa.*
2. *5 satsu mo kashite kureta wa.*
3. *Kinoo saifu o otoshichatta.*
4. *Kinoo Takashi kun kara Nihon no bideo o 3 bon mo karichatte sa.*
5. *Mada mitsukaranai n da yo.*
6. *Masako san ni manga no hon o kashite to tanonda no.*
7. *Onaka ga itaku natte oisha san ni mite moratta no.*
8. *Omise ga shimatte ite dame datta yo.*
9. *Tetsuya de zenbu michatta yo.*
10. *Udon ga tabetaku natte Nihon resutoran ni itta n da.*

5 Conveying information

In groups of three: This activity involves passing on or conveying information that one has received to someone else. For each of the following situations, the first two lines are given. A asks B a question, and B answers. Then C asks A about what B said. (C is sitting near A but far from B. C cannot hear what B is saying.) A conveys to C what B has said. In groups of three, complete the following dialogues following the example. Afterward, each group should demonstrate one or two dialogues in front of the class, depending on time.

Example: A: *Chokoreeto ikutsu moratta no?* (given)
         B: *20 ko da yo.* (given)
         C: *Ikutsu moratta <u>tte</u>?*
         A: *20 ko <u>datte</u>.*

Situation 1
A: *Zenbu de ikura desu ka?*
B: *1,387 en desu.*

Situation 2
A: *Otoosan, biiru nanbon hoshii?*
B: *Gohon de ii yo.*

Situation 3
A: *Maiku san, ringo nanko hoshii?*
B: *Ikko de ii yo.*

Situation 4
A: *Denwa dare kara?*
B: *Ojiichan da yo.*

Situation 5
A: *Otoosan, nani ga tabetai?*
B: *Takoyaki katte kite moraoo ka.*

Situation 6
A: *Haikingu ni wa nan de iku?*
B: *Densha de iku yo.*

6 The biggest in America

In pairs: Using adjectives that you have learned, use the superlative to describe several states, cities, rivers, mountains, and so on. in America.

Example: *Arasuka wa Amerika de <u>ichiban</u> ookii shuu <u>desu</u>.* (Alaska is the largest state in America.)

7 U.S. vs Japan

In pairs: Write three sentences to compare the United States with Japan.

Example: *Amerika <u>wa</u> Nihon <u>yori</u> ookii desu.* (America is bigger than Japan.)

8 Free trip to Japan

Individually: Imagine that you just won a roundtrip ticket to Japan. Write three sentences stating what you definitely want to do once you get to Japan.

Example: *<u>Zettai</u> shinkansen* (bullet train) *ni nor<u>itai desu ne</u>.*
        (I definitely want to ride on the *shinkansen*.)

Lesson 20   163

Lesson 21: Review & Application

IV. PERFORMANCE

1. Application

1 **Conversation completion**

In small groups: The following is a conversation between students A and B. They are talking about things native to Japan and China. Guess what student B would say. Choose the most appropriate sentence from below.

A: *Ajia to ieba, kome da ne. Ajia no hito wa minna kome o taberu daroo.*
(Speaking of Asia, I think of rice. All Asians eat rice, don't they?)

B: *Soo ne. Tabemono ni kankei ga aru kedo,* ( ).
(Right. With regards to food, chopsticks and tea are also Asian things, right?)

A: *Un. Jaa, Ajia no kuni to ittara, doko o omoidasu?*
(Right. So, what Asian countries do you think of?)

B: ( ) (Japan, China ...)

A: *Nihon to ieba, denkiseihin to kuruma da ne.*
(Speaking of Japan, I think of electrical appliances and cars.)

B: ( ) (Japan is also known for *kimono*, *ukiyoe*, and sumo.)

A: *Soo datta ne.* (Yeah.)

B: ( ) (China has a very large population. I hear that there are 1.2 billion people.)

A: *Un. Amerika no 5 bai dakara na.* (Yeah. It's five times America's population.)

B: ( ) (We see lots of things made in China these days. It seems that cheap clothing is made mostly in China.)

A: *Boku no shatsu mo chuugokusei da yo.* (My shirt was made in China.)

B: ( ) (China is the country where *kanji* was created. Japan learned *kanji* from China and made *hiragana* and *katakana* from it.)

A: *Aa, wasureteta! Ashita nihongo no tesuto ga aru n da!*
(I almost forgot! I have a Japanese test tomorrow.)

1. *Nihon toka Chuugoku toka ...*
2. *Chuugoku wa jinkoo ga ooi wa ne. 12 oku nin iru soo yo.*
3. *Chuugoku wa kanji o tsukutta kuni yo. Nihon wa Chuugoku kara kanji o manande, hiragana to katakana mo kanji kara tsukutta soo yo.*
4. *Hashi toka ocha mo Ajia no mono deshoo.*
5. *Saikin, chuugokusei ga ooi deshoo. Yasui fuku wa hotondo chuugokusei rashii wa.*
6. *Kimono ya ukiyoe ya sumoo mo yuumei yo.*

2 **Conversation completion**

In small groups: The following is a conversation between an American student (A) and a Japanese student (J) who is studying in America. They are talking about Asian countries. Guess what the American student would say in the underlined parts in the conversation. Each group presents their conversation to the class.

J: *Nihon ni chikai Ajia no kuni tte shitteru?* (Do you know any Asian countries near Japan?)

A: *Eeto, _____ toka _____ toka.* (Um, _____ and _____ .)

J: *Jaa, Ajia de 1nenjuu atsui kuni wa?*

(Do you know any Asian countries where it is hot all year round?)

A: *_____ toka _____ toka.* (_____ and _____ .)

J: *Ajia no omo na shuukyoo wa?* (What is a major religion in Asia?)

A: *Uun, bukkyoo ka na?* (Um, perhaps Buddhism?)

J: *Kirisutokyoo ga sakan na kuni mo aru wa yo.*

(There are also some countries where Christianity is well respected.)

A: *Sore, _____ no koto daro.* (You must be talking about _____ .)

J: *Ee. Kankoku ni kirisutokyoo o shinjite iru hito ga takusan iru rashii wa.*

(Yes. I heard that there are a lot of people in Korea who follow Christianity.)

A: *Hee, soo nano.* (Really?)

J: *Sorekara, isuramukyoo ga chuushin no kuni mo ooi no yo.*

(There are many countries that put Islam at the center, too.)

A: *_____ toka, _____ daro.* (Such as _____ and _____ .)

J: *Ee. Mada aru wa. Iran toka Iraku toka Saujiarabia toka, Chuutoo no kuni mo isuramukyoo no kuni yo.*

(Yes. There are more: Middle Eastern countries such as Iran, Iraq, and Saudi Arabia.)

A: *Ee, Chuutoo mo Ajia nano?* (What? The Middle East is also part of Asia?)

3 Making sentences

In groups of three: Each group receives a set of adjective cards. Place the cards face down. Take turns drawing cards and making sentences in the form --- (verb in dictionary form) *no wa* (adjective or adjectival noun). Use the adjective on the card.

Example: A: *tanoshii*   →   *Bon'odori o odoru <u>no wa tanoshii</u> desu ne.*
         (fun)   →   (It is fun to dance *bon'odori*.)
       B: *tsumaranai* → *Nichiyoobi hitori de uchi ni iru <u>no wa tsumaranai</u>.*
         (boring)   →   (It is boring to stay home alone on Sunday.)

List of adjectives and adjectival nouns: *tanoshii, tsurai, muzukashii, kanashii, isogashii*
                                                tsumaranai, kantan, taihen, ureshii, taisetsu

4 The four seasons

① In four groups: Each group represents one of the four seasons and thinks about what happens in that season. Use the expression --- *ni naru to*.

Example: Spring   A: *Haru <u>ni naru to</u>, chuurippu ga sakimasu.*

                    (When spring comes, tulips bloom.)

              B: *Haru <u>ni naru to</u>, tanpopo mo sakimasu.*

                    (When spring comes, dandelions bloom, too.)

C: *Haru <u>ni naru to</u>, atatakaku narimasu.*
 (When spring comes, it gets warm.)

D: *Haru <u>ni naru to</u>, yuki ga tokemasu.* (When spring comes, snow melts.)

② A representative from each group presents its discussion to the class.

Example: <u>*Haru ni naru to*</u>, *atatakaku narimasu. Soshite, yuki ga tokete, iroiro na hana ga sakimasu. Chuurippu ya tanpopo ya sumire ya sakura ga sakimasu.*
 (When spring comes, it gets warm. Snow melts, and many flowers bloom, such as tulips, dandelions, violets, and cherry blossoms.)

5 Famous people

① In groups of four or five: Each group chooses one of the professions written below. Make a list of as many famous people in that profession as possible. Each member chooses one of the famous people and asks ten to fifteen classmates if they like the person. Students should express degrees of like and dislike by using one of the following expressions: *totemo* (very much); *maa maa* (so-so); *amari ---nai* (not so much); *zenzen ---nai* (not at all). Students who are indifferent should use the expression *Nan tomo omowanai*, and those who don't know the famous person should say *Shiranai*. Practice using *un* or *uun* to informally say yes or no.

Professions: musician, actor/actress, news reporter, politician, athlete

Example: musicians A: *B san, Madonna wa suki?* (B, do you like Madonna?)

B: *Un, <u>totemo</u> suki.* (Yes, very much.)

A: *C san, Madonna wa suki?* (C, do you like Madonna?)

C: *Uun, <u>zenzen</u> suki ja <u>nai</u>.* (No, not at all.)

A: *D san, Madonna wa suki?* (D, do you like Madonna?)

D: <u>*Nan tomo omowanai.*</u> (I have no interest.)

② When the interview is finished, each group makes a chart of the results. A representative from each group reports the results to the class. Follow the example.

Example: musicians

	totemo	*maa maa*	*amari*	*zenzen*	*nan tomo*	*shiranai*
Madonna	1	2	3	2	6	1
Beatles	3	5	2	2	3	0
Elvis	1	3	4	3	4	0

Example: *Watashitachi no guruupu wa myuujishan ni tsuite shirabemashita. Myuujishan wa Madonna to Biitoruzu to Puresurii to --- desu. Kono naka de Biitoruzu ga ichiban ninki ga arimasu. Niban wa ---*
 (Our group asked about musicians. The musicians we chose were Madonna, the Beatles, Elvis, ... Among them, the most popular is the Beatles. The next is ...)

6 Asking the price

① In pairs: Students ask their partner about the prices of the following things.

casette tape (100 minutes)	¥260
videotape (120 minutes)	¥620
electronic calculator	¥1,280
electric mixer	¥3,900
coffeemaker	¥4,500
walkman	¥29,800
television	¥88,000
refrigerator	¥149,000

Example: A: *Kono kasettoteepu wa ikura?* (How much is this cassette tape?)
B: 260 *en. Kono bideoteepu wa ikura?* (260 yen. How much is this videotape?)
A: 620 *en.* (620 yen.)

② Each pair receives an advertisement and discusses the prices of the goods listed in it.

7 That expensive? That cheap?

In pairs: Each pair needs an advertisement or a mail order catalog. Students tell their partner the price of an item. The partner responds by saying *E, sonna ni takai no?* if they think that the item is expensive, *E, sonna ni yasui no?* if they think it is cheap, or *Soo* if they think it is average.

Example: 1) A: *T shatsu ga 20 doru datte.* (This T-shirt costs 20 dollars.)
B: <u>*Soo*</u>. (Is that so?)

2) A: *T shatsu ga 50 doru datte.* (This T-shirt costs 50 dollars.)
B: *E, <u>sonna ni</u> takai no?* (Really? That expensive?)

3) A: *T shatsu ga 6 doru datte.* (This T-shirt costs 6 dollars.)
B: *E, <u>sonna ni</u> yasui no?* (Really? That cheap?)

8 How big is ...?

In pairs: Take turns asking each other about the height of the following structures.
Example: A: *Nara no daibutsu wa <u>dono kurai</u> takai <u>n desu ka</u>?*
(About how tall is the Great Buddha in Nara?)
B: *15 meetoru <u>gurai desu</u>.* (It's about 15 meters.)

(1) *Jiyuu no megami*
(2) *Ejiputo no piramiddo*
(3) *Washinton monyumento*
(4) *Waarudo Toreedo Sentaa Biru*

9 **Team competition: Whisper game**

Two or three teams: Each team makes a single-file line. The teacher gives the person at the end of each line a card with a news event written on it. Students whisper the news to the person in front of them until the news reaches the person at the front of the line. After the person at the front receives the news, he/she repeats it to the teacher, who will determine if the news has been conveyed correctly. If it is right, the person at the front of the line may leave. If it is not correct, no one may leave. The first person in line receives a new card and goes to the back of the line to start the next round. After four or five rounds, the team with the least number of members left in line is the winner.

2. Actualization

1 Practice the following conversation and develop your own dialogue on a similar subject with your partners.

4 nen 4 kumi wa shakaika no jugyoo de, Nihon no noogyoo ni tsuite manande imasu.
(The 4th grade, class 4 students are learning about Japan's agriculture in social studies.)

Ooyama sensei:	*Hokkaidoo wa, noogyoo ga sakan desu ne. Donna sakumotsu ga saibai sarete imasu ka?*
	(Agriculture is prosperous in Hokkaido. What kinds of crops are grown there?)
Hirota san:	*Jagaimo, azuki ...* (Potatoes, azuki [red] beans, ...)
Suzuki kun:	*Daizu to tensai.* (Soybeans and sugar beets.)
Ooyama sensei:	*Hoka ni wa?* (What else?)
Tanaka kun:	*Okome mo takusan toreru yo.* (They grow a lot of rice, too.)
Ooyama sensei:	*Soo desu ne. Dewa, Okinawa wa?* (That's right. How about Okinawa?)
Yoshida san:	*Painappuru ga yuumei da wa.* (Its pineapples are famous.)
Takeda kun:	*Satookibi mo.* (Sugar cane, too.)
Ooyama sensei:	*Okome wa?* (How about rice?)
Yamada san:	*Okome wa hotondo saibai sarete imasen.* (Not much rice grown there.)

2 Practice the following conversation and develop your own dialogue on a similar subject with your partners.

4 nen 6 kumi no seito wa, shakaika no jugyoo de, sankinkootai ni tsuite manande imasu.
(The 4th grade, class 6 students are learning about *sankinkootai* in social studies.)

Suzuki sensei:	*Sankinkootai to wa nan desu ka?* (What is *sankinkootai*?)
Hirota san:	*Daimyoo ga, 1nen oki ni Edo to jibun no ryoochi ni sumu koto desu.*
	(It was the system in which *daimyoo*, or fuedal lords, spent alternate years living in Edo and their own territory.)
Suzuki sensei:	*Soo desu ne. Dewa, Tokugawabakufu wa, dooshite soo saseta no deshoo?*
	(That's right. Why did the Tokugawa shogunate make this system?)

Tanaka kun: *Daimyoo ni okane o tsukawasete, somuku koto ga dekinai yoo ni suru tame desu.*
(To make *daimyoo* spend money traveling to Edo to prevent them from betraying the shogunate.)

Suzuki sensei: *Yoku wakarimashita ne. Dewa, kono jiki ni dooro ga hattatsu shita riyuu wa?*
(You understand it very well. Well then, why was the road system developed in this period?)

Yamada san: *Takusan no daimyoo ga, Edo to chihoo o ittari kitari shita kara desu.*
(Because many *daimyoo* traveled back and forth between Edo and their own territories.)

3 Practice the following conversation and develop your own dialogue on a similar subject with your partners.

Shakaika no jugyoo de, ima to mukashi no ryokoo no chigai o manande imasu.
(In social studies, students are learning the differences between past and present ways of traveling.)

Yokoyama sensei: *Tookyoo kara Oosaka made wa dono gurai kakarimasu ka?*
(About how long does it take to go from Tokyo to Osaka?)

Hirota san: *Shinkansen de 3jikan gurai desu.* (It takes about 3 hours by *shinkansen*.)

Yamada kun: *Koosokudooro da to 7jikan gurai ka na.*
(If you go by highway, it takes about 7 hours.)

Yokoyama sensei: *Edojidai wa doo yatte tabi o shimashita ka?*
(How did people travel in the Edo Period?)

Kobayashi kun: *Aruite desu ka?* (On foot?)

Yokoyama sensei: *Aruitari, uma ni noru hito mo imashita.*
(Some traveled on foot and some on horseback.)

Yamada kun: *Dono gurai kakatta n desu ka?* (How long did it take?)

Yokoyama sensei: *15nichi gurai desu.* (About 15 days.)

Nakamura kun: *Hee. Sonna ni kakatta n da.* (Really? It took that long!?)

4 Conversation completion

In small groups: The following is a conversation between students A and B. They are talking about international problems. Guess what student B would say. Choose the most appropriate sentence from below.

A: *Kokusai mondai wa iroiro na tokoro ni aru ne.*
(There are international problems in various areas.)

B: (   ) (There are problems in the world of sports, too.)

A: *Orinpikku toka sekaisenshuken no koto deshoo.*
(You're talking about the Olympic Games or world championships, right?)

B: (   ) (Yes. The Soviet Union didn't participate in the Los Angeles Olympics.)

A: *Mosukuwa Orinpikku ni wa Nihon mo America mo sanka shinakatta wa ne.*
(Both America and Japan didn't participate in the Moscow Olympics.)

B: (   ) (Another problem I have heard about is that some athletes are using drugs to enhance their performance.)

A: *Nan toka iu doraggu no koto ne. Soo iu kuni wa hoka no kuni ni katsu tame ni wa, warui to wakatte ite mo, senshu ni kusuri o tsukawaseru no ne.*
(I know what you're talking about. Those countries make their athletes use drugs to beat other countries' athletes, even though they know it's wrong.)

B: ( ) (I heard that athletes from such countries who have won gold medals can live wealthy lives.)

A: *Supootsu ni tai suru kangaekata ga chotto chigau no kamo shirenai wa.*
(They have slightly different way of thinking about sports.)

B: ( ) (It's horrible. They don't know the real purpose of sports.)

A: *Supootsu o tsuujite, sekaijuu no kuni no hitobito ga nakayoku naroo to iu no ga Orinpikku no mokuteki deshoo?*
(Bringing people of different countries of the world together through sports is a goal of the Olympics, isn't it?)

B: ( ) (That's right. I hope that people don't use sports for money and politics.)

A: *Sekaijuu no hito ga moo ichido supootsu no mokuteki o kangaenaoshita hoo ga ii wa ne.*
(It's necessary for the people of the world to reconsider the purpose of sports.)

B: ( ) (Originally, sports existed just for fun.)

1. *Soo iu kuni de wa, kin medaru o totta senshu wa isshoo yutaka na seikatsu ga dekiru soo yo.*
2. *Soo da yo. Supootsu o seiji ya okane no tame ni riyoo shinai de moraitai na.*
3. *Supootsu no sekai ni mo aru ne.*
4. *Iya da ne. Supootsu no hontoo no mokuteki ga wakatte nai yo.*
5. *Moo hitotsu no mondai wa jibun no seiseki o ageru tame ni doraggu o tsukau senshu ga iru koto da soo yo.*
6. *Sore ni moto moto supootsu wa tanoshimu mono nan da yo.*
7. *Un. Rosanzerusu Orinpikku de wa, Soren ga sanka shinakatta daro.*

5 Discussing current events

In pairs: One student in each pair receives current events Group A and the other gets Group B. The first topic in Group A should be related to the first one in Group B, as should the second and third current events in each group. Partners take turns discussing their news using the expression --- *to iu koto desu*. Follow the example.

Examples of recent news:

(A) 1. *1995nen ni Tookyoo no chikatetsu de tero ga atte, 12nin no hito ga nakunarimashita.*
(There was terrorism on the subway in Tokyo in 1995, and 12 people were killed.)

2. *Madonna wa Nihon de osake no senden ni dete imasu.*
(Madonna appears in a Japanese TV advertisement for a liquor company.)

3. *Hawai kara Nihon e itta Akebono wa yokozuna ni narimashita.*
(Akebono, who went from Hawaii to Japan, became a *yokozuna* in sumo wrestling.)

(B) 1. *1995nen ni Okurahoma de tero ga atte, oozei no hito ga nakunarimashita.*
(Many people were killed in the terrorist attack that happened in Oklahoma in 1995.)

2. *Sharon Sutoon wa Nihon de keshoohin no CM ni dete imasu.*
(Sharon Stone appears in a Japanese TV commercial for a cosmetics company.)

3. *Nihon kara Amerika ni kita Nomo wa Dojaazu no pitchaa ni narimashita.*
(Nomo, who came to America from Japan, became a pitcher for the Dodgers.)

Example: A: *Madonna wa Nihon de osake no senden ni dete iru <u>to iu koto desu</u>.*
B: *Sharon Sutoon wa Nihon de keshoohin no CM ni dete iru <u>to iu koto desu</u>.*

6 On the last day of ...

In pairs: Think and write about what you would like to do on the last day of an event. Choose an event from the following:

(1) The last day of Japanese class.
(2) The last day of high school.
(3) The last day of summer vacation.

Example: The last day of my trip to Japan → *Nihonryokoo no saigo no hi wa nihonryoori o tabetai desu. Sore kara omiyage o kaitai desu. Osewa ni natta Nihon no hitotachi ni, denwa o kakete "Arigatoo gozaimashita" to iitai desu.*
(On the last day of my trip to Japan, I would like to eat Japanese food. I want to buy souvenirs, and I would like to call the people who were nice to me to say, "Thank you very much.")

3. Enrichment

1 *Kanji* for Lesson 19

米	箸	中国	自動車	韓国
宗教	仏教	国	南	東南
東	香港	台湾		

2 *Kanji* for Lesson 20

眠い	夜中	電話	寝る	友達
熱心	数	個	義理	詳しい
教える				

3 Other useful *kanji*

甘、咲、上、下、軽、深、浅、広、細、若、引、押、置、倍、仕事、渡

4 Strategies

For those *kanji* that were formed to represent abstract concepts, the separate components do not have any specific meanings. For example 上 and 下 were formed on the basis of contrast; 上 represents "up," and 下 "represents down." The abstract meanings of some *kanji* may have been derived or borrowed from concrete meanings.

5 Exercise

Check all *kanji* appearing in the previous lessons and point out which ones fall into the various formation categories described in the previous lessons. Try to figure out why.

Lesson 22: Basketball game[1]

I. PERSPECTIVE

1. Objectives

1 Function:

(1) Describing what someone is doing or what is happening presently:
   (Nobuo ga te) o (fut)te iru yo/wa.
(2) Implying/Guessing a condition or something that may happen: *(Jishin ga aru) no kamo shirenai ne.*
(3) Expressing hearsay: *(Umai) rashii no.*
(4) Expressing surprise: *Hee ...*
(5) Stating that one has done something before: *(Mi ni it)ta koto ga aru no.*
(6) Attracting someone's attention: *A, mite mite.*
(7) Guessing someone's condition: *(Chooshi) ga (ii) mitai.*

2 Language:

(1) *(Nobuo) ga (te) o (fut)te iru wa.*
(2) *(Jishin ga aru) no kamo shirenai ne.*
(3) *(Kare) tte (shuuto) ga (umai) rashii no.*
(4) *(Sugoi) ja nai.*
(5) *(Boku wa kyoo) hajimete (mir)u yo.*
(6) *Mite mite.*
(7) *(Chooshi) ga (ii) mitai.*
(8) *(Maaku sa)reteru yo.*

3 Culture:

(1) Sports tournaments in high school

II. PREPARATION

1. Context

バスケットボールの試合

のぶおが、バスケットボールの試合に出場する。対戦相手は同じ学区の高校だ。強敵ともいえる長年のライバル校だ。ピーターはよしこと一緒に体育館へ応援に行った。のぶおは観客席にピーターとよしこを見つけると、手を振った。二人はのぶおのシュートが決まると、歓声を上げた。勝てるかもしれない、そんな試合になりそうだった。

Nobuo was going to play in a basketball game. The opposing team was from another high school in the same school district. This strong team and Nobuo's school have been rivals for many, many years. Peter went to the gymnasium with Yoshiko to cheer for Nobuo. Nobuo saw Peter and Yoshiko in the bleachers and waved to them. Peter and Yoshiko cheered when Nobuo made a basket. It seemed that their team could win the game.

2. Sample Conversation

Y: のぶおが手を振っているわ。
P: 今日の試合は自信があるのかもしれないね。
Y: 彼ってシュートがうまいらしいの。
P: へええ、すごいじゃない。僕は今日初めて見るよ。
Y: わたし、練習を見に行った事があるの。
P: あ、見て見て。あのカットイン、うまいなあ。
Y: 今日は本当に調子がいいみたい。
P: のぶおがマークされてるよ。あのディフェンスは手ごわいぞ。
Y: 声援送ってあげましょうよ。
P: そうだな。フレー、フレー、のぶお！

Y: *Nobuo ga te o futte iru wa.*
P: *Kyoo no shiai wa jishin ga aru no kamo shirenai ne.*
Y: *Kare tte shuuto ga umai rashii no.*
P: *Hee, sugoi ja nai. Boku wa kyoo hajimete miru yo.*
Y: *Watashi, renshuu o mi ni itta koto ga aru no.*
P: *A, mite mite[2]. Ano kattoin, umai naa.*
Y: *Kyoo wa hontoo ni chooshi ga ii mitai[3].*
P: *Nobuo ga maaku sareteru[4] yo. Ano difensu wa tegowai zo[5].*
Y: *Seien okutte agemashoo yo.*
P: *Soo da na. Furee, furee, Nobuo!*

Y: Nobuo is waving to us.
P: He must feel good about today's game.
Y: I hear that he's good at shooting.
P: Really? That's cool. This is my first time to watch one of his games.
Y: I've seen him practice before.
P: Look! That cut-in was excellent.
Y: He seems to be in very good shape today.
P: Nobuo is marked. That guy is a tough guard.
Y: Let's cheer him on.
P: Yeah! Hip hip hurray! Nobuo!

Y: やまだ よしこ   *Yamada Yoshiko*   Yoshiko Yamada
P: ピーター スミス   *Piitaa Sumisu*   Peter Smith

3. Language & Culture Notes

1 Sports tournaments are very popular in Japanese junior high and high schools. They may be held between teams in the school or between several schools in the same town or county. The most common tournament sports are baseball, soccer, volleyball, basketball, tennis, and table tennis. These games teach students both team and school spirit as well as how to work together as a team. In addition to the tournaments, sports festivals are held once or twice a year. Students who are not participating in the sports competition show their spirit by attending the games and cheering for their school, team, or town. Most of the spectators are from the school or town in which the event is being held. It is not very common for teams to bring fans along with the players to a sports event.

2 *Mite* is a shortened, less formal way of saying *mite kudasai*.

3 The expression --- *mitai* has various meanings that depend on the words that precede it. When following a noun (e.g. *saru mitai*), --- *mitai* means "looks like" or "resembles." (It looks like a monkey.) After an adjective (e.g. *ii mitai*), it means "seems to be." (It seems good.) Following a verb (e.g. *iku mitai*), --- *mitai* means "looks like [doing something]." (It looks like it's going.)

4 *Sareteru* has been abbreviated from *sarete iru*. *Sarete* is the -*te* form of the verb *sareru*, the passive form of *suru*.

5 *zo* is a sentence function marker that signifies a strong reminder.

III. PARTICIPATION

1. Vocabulary

1 From sample conversation:

chooshi (condition)
kamo (may, might)
maaku sareteru (be marked)
okutte (give)
seien (encouragement, support, cheer)
shuuto (shoot [basketball])
tegowai (tough)
umai (good at, great)

jishin (confidence)
kare tte (he is)
mite (look)
renshuu (practice, exercise, training)
shiai (game)
sugoi (great)
te o futte iru (waving)

2 Useful for activities:

arau (to wash)
choocho (butterfly)
gorufu (golf)
Hontoo da. (It's true.)
kanashisoo (look sad)
mezurashii (rare, unusual)
okotte iru (be angry)
shoosan (admiration)
tazuneru (to visit)

buchoo (director, department head)
chuushoku (lunch)
hohoemu (to smile)
kamu (to chew)
koshoo (trouble)
nodo ga kawaku (be thirsty)
onaka ga suku (be hungry)
tako o ageru (to fly a kite)
te o furu (to wave)

2. Activity, Practice, & Exercise

1 Guessing the reason

In groups of three: The sentences in this activity describe how someone looks or seems. For each sentence, write a short dialogue in which two people guess why the third person might feel a certain way. Use the expression --- *no kamo (shiremasen) ne*, or --- *no kamo (shirenai) ne*. Follow the example.

Example: Father has been smiling since he came home this evening.

    ane (my sister): *Otoosan, dooshita no kashira?* (What happened to Dad?)
    watashi (me):   *Kaisha de ii koto ga atta <u>no kamo ne</u>.*
                    (Maybe something good happened at work.)

1. The teacher has been smiling since early this morning.
2. The teacher has looked angry since early this morning.
3. --- looks happy. (Choose a classmate.)
4. --- looks sad. (Choose a classmate.)

2 That's great!

In pairs: Students tell their partner something exceptional or outstanding about a friend or family member. The partner responds with *Hee, sugoi ja nai*.

Example: A: *Nobuo tte, shuuto ga umai n da yo/no yo.* (Nobuo is good at shooting [basketballs].)
B: *Hee, sugoi ja nai.* (Really? That's great!)

3 Oh! Take a look.

In small groups: Find something interesting or strange in or around the classroom. Ask the other group members to notice it by saying *A, mite mite*. The others respond with their own comments. Follow the example.

Example: A: *A, mite mite.* (Oh! Take a look.)
B: *Nani?* (What?)
A: *Kirei na ookii choocho.* (The big, pretty butterflies.)
C: *Hontoo da. Mezurashii choocho da ne/ne.*
(Oh, yeah. They're rare butterflies, aren't they?)

4 Substitution

In pairs: Replace the underlined words in the following sentence with original ideas. Try to make as many new sentences as possible.

Yamada san wa nihongo ga umai rashii.

5 Translation

Individually: Use the expression *-ta koto ga aru* to translate the following sentences into Japanese.

1. I have eaten Japanese food.
2. Mr. Hayashi has visited Canada.
3. Ms. Smith has studied French.
4. Professor Matsunaga has taught here.
5. Lisa has been hospitalized.

6 Matching phrases

In groups of three: The teacher makes two sets of cards, Set A and Set B, for each group of students. The two sets of cards should be scrambled separately. Each group works together to match the phrases in Set A with the phrases in Set B to make correct, complete sentences. The groups have 10 minutes to complete the task. When time is up, the teacher asks each group to read a few of their sentences. The teacher should write the correct sentences on the blackboard.

Set A	Set B
Kaze o	hiita mitai
Chooshi ga	warui mitai
Ashi o	kitta mitai
Onaka ga	suita mitai
Koshoo ga	naotta mitai
Nodo ga	kawaita mitai
Atarashii eiga wa	omoshirokatta mitai
Ashita no tesuto wa	muzukashii mitai
Konpyuutaa ga	kowareta mitai
Kyoo no chuushoku wa	oishii mitai
Kondo no buchoo wa	yasashii mitai
Asu wa	hareru mitai

7 Verb conjugation: causative form

In pairs: Using verb cards, change verbs from the dictionary form into the causative form.

Example:
kaku	→	kakaseru	oyogu	→	oyogaseru
tsukau	→	tsukawaseru			
hanasu	→	hanasaseru			
nomu	→	nomaseru			
taberu	→	tabesaseru			
denwa suru	→	denwa saseru			
kuru	→	kosaseru			

8 Describing illustrations

In class: The teacher makes several illustrations or copies some from a book or other sources, puts them on the blackboard, and numbers each illustration. The teacher then randomly calls an illustration by number in Japanese. As a class, the students describe the picture using the form --- *o -te iru*. Following are some examples. They may be changed if they cannot be drawn or if illustrations cannot be found.

Example:
1. Nobuo is waving at us.
2. Some kids are flying kites.
3. Your brother is singing karaoke.
4. Your father is practicing golf.
5. Your little sister is reading the newspaper.
6. A dog is chewing on a bone.
7. A cat is washing its face.

9 Write five sentences using *hajimete miru yo*. Then substitute *miru* with other verbs.

Lesson 23: An accident during the game

I. PERSPECTIVE

1. Objectives

1 Function:

(1) Worrying about whether someone is all right: *(Nobuo), daijoobu kashira.*
(2) Guessing who, what or how: *(Hone o ot)te iru kamo shirenai.*
(3) Sympathizing with someone: *Kawaisoo.*
(4) Reporting circumstances: *(Kinoshita) wa (nenza), (Miraa) wa (kossetsu) no yoo desu.*
(5) Inviting someone to go somewhere together: *(Imushitsu) e ikanai?*
(6) Expressing feelings: *(Shinpai) da mon na/ne.*
(7) Guessing someone's feelings: *Kitto, (zannen gat)teru yo/wa yo*

2 Language:

(1) *(Ita)i n deshoo ne.* (2) *(Kossetsu) no yoo desu.*
(3) *Nee, (imushitsu) e ikanai?* (4) *(Shinpai) da mon na.*
(5) *Kitto, (zannen gat)teru wa yo.*

3 Culture:

(1) School nurses

II. PREPARATION

1. Context

試合中の事故

試合中に事故が起こった。シュートに向かうのぶおから相手側の選手がボールを取ろうとしてぶつかり、二人一緒に床に叩きつけられた。しかし、その後二人ともしばらく起き上がらなかった。コーチが急いで近寄った。また、医務室の先生もやってきた。試合はしばらく中断となった。

There was an accident during the game. Nobuo tried to shoot the ball while a player from the other team tried to steal it. Nobuo and the other player collided, and both of them fell to the floor. Neither of them were able to get up right away. The coach and the school doctor rushed over. The game was suspended for a while.

2. Sample Conversation

P: 選手がけがをしたようだよ。
Y: のぶお、大丈夫かしら。
P: 骨を折っているかもしれない。
Y: 本当。痛いんでしょうね。かわいそう。
P: 担架がやって来たよ。
Q: 木下選手はねんざ、ミラー選手は骨折のようです。選手交代後、試合を続けます。
Y: レフリーは何て言ったの。
P: のぶおはねんざだって。
Y: ねえ、医務室へ行かない。
P: そうだね、心配だもんな。
Y: きっと残念がってるわよ。

P: *Senshu ga kega o shita yoo da yo.*
Y: *Nobuo, daijoobu kashira[1].*
P: *Hone o otte iru kamo shirenai.*
Y: *Hontoo? Itai n deshoo ne. Kawaisoo.*

P: *Tanka ga yatte kita yo.*
Q: *Kinoshita senshu wa nenza, Miraa senshu wa kossetsu no yoo desu. Senshu kootai go, shiai o tsuzukemasu.*
Y: *Refurii wa nan te itta no?*
P: *Nobuo wa nenza datte.*
Y: *Nee, imushitsu[2] e ikanai?*
P: *Soo da ne, shinpai da mon na[3].*
Y: *Kitto, zannen gatteru wa yo.*

P: It looks like some players got hurt.
Y: Do you think Nobuo is OK?
P: Maybe he broke a bone.
Y: Do you think so? It must be so painful. Poor Nobuo!
P: They're bringing the stretcher.
Q: It seems that Kinoshita has a sprain and Miller has a bone fracture. We'll continue the game after the player change.
Y: What did the referee say?
P: He said that Nobuo has a sprain.
Y: Why don't we go to the nurse's office?
P: That's a good idea. I'm worried about Nobuo.
Y: He must be disappointed.

Q:	レフリー	*Refurii*	Referee
P:	ピーター スミス	*Piitaa Sumisu*	Peter Smith
Y:	やまだ よしこ	*Yamada Yoshiko*	Yoshiko Yamada

3. Language & Culture Notes

1 *Kashira*, which comes at the end of a sentence, is a marker that shows some doubt about something.

2 Certified nurses are always on duty at American schools. In Japanese schools, however, a certified teacher who was trained in health education takes the place of a nurse. Usually female, health teachers are responsible for tending to students' general health and general health problems, such as colds, fevers, cuts, and bruises. Although perfectly capable of handling minor incidents, school health teachers cannot administer shots or draw blood like a certified nurse. The "health teacher" is a staff member with a desk in the staff room, but she usually takes care of students' needs in the Health Room.

3 --- *da mon na/ne*, which follows nouns or adjectival nouns, such as *shinpai*, is an expression that is used to express one's feelings about someone or something. The expression may also follow adjectives. In this case, however, *da* is omitted.

III. PARTICIPATION

1. Vocabulary

1 **From sample conversation:**

go (after)
hone (bone)
ikanai? (How about going/Would you like to go to ...?)
imushitsu (health room)
itai (hurt, be painful)
kega (injury)
kossetsu (bone fracture)
nenza (sprain)
otte iru (broken)
refurii (referee)
senshu (player)
senshu kootai (player change)
shinpai (worry, concern)
tanka (stretcher)
tsuzukemasu (continue)
yatte kita (arrived, came)
zannen (unfortunate, regrettable)
zannen gatteru (feel/be disappointed, regretful, sorry)

2 **Useful for activities:**

Foodo (Ford)
hakiyasui (comfortable, easy to wear)
kawaisoo (feel sorry for [someone])
kootsuujiko (auto accident)
kozutsumi (package)
kuyashii (disappointed)
Matsuda (Mazda)
mukoo (over there)
nokku suru (to knock)
okonomiyaki (a pancake-like pizza)
ooame (heavy rain)
oru (to break)
oto (sound)
Soo kanaa. (Is that so?)
tsukiyubi o suru (to sprain one's finger)
zenzen chigau (totally different)

2. Activity, Practice, & Exercise

1 Giving reasons

In pairs: Students ask their partner why they do or did something. The partners respond with a reason using the expression --- *mon na/ne*. Follow the example.

Example: A: *Dooshite itsumo jiinzu o haite iru no?* (Why do you always wear jeans?)
B: *Soryaa hakiyasui mon ne.* (Because they're comfortable.)

2 Past injuries

In pairs: Tell your partner about an injury that has happened to you, someone in your family, or one of your friends. Your partner responds by expressing sympathy.

Example: 1) A: *Kono mae, bareebooru o shite iru toki ni tsukiyubi shichatta no.*
(I sprained my finger while playing volleyball the other day.)
B: *Hontoo! Itakatta deshoo. Kawaisoo.* (Really! It must have hurt. I feel for you.)

2) A: *Sengetsu ani wa kootsuujiko de ashi to ude no hone o otta n da.*
(My brother was in a car accident last month and broke his arm and leg.)
B: *Hontoo! Taihen datta ne. Ima wa doo?*
(Really! It must have been tough. How is he now?)
A: *Sanshuukan nyuuin shite, ima wa moo daijoobu da yo.*
(He was in the hospital for three weeks, but he's OK now.)
B: *Soo. Sore wa yokatta.* (That's good.)

3 I wonder if ...

In pairs: Tell your partner what you wonder about. Use the expression --- *kashira* or --- *daroo ka*.

Example: 1) A: *Kumo ga dete kita wa. Ame ga furu kashira.*
(Clouds are coming out. I wonder if it will rain.)
B: *Furu kamo ne. Kasa motteru?* (It might. Do you have an umbrella?)
A: *Uun. Mottenai. Komatta wa.* (No, I don't. What should I do?)

2) A: *Ashita no tesuto, daijoobu daroo ka.*
(I wonder if I'll do OK on tomorrow's exam.)
B: *Kon'ya isshookenmei benkyoo sureba, daijoobu da yo.*
(You'll do OK if you study hard tonight.)
A: *Soo kanaa.* (You can't be so sure.)

4 Describing pictures

In pairs: Partners describe how the people in the following situations might feel. Use the expression --- *n daroo na* or --- *n deshoo ne*.

Example: A little boy who is learning how to ride a bicycle and keeps falling off of it.
A: *Itai n daroo na/deshoo ne. Kawaisoo.* (It must hurt. The poor boy.)
B: *Sore ni, kuyashii daroo na/deshoo ne.* (He must be disappointed, too.)

1. A high school student studying hard late at night
2. A woman whose eyes are filled with tears over a broken love
3. A child with his head hanging down. He broke a plate and his mother is angry at him
4. A homeless person who is lying on the street on a cold winter's day

5 Combining and matching conversation parts

In groups of fourteen: Following are seven 4-line conversations between two people. There are 14 cards: seven cards with A's part in a dialogue and seven cards with B's part. The teacher mixes the cards and randomly gives one to each student. Students will know which part they have, but they will not know which students have A parts or B parts. Students will go around the room trying to find the student who has the card that completes their conversation. When pairing up with a student, do not show each other the cards. Students will determine whether or not their cards match by reading their cards out loud. Once students think they have found their match, they should go to the teacher and recite the conversation. If the match is incorrect, the students must continue trying to find the correct one. The first pair of students to find the correct match is the winner. (Note: If there are less than fourteen students in the class, simply eliminate cards as necessary. If there are more than fourteen students in the class, more conversations can be made, or split the class into two smaller groups and give each group the same set of conversations to use.)

Conversations:

Part A

1. A: *Doa o nokku suru oto ga shita yo.*
   B:
   A: *Otoosan kamo shirenai.*
   B:

2. A: *Ojisan kara kozutsumi ga todoita wa yo.*
   B:
   A: *Okashi kamo shirenai.*
   B:

Part B

A:
B: *Dare kashira.*
A:
B: *Yappari otoosan datta wa ne.*

A:
B: *Nani kashira.*
A:
B: *Yappari soo da wa.*

3. A: *Kochira ni hashitte kuru ano kuruma nan daroo?*
   B:
   A: *Matsuda kamo shirenai yo.*
   B:

4. A: *Okaasan, denwa.*
   B:
   A: *Satoko obasan kamo shirenai.*
   B:

5. A: *Ano ryoori nan daroo?*
   B:
   A: *Kureepu kamo shirenai.*
   B:

6. A: *A, kore wa Nihon no nyuusu da.*
   B:
   A: *Tookyoo kamo shirenai yo.*
   B:

7. A: *Sora ga kumotte kita na.*
   B:
   A: *Ooame ni naru kamo shirenai yo.*
   B:

A:
B: *Foodo kashira.*
A:
B: *Zenzen chigatta. Nissan da.*

A:
B: *Dare kashira.*
A:
B: *Moshi moshi. Aa yappari Satoko datta no.*

A:
B: *Piza kashira.*
A:
B: *Okonomiyaki to kaite aru wa yo.*

A:
B: *Doko kashira.*
A:
B: *Tookyoo ja nakutte, Oosaka deshita.*

A:
B: *Ame kashira.*
A:
B: *Hora, mukoo kara futte kita yo.*

6 How about ...?

In class: Change the following question into new questions. Try to find as many people as possible who want to do something with you. Ask everyone the same question.

   Imushitsu e ikanai? (Why don't we go to the nurse's office?)

7 It seems that ...

In pairs: Change the underlined part in the following sentence. Try to make as many sentences as possible that express "It seems that ---," by using --- *no yoo desu*.

   <u>*Miraa san wa kossetsu*</u> *no yoo desu.* (It seems that Miller has a bone fracture.)

8 Expressing regret

Individually: Use the expression *zannen gatte iru* to express regret or disappointment at not being able to do or achieve something. Try to write at least two sentences.

Lesson 23

Lesson 24: Review & Application

IV. PERFORMANCE

1. Application

1 TV and movie actors

In pairs: Talk about your favorite TV programs and movies and the actors and actresses who star in them. Use the following conversation as an example. (T = Toshio, S = Sachiko)

Example: T: *Sachiko san wa donna terebi bangumi o mimasu ka?*
(Sachiko, what kind of TV programs do you watch?)

S: *Iroiro mimasu. Ichiban suki na bangumi wa "C" desu.*
(Many kinds. My favorite is "C")

T: *Dare ga dete imasu ka?* (Who's in it?)

S: *D ga dete imasu. Watashi wa D no fan nan desu. Toshio kun wa donna bangumi ga suki desu ka?*
(D stars in it. I really like D. Toshio, what kind of programs do you like?)

T: *Boku wa "E" ga suki desu. Omoshirokute, itsumo waraimasu.*
(I like "E." It's interesting and makes me laugh.)

S: *Dare ga dete imasu ka?* (Who's in it?)

T: *F to G ga dete imasu.* (F and G)

S: *Toshio kun wa eiga mo suki desu ka?* (Toshio, do you like movies, too?)

T: *Mochiron. Atarashii eiga no naka de wa "H" ga yokatta desu. I to J ga "H" ni demashita. I wa keikan no yaku de kakko yokatta desu.*
(Of course. Among the new movies, H was good. I and J are in it. I was good at playing the role of a policeman.)

S: *Watashi wa senshuu "K" o mimashita. L to M ga demashita. L to M wa koibito no yaku deshita.*
(Last week I saw *K* with L and M. They played the roles of lovers.)

2 My schools

In pairs: Tell your partner about the different schools that you have attended. Specify the names of the schools and the years in which you entered and graduated each school.

Example: *Watashi wa 1986 nen ni A shoogakkoo ni hairimashita. Soshite, 1991 nen ni soko o demashita. 1991 nen ni B chuugakkoo ni hairi, 1994 nen ni sotsugyoo shimashita. Sorekara, 1994 nen ni C kookoo ni hairimashita.*
(I entered A Elementary School in 1986 and graduated in 1991. I entered B Junior High School in 1991 and graduated in 1994. Then I entered C High School in 1994.)

3 Did you go anywhere last Sunday?

In groups of three: Each group needs a copy of the two cards written below: *Shitsumon Kaado* and *Kotae Kaado*. Student A has about one minute to study and try to memorize the questions on the *Shitsumon Kaado*. Student B will then take the *Shitsumon Kaado* and help Student A when he/she has trouble remembering a question. Student C takes the *Kotae Kaado* and answers Student A's questions. The answer to the first question will always be *mooru*. For question 2, Student C should choose one of the three options listed. Student C may answer questions 3 through 7 any way he/she wishes. The activity should be done three times so that each group member has the opportunity to do each part.

Shitsumon Kaado	Kotae Kaado
1. *Senshuu no nichiyoobi wa doko ka e ikimashita ka?*	1. *mooru*
2. *Nani o shi ni ikimashita ka?*	2. *shokuji/kaimono/eiga*
3. *Nanji goro dekakemashita ka?*	3.
4. *Dare to ikimashita ka?*	4.
5. *Nani o tabemashita/kaimashita ka/mimashita ka?*	5.
6. *Nanji goro ie ni kaerimashita ka?*	6.
7. *Tanoshii ichinichi deshita ka?*	7.

4 Take a look.

In small groups: On a piece of paper, each student draws a picture of something or cuts a picture out of a magazine. Students take turns showing their picture to the group saying *Mite, mite,* and describing the picture. Others comment on the description.

Example: A: <u>*Mite, mite*</u>. *Boku no shoorai no gaarufurendo da.*
(Take a look. This is my future girlfriend.)
B: *Hee, totemo kirei na hito ja nai.* (Really? She's very pretty.)
A: *Totemo se ga takai daroo.* (She's very tall, don't you think?)
C: *Atama mo yosasoo da ne.* (She looks smart, too.)

5 Sake is made from rice.

In pairs: Below is a list of products and materials. Match each product with the material from which it is made. Make sentences using the expression --- *wa* --- *kara* or --- *wa* --- *de tsukurareru*. *Kara* is used when something is made from raw materials.

products: *furui Nihon no ie* (old Japanese houses), *osake* (Japanese rice wine), *biiru* (beer), --- *san no kutsu* (---'s shoes), *hon* (book), *chiizu* (cheese), *koora no kan* (can of soda), *yukata*, *purasuchikku* (plastic)

materials: *arumi* (aluminum), *kawa* (leather), *budoo* (grapes), *sekiyu* (oil), *ki* (wood), *gyuunyuu* (milk), *mugi* (wheat), *momen* (cotton), *kami* (paper), *kome* (rice)

Example: • *Furui Nihon no ie <u>wa</u> ki <u>de tsukurareta</u>.* (Old Japanese houses were made of wood.)
• *Osake <u>wa</u> kome <u>kara tsukurareru</u>.* (Japanese wine is made from rice.)

6 Listening comprehension and/or oral production

Individually: Listen to the conversations between two people. Complete the sentences by writing what one person did for the other.

Example: A: *Tomu, denwa da yo.* (Tom, telephone.)
B: *Ima chotto te ga hanasenai n da. Jimii kun, warui kedo, tanomu yo.*
   (My hands are full. Jimmy, can you answer it?)
A: *Ja, boku ga deru yo ... Moshi moshi.* (I'll get it ... Hello?)
Answer:
→ <u>*Jimii*</u> ga <u>*denwa ni dete*</u> *kuremashita.* (Jimmy answered the telephone for Tom.)

1. A: *Aa, shimatta. Terehonkaado, wasurechatta yo.* (Oh no. I forgot my telephone card.)
   B: *Ken, ja, watashi no o tsukatte.* (Ken, use mine.)
   A: *Arigatoo, Nanshii. Ja, kariru yo.* (Thanks for letting me borrow it, Nancy.)
   B: *Doozo.* (Go ahead.)
   (→ Nancy let Ken use her telephone card.)

2. A: *Midori san, isogashisoo desu ne.* (Midori, you seem busy.)
   B: *Ee, chotto keisan ga takusan atte.* (Yeah. I have a lot of calculations to do.)
   A: *Watashi, tetsudaimashoo ka? Keisan wa tokui desu kara.*
      (Shall I help you? I'm good at calculating.)
   B: *Maa, Keiko san. Sooshite kureru to tasukaru wa. Ja, onegai ne.*
      (Oh, Keiko, it would be a great help. Could you do that?)
   (→ Keiko helped Midori do calculations.)

3. A: *An, uchi made okuru yo.* (Ann, I'll drive you home.)
   B: *Demo, Bobu no uchi, hoogaku ga chigau deshoo. Warui wa.*
      (But, Bob, you're going a different direction. I hate to bother you.)
   A: *Ii yo. Enryo shinai de.* (It's OK. Don't be silly.)
   B: *Arigatoo.* (Thank you.)
   (→ Bob drove Ann home.)

4. A: *Hiroshi san, uta ga joozu deshoo.* (Hiroshi, you're good at singing, aren't you?)
   B: *Sonna koto nai yo. Karaoke wa suki dakedo ...* (Not at all. I like karaoke, but ...)
   A: *Nee, Nihon no uta o utatte yo.* (Would you sing a Japanese song?)
   B: *Hazukashii na.* (I'm too shy.)
   A: *Onegai.* (Please?)
   B: *Jaa ...* (Well, ...)
   (→ Hiroshi sang a Japanese song for his friend.)

Answers:
1. _____ ga _____ kuremashita.
2. _____ ga _____ kuremashita.
3. _____ ga _____ kuremashita.
4. _____ ga _____ kuremashita.

7 Listening comprehension and/or oral production

Individually: Listen to the conversations and decide what is likely to happen. Circle the correct choice.

Example: A: *Atarashii seitokaichoo wa Timu kana. Ninki ga aru kara ne.*
(I wonder if Tim will be the new student council president. He's popular.)
B: *Jon wa doo na no?* (How about John?)
A: *Jon wa chotto ne ...* (John seems a little, well ...)
B: *Dame kamo shirenai no?* (He may lose?)
A: *Maa ne.* (It seems so.)
Answer:
→ *Atarashii seitokaichoo ni naru no wa [**Timu**/Jon]da to omoimasu.*
(I think the new student council president will be [**Tim**/John].)

1. A: *Saikin ame ga furanai kara, mizu ga tarinaku natteru n datte. Asu wa doo daroo?*
   (I heard that we're running out of water because it hasn't rained recently. What about tomorrow?)
   B: *Furu kamo shirenai kedo, tenkiyohoo dewa, 10% datte.*
   (It may rain, but according to the weather forecast the possibility is only 10%.)
   A: *Soo ka. Komatta na.* (Really? That's not good.)
   (→ I think it [will/will not] rain tomorrow.)

2. A: *Asu no Jaiantsu to Dojaazu no shiai, dotchi ga katsu ka na?*
   (Who do you think will win tomorrow's Giants-Dodgers game?)
   B: *Dotchi daroo? Jaiantsu kamo shirenai kedo ...* (I wonder. The Giants may win, but ...)
   A: *Demo, Dojaazu wa saikin nakanaka ganbatteru yo.*
   (But the Dodgers have been playing well lately.)
   B: *Soo da ne. Kantoku mo ii shi, pitchaa mo battaa mo sorotteru shi ne.*
   (Yeah. The manager is good, and the team's batters and pitchers are all in good shape.)
   A: *Soo da ne.* (I agree.)
   (→ I think the [Giants / Dodgers] will win the game tomorrow.)

3. A: *Raishuu no nihongo no tesuto, chotto shinpai ne.*
   (I'm a little worried about the Japanese test next week.)
   B: *Soo ne. Kaku mondai ga aru kara ne.* (Yeah. We have writing questions.)
   C: *Demo, Hayashi sensei wa itsumo muzukashii mondai wa dasanai deshoo.*
   (But Hayashi *sensei* usually doesn't give us difficult questions, right?)
   A: *Sore mo soo ne. Jugyoo de yatta koto o fukushuu sureba daijoobu kamo shirenai wa.*
   (Right. We'll be OK if we review what we learned in class.)
   B: *Ee. Ja, shuumatsu issho ni benkyoo shinai?*
   (Yeah. Should we study together over the weekend?)
   AC: *Ii wa ne.* (Sounds good.)
   (→ I think Mrs. Hayashi's Japanese exam will [be difficult/not be so difficult.])

Answers:
1. *Asu wa ame ga (furu/furanai) to omoimasu.*
2. *Asu no shiai wa (Jaiantsu/Dojaazu) ga katsu to omoimasu.*
3. *Hayashi sensei no nihongo no tesuto wa (muzukashii/amari muzukashikunai) to omoimasu.*

8 Giving advice

In pairs: Using the expression --- *yoo ni*, give advice to friends who have the following problems.
   (1) Angela eats too much.
   (2) Tom drinks too much.
   (3) Stephanie watches too much TV.
   (4) Frank drives too fast.
   (5) Lucy works too hard.

9 Making sentences

In class: The teacher makes a flashcard for each of the seven verbs listed below. The teacher first shows the students a flashcard for a few seconds and then puts it down. The teacher then demonstrates the action or situation that is described in parenthesis. Students write a sentence using the verb on the flashcard to express the situation. Note: Before beginning the activity, the teacher should explain the sentence structure to the students.

   Procedure: flash card → (teacher's gesture) → students' sentence
   1. <u>ochiru</u>   → (dropping a ball-point pen) → *Boorupen ga ochimashita.*
   2. <u>taoreru</u>   → (knocking a chair over) → *Isu ga taoremashita.*
   3. <u>yabureru</u>   → (showing a ripped piece of paper) → *Kami ga yaburemashita.*
   4. <u>wareru</u>   → (showing a broken glass) → *Koppu ga waremashita.*
   5. <u>kireru</u>   → (showing a piece of rope that ripped into two pieces) → *Himo ga kiremashita.*
   6. <u>nakunaru</u>   → (showing an empty wallet) → *Okane ga nakunarimashita.*
   7. <u>kieru</u>   → (lighting a candle and blowing it out) → *Hi ga kiemashita.*

10 Conversation completion

The following is a conversation between students A and B. They are watching a basketball game at school. From the list below, fill in the parentheses with the most appropriate responses for student B.

A: *Hora, Kenji kun ga te o futteru wa.* (Look! Kenji is waving.)
B: ( ) (He looks confident.)
A: *Soo ne. Kenji kun wa shuuto ga tokui dakara.* (Yeah. He is really good at shooting.)
B: ( ) (Wow! That's great!)
A: *Mae ni chiimu no renshuu o mi ni itta koto ga aru no yo.*
   (I've seen the team practice before.)
B: *Hee, soo?* ( ) (Really? This is my first time seeing them.)
A: *Aa, shiai ga hajimatta wa.* (Oh, the game has started.)
B: ( ) (Look, look! He made a good cut-in.)
A: *Ee, nakanaka umai wa ne.* (Yeah. It was pretty good.)
B: ( ) (Oh, they're keeping an eye on Kenji.)
A: *Jaa, ooen shimashoo.* (Let's cheer for him.)
B: *Yoshi!* ( ) (Yes. Hurray! Hurray! Kenji!)

   1. *Mite, mite. Ano kattoin, umai naa.*
   2. *Furee, furee, Kenji!*
   3. *Fuun, sugoi ja nai ka?*
   4. *Boku wa kyoo hajimete da yo.*
   5. *Jishin ga arisoo ne.*
   6. *Aa, kenji ga maaku sarehajimeta.*

2. Actualization

1 Practice the following conversation and develop your own dialogue on a similar subject with your partners.

Kayoobi no 2jikanme, taiiku no jugyoo desu. Kondo no nichiyoobi wa undookai desu. Danjokongoo 400meetoru riree (Danjo kaku futari) no senshu o erabu tame seito wa kootai de 50 meetoru soo no kiroku o totte imasu.

(Second period on Tuesday is physical education. There is an athletic meet this Sunday, so students are selecting the representatives of the boys and girls mixed 400-meter relay race. The students are timing each other in the 50-meter dash.)

Hirayama sensei:	*Ichi ni tsuite, yooi, don.* (Ready, get set, go!)
Ooyama san:	*Tanaka kun, 7 byoo 8.* (Tanaka, 7.8 seconds.)
Yamamoto san:	*Suzuki kun, 8 byoo choodo.* (Suzuki, exactly eight seconds.)
Hirayama sensei:	*Ichi ni tsuite, yooi, don.* (Ready, get set, go!)
Ooyama san:	*Iida san, 8 byoo 4.* (Iida, 8.4 seconds.)
Yamamoto san:	*Yamada san wa 8 byoo 6.* (Yamada, 8.6.)
Hirayama sensei:	*Kore de, zen'in owarimashita ne. Danshi wa, ichiban hayakatta no ga Kobayashi kun. 2 banme ga Tanaka kun desu ne. Joshi wa Yamamoto san to Iida san. Kono 4 nin ni kimarimashita.* (Everyone has finished. The fastest boy is Kobayashi. Next is Tanaka. As for the girls, Yamada and Iida are the fastest. These four students will run in the relay race.)
Seito zen'in:	*[Hakushu]* (Applause)

2 Practice the following conversation and develop your own dialogue on a similar subject with your partners.

Suiyoobi no 3jikanme, taiiku no jugyoo desu. 4 nen 1 kumi no seito wa hashirihabatobi no kiroku o totte imasu.

(Third period on Wednesday is physical education. The 4th grade, class 1 students are doing the long jump.)

Akiyama sensei:	*2 meetoru 53. Hai, tsugi.* (2.53 meters. OK. Next.)
Tanaka kun:	*Itai. [Shirimochi o tsuku]* (Ouch! [He fell on his behind.])
Akiyama sensei:	*Daijoobu?* (Are you all right?)
Tanaka kun:	*Hai.* (Yes.)
Akiyama sensei:	*Eeto. 2 meetoru 86.* (Well, 2.86 meters.)
Tanaka kun:	*Zannen datta naa. Shirimochi o tsukanakattara, 3 meetoru koeteta noni.* (What a pity. I would have gotten over 3 meters if I hadn't fallen.)
Akiyama sensei:	*Moo ichido tonde ii wa yo. [Tanaka kun moo ichido tobu.]* (You can do it again.) [Tanaka jumps again.]
Tanaka kun:	*Sensei, nan meetoru desu ka?* (Mrs. Akiyama, how many meters was it?)

Lesson 24   189

Akiyama sensei:	*3 meetoru 5.* (3.5 meters.)
Tanaka kun:	*Yatta.* (I did it!)
Akiyama sensei:	*Kondo wa umaku itta wa ne.* (You did great this time.)
Tanaka kun:	*Hai.* (Thanks.)

3 Practice the following conversation and develop your own dialogue on a similar subject with your partners.

Getsuyoobi no 1jikanme, 4 nen 2 kumi no seito wa, taiiku no jugyoo de sakaagari no renshuu o shite imasu.
(In first period on Wednesday, the 4th grade, class 2 students are practicing backward rotations around a bar.)

Ooki sensei:	*10 byookan ni minasan dekirudake sakaagari o shite kudasai. Soredewa hajime...* [*Mina, sakaagari o suru.*] *... Yame.* (Everyone, do as many backward rotations around the bar as you can in ten seconds. Start ... Stop.)
Tanaka san:	*Sensei, watashi ikkai mo dekimasen deshita.* (Mr. Oki, I couldn't even do it once.)
Ooki sensei:	*Daijoobu. Renshuu sureba kanarazu dekiru yoo ni naru kara. Dewa, 1 kai no hito ... Hai, te o oroshite. 2 kai no hito wa ... Hai, 3 kai no hito wa ... Takusan imasu ne. 4 kai no hito wa ... Ooyama san to Suzuki kun to Tanaka kun no 3 nin desu ne.* (Don't worry. You'll be able to do it if you practice more. Well, how many of you did it once? ... I see. Put your hands down. How about twice? ... OK. How about three times? ... Many of you. How about four times? ... Ooyama, Suzuki, and Tanaka. Three people.)
Yamamoto kun:	*Sensei, boku 5 kai dekimashita.* (Mr. Oki, I did it five times.)
Ooki sensei:	*Hoka ni 5 kai ijoo dekita hito, imasu ka. Imasen ne. Yamamoto kun ga ichiban takusan dekimashita ne.* (Did anyone else do five or more? ... None. Yamamoto did the most.)
Yoshida san:	*Sugoi wa ne, Yamamoto kun.* (That's great, Yamamoto.)
Yamamoto kun:	*Arigatoo.* (Thanks.)

4 Perform Japanese *rajio taisoo* in class.

5 Greetings

In pairs: Practice exchanging New Year's greetings as well as cards on other occasions, such as graduation, recovery from illness, and condolences.
Example: a) When greeting seniors:
        A: *Akemashite omedetoo gozaimasu. Kotoshi mo doozo yoroshiku onegaishimasu.*
        B: *Akemashite omedetoo gozaimasu. Kochira koso doozo yoroshiku.*
   b) When greeting friends:
        A: *Akemashite omedetoo. Kotoshi mo doozo yoroshiku.*
        B: *Akemashite omedetoo. Kochira koso yoroshiku.*

3. Enrichment

1 *Kanji* for Lesson 22

| 振る | 試合 | 自信 | 彼 | 初めて |
| 練習 | 事 | 調子 | 声援 | |

2 *Kanji* for Lesson 23

選手	骨	折る	痛い	担架
骨折	交代	後	続ける	医務室
心配	残念			

3 Other useful *kanji*

席、室、客、犬、誘、怒、逃、県

4 Strategies

Determining the phonetic component of a particular *kanji* may be useful in figuring out the pronunciation of another *kanji* with the same semantic component or classifier. As previously stated, each *kanji* has two types of pronunciation. The *on* pronunciation came from various regions of China over different periods of time and was imitated by the Japanese who introduced *kanji* to Japan. The *kun* reading is the pronunciation of a Japanese word with an equivalent meaning that the original *kanji* has. Only the *on* pronunciation can be identified through this strategy.

5 Exercise

To the best of your knowledge, try to identify the *on* pronunciation of the *kanji* learned in previous lessons.

Lesson 25: Health checks

I. PERSPECTIVE

1. Objectives

1 Function:
(1) Stating a small quantity, size, number: *Tatta, (futari) desu.*
(2) Implying that actions have been taken: *(Boku wa dashi)ta.*
(3) Indicating approval as a result of something: *(Her)u kara ii desu ne.*
(4) Indicating that if something happens, or if someone does something, it would be unfortunate or a loss: *(Her)u to son desu yo.*

2 Language:
(1) *Moo ichido (kakunin) shimasu.*
(2) *Tatta, (futari) desu.*
(3) *(Boku) wa (dashi)ta.*
(4) *Wasurenai de kudasai.*
(5) *(Jikan) ga (her)u kara, (ii) desu ne.*
(6) *(Jikan) ga (her)u to (son) desu yo.*

3 Culture:
(1) Student physical examinations and physical fitness tests
(2) Canceling classes for non-academic purposes

II. PREPARATION

1. Context

健康診断

健康診断書の提出日が近づいてきた。ホームルームの時間に担任の先生が提出期限の確認をした。まだほとんどの学生が提出していなかった。よしこは、日本での健康診断の仕方を話した。学校で全員そろって検査をする方法である。

The date for submitting health certificates is approaching. The teacher in charge made sure that the certificates would be turned in during homeroom. Most of the students have not submitted them yet. Yoshiko explained how health checks are done in Japan. Everyone gets their health examinations done together at school.

2. Sample Conversation

W: もう一度、確認します。締切りは来週の金曜日です。
P: 先生、何人出しましたか。
W: たった、二人です。少ないですよ。
N: 僕は出したと思うんですが。
W: いいえ、まだですよ。忘れないで下さい。
Y: 日本では学校でいっせいに健康診断をします。
W: 授業はどうなるんですか。
Y: その時は休みになるんです。
P: 勉強時間が減るから、いいですね。
W: 勉強時間が減ると損ですよ。

W: *Moo ichido, kakunin shimasu. Shimekiri wa raishuu no kin'yoobi desu.*
P: *Sensei, nannin dashimashita ka?*
W: *Tatta, futari desu. Sukunai desu yo.*
N: *Boku wa dashita to omou n desu ga.*
W: *Iie, mada desu yo. Wasurenai de kudasai.*
Y: *Nihon de wa gakkoo de issei ni kenkooshindan[1] o shimasu.*
W: *Jugyoo wa doo naru n desu ka?*
Y: *Sono toki wa yasumi[2] ni naru n desu.*
P: *Benkyoo jikan ga heru kara, ii desu ne.*
W: *Benkyoo jikan ga heru to son desu yo.*

W: I'm confirming again. The due date is next Friday.
P: How many students have submitted them?
W: Only two students. Very few.
N: I think I submitted mine.
W: No, not yet. Please don't forget.
Y: In Japan we all have our medical check-ups done at the same time at school.
W: What about classes?
Y: We don't have them on that day.
P: It's nice because they have fewer class hours.
W: Fewer class hours is a loss.

W: ウィンストン ブラウン（先生）　*Winsuton Buraun (sensei)*　Winston Brown (teacher)
P: ピーター スミス　*Piitaa Sumisu*　Peter Smith
N: きのした のぶお　*Kinoshita Nobuo*　Nobuo Kinoshita
Y: やまだ よしこ　*Yamada Yoshiko*　Yoshiko Yamada

3. Language & Culture Notes

1 Instead of going to see the family physician, Japanese students get their physical examinations done at school usually by a visiting doctor. All students have their health check on the same day. One at a time, each class visits the health room. Teachers also get their health checks done together; however, they usually go to a central place, such as a community center, in the town where they work. Their health checks are performed by a local doctor. At a different time, students have their physical fitness tests, where they are tested in fields from the high jump and the shot put to cardio-vascular activities.

2 In the United States, when a special school event occurs, either it is held after school, or classes are shortened to save time in the afternoon for the activity. On the contrary, classes in Japanese schools are often canceled for such events. For example, on the day of physical examinations, all or most classes are canceled. Classes are also canceled for sports festivals and often for school sports tournaments, too. Cultural festivals are usually held on a Sunday, but then school is usually canceled on Monday because teachers and students had to work and go to school over the weekend.

III. PARTICIPATION

1. Vocabulary

1 **From sample conversation:**

benkyoo jikan (study hour)
futari (two people)
ichido (once, one time)
kakunin shimasu (confirm)
kenkooshindan (medical/physical examination, health check)
nannin (how many people)
raishuu (next week)
son (loss, disadvantage)
tatta (only, small amount)
yasumi (day off, holiday, vacation)

dashimashita, dashita (submitted)
heru (to reduce, become less)
issei (at the same time)

omou (to think)
shimekiri (deadline, closing)
sukunai (few)
wasurenai (do not forget)

2 **Useful for activities:**

booru (ball)
chika (basement)
dasu (to send)
haitte iru (be in, be contained)
ijoo (over, more than)
kesu (to turn off)
kotae (an answer)
mazeru (to mix)

chansu (chance)
daijishin (big earthquake)
gifuto (gift)
haru (to put on, to stick)
keeki (cake)
kippu (ticket)
kyanseru suru (to cancel)
mo (as many as, no less than)

nandai (how many [cars])
oyu (hot water)
rajikase (radio cassette player)
shika (only)
shooyu (soy sauce)
suteru (to throw away)
tsuushinhanbai (mail-order)
yoofuku (clothes)

nedan (price)
raito (light)
satoo (sugar)
shinchoo (height)
shurui (kind, sort)
taifuu (typhoon)
yaku (to bake)

2. Activity, Practice, & Exercise

1 I think ...

In small groups: One person asks when a certain event took place. Other group members answer the question using the expression --- *to omou n desu ga*, to imply that they are not sure.

Example: A: *Koobe de daijishin ga okotta no wa itsu deshita ka?*
(When was the big earthquake in Kobe?)
B: *1995 nen no 2 gatsu datta to omou n desu ga.* (I think it was February 1995.)
C: *Iie, are wa 1 gatsu deshita yo.* (No. It was in January.)

2 I think you should

In pairs: Partners tell each other what they would like to buy. Suggest a good store or company using the expression --- *to omou n desu ga* or --- *to omou n dakedo*. State why the store is recommended.

Example: A: *Atarashii rajikase ga hoshii naa/wa.* (I want a new radio cassette player.)
B: *Rajikase nara ---* (name of a store) *ga ii to omou n dakedo. Shurui mo ooi shi, nedan mo yasui shi.*
(I think you should go to --- for a radio cassette recorder. The store has many kinds, and the prices are reasonable.)
A: *Jaa, soko de mite miru yo/wa.* (Well then, I'll go there and look at them.)

3 Advantage or disadvantage?

In pairs: Partners discuss the following situations and give their opinions. Use the expression --- *to toku desu yo* if the situation is an advantage, or --- *to son desu yo* if it is a disadvantage. Students should include a reason.

Example: *Jugyoo no jikan ga heru.* →
A: *Jugyoo no jikan ga heru to son desu yo.*
(If class hours are shortened, it will be a disadvantage.)
B: *Dooshite desu ka?* (Why is that?)
A: *Benkyoo no chansu ga heru kara desu.*
(Because we will have fewer opportunities to learn.)

1. *Taifuu de gakkoo ga yasumi ni naru.* (Schools will close because of a typhoon.)
2. *Tsuushinhanbai de yoofuku o kau.* (Buying clothes from a mail-order catalogue.)
3. *Shinchoo ga 190 cm ijoo aru.* (Being over 190 cm tall.)

4 Large amount – small amount

In class: Partners ask each other about the number or amount of something. Answer the question using the expression *tatta* if the number seems very small or --- *mo imasu/arimasu* if it seems very large. If the number is average, then the above expressions are not necessary.

Example: 1) A: *Ie ni terebi ga nandai arimasu ka?* (How many televisions do you have at home?)
B: *2 dai desu.* (Two.)

2) A: *Itoko wa nannin imasu ka?* (How many cousins do you have?)
B: *Tatta 3nin desu.* (Only three.)

3) A: *Ie ni wa kuruma ga nandai arimasu ka?* (How many cars does your family have?)
B: *4 dai mo arimasu.* (We have four cars!)

5 Sentence completion

In small groups: Fill in each blank with an appropriate word. Pay attention to the expression *tatta --- shika nai*.

Example: 1) *Kono gakkoo ni wa ryuugakusei ga tatta hitori shika imasen.*
(There is only one international student in this school.)
2) *Watashi no ie ni wa terebi ga tatta 1 dai shika arimasen.*
(There is only one TV in my home.)

1. *Kono gakkoo ni wa _____ ga tatta _____ shika arimasen.*
   (There is/are only _____ _____ in this school.)
2. *Watashi no ie ni wa _____ ga tatta _____ shika arimasen.*
   (There is/are only _____ _____ in my home.)
3. *Saifu no naka ni wa tatta _____ shika haitte imasen.*
   (Only _____ is in my wallet.)
4. *Tesuto de tatta _____ shika toremasen deshita.*
   (I got only _____ on the exam.)

6 Substitution

In pairs: Change the underlined part in the following sentence. Make at least five sentences that ask someone not to do something.

Wasurenai de kudasai. (Please don't forget.)

7 I'm sorry. I already ...

In class: Everyone sits in a circle. Students take turns making a statement, choosing from the list below. Students may call on any one of their classmates; however, they should use their name. The student called responds to the statement using *-te shimaimashita*, following the example. Then that student will call on someone else. The teacher will correct the student's usage of *-te shimaimashita* if necessary. The activity continues until each student has had a chance to both give and respond to a statement.

Example: A: *Sutiibu san, chokoreeto wa mada tabenai de kudasai.*
(Steve, please don't eat the chocolate yet.)
B: *Sumimasen, moo tabete shimaimashita.* (I'm sorry. I already ate it.)

Statements:
1. *XX san, dezaato wa mada tabenai de kudasai.* (dessert/eat)
2. *XX san, eiga no kippu wa mada kawanai de kudasai.* (movie ticket/buy)
3. *XX san, chika no raito wa mada kesanai de kudasai.* (basement light/turn off)
4. *XX san, juusu wa mada nomanai de kudasai.* (juice/drink)
5. *XX san, gifuto wa mada akenai de kudasai.* (gift/open)
6. *XX san, mada satoo to shooyu o mazenai de kudasai.* (sugar and soy sauce/mix)
7. *XX san, Furorida no tsuaa wa mada kyanseru shinai de kudasai.* (tour/cancel)
8. *XX san, takoyaki wa mada yakanai de kudasai.* (*takoyaki*/cook)
9. *XX san, sono oyu wa mada sutenai de kudasai.* (hot water/throw away)
10. *XX san, hagaki ni wa mada kitte o haranai de kudasai.* (stamp/affix)
11. *XX san, tegami wa mada dasanai de kudasai.* (letter/send)
12. *XX san, sono keeki wa mada kiranai de kudasai.* (cake/cut)
13. *XX san, mada kotae wa kakanai de kudasai.* (answer/write)
14. *XX san, watashi ga kega o shita koto o mada sensei ni iwanai de kudasai.* (injury/tell)
15. *XX san, kinoo katta atarashii booru wa mada tsukawanai de kudasai.* (new ball/use)

8 Use *-te shimaimashita* and *Moo ichido kakunin shite kudasai* to write five sentences.
Example: *Yamada san ga makete shimaimashita. Moo ichido kakunin shite kudasai.*

Lesson 26: Thermometer

I. PERSPECTIVE

1. Objectives

1 Function:

(1) Thinking that something might have happened due to something else:
  (Watashi wa koonetsu) de (shinu) to omotta (wa).
(2) Encouraging or urging the speaker to continue speaking: *Sorede,*
(3) Describing one's appearance: *(Shinpai)soo na kao o shite,*
(4) Conveying what another person has said: *(Daijoobu) tte itte kureta.*
(5) Mathematical calculations:
  (Hyakudo) kara mazu (sanjuuni) o hiite, sorekara (go) o kakete, (kyuu) de waru.
(6) Describing an "if ... then" situation: *Soo suru to (---) ni naru.*

2 Language:

(1) *(Shinpai)soo na (kao) o shite.*   (2) *(Daijoobu) tte itte kureta.*
(3) *Soo suru to (---) ni naru wa.*

3 Culture:

(1) Systems of measurement   (2) Mathematical vocabulary

II. PREPARATION

1. Context

体温計

れいこがよしこの家へ遊びに来た。れいこは子供の時かかった病気の経験話をした。れいこは小さい頃病気にかかり、高い熱を出した。れいこのお母さんは体温を計りなさいと言って部屋を出て行った。れいこは自分で体温計の温度を読むことにした。体温は１００度だった。

Reiko went to Yoshiko's house to visit. She told Yoshiko about an experience that she had when she was a little girl. Reiko was sick and had a high fever. Her mother asked her to take her temperature herself and left the room. Reiko checked the thermometer herself. It was 100 degrees.

2. Sample Conversation

R: お母さんのいない時、体温計を読んだの。
Y: 何度だったの。
R: １００度だったのよ。私は高熱で死ぬと思った。
Y: それは摂氏じゃないわよ。
R: アメリカへ来たばかりだったから知らなかったの。
Y: それで。
R: 私は怖くなって泣き始めた。
Y: そこへお母さんがやって来た。
R: うん。心配そうな顔をして私を見るの。
Y: １００度だったことを話したの。
R: 大丈夫って言ってくれた。そして、摂氏に計算してくれた。
Y: 華氏の１００度からまず３２を引いて、それから５を掛けて、９で割る。そうすると約３７．８度になるわ。

R: *Okaasan no¹ inai toki, taionkei o yonda no.*
Y: *Nando datta no?*
R: *Hyakudo² datta no yo. Watashi wa koonetsu de³ shinu to omotta.*
Y: *Sore wa sesshi ja nai⁴ wa yo.*
R: *Amerika e kita bakari⁵ datta kara shiranakatta⁶ no.*
Y: *Sorede⁷,*
R: *Watashi wa kowaku natte nakihajimeta⁸.*
Y: *Soko e okaasan ga yatte kita?*
R: *Un. Shinpaisoo⁹ na kao o shite watashi o miru no.*
Y: *Hyakudo datta koto o hanashita no?*
R: *Daijoobu tte¹⁰ itte kureta¹¹. Soshite, sesshi ni keisan shite kureta.*
Y: *Kashi no hyakudo kara mazu sanjuuni o hiite, sorekara go o kakete, kyuu de waru¹². Soo suru to yaku sanjuunana ten hachi do ni naru wa.*

R: When my mother wasn't there, I read my thermometer myself.
Y: How many degrees was it?
R: It was 100 degrees! I thought I was going to die from a high fever.
Y: It wasn't a centigrade thermometer.
R: I had just come to America, so I didn't know.
Y: Then?
R: I got scared and began to cry.
Y: Did your mother come back to your room?
R: Yeah. She looked at me with a worried look on her face.
Y: You told her it was 100 degrees, right?
R: She told me it was OK. Then she calculated it into Celsius for me.
Y: First subtract 32 from 100 degrees Fahrenheit, then multiply it by 5 and divide by 9. You get about 37.8 degrees centigrade.

R: きのした　れいこ　　　　　*Kinoshita Reiko*　　　　Reiko Kinoshita
　　（のぶおのお姉さん）　　*(Noboru no oneesan)*　　(Nobuo's older sister)
Y: やまだ　よしこ　　　　　*Yamada Yoshiko*　　　　Yoshiko Yamada

3. Language & Culture Notes

1 *No* may replace *ga* in subordinate clauses.
   Okaasan no/ga inai toki, taionkei o yonda no.
   (When my mother wasn't there, I read the thermometer myself.)

2 In Japan, the metric system is the official method of measurement. Length is measured in meters, distance in kilometers, weight in grams, and volume in liters. Although it is not widely used in the United States, many Americans are familiar with the metric system. There are also some traditional units of measurement that are unique to Japan. For example, the area of a room is not measured in square meters but by *joo*, the area of one *tatami* mat (the woven floor covering of traditional Japanese rooms). One *joo* is about one by two meters. Most rooms are 4, 6 or 8 *joo*. Land is measured in *tsubo*. One *tsubo* is about 3.3 square meters or 35 square feet. Another traditional Japanese measurement is a *ri*, a distance of about 4 kilometers, or 2.5 miles. However, *ri* are rarely used today to measure distance.

3 *De* signifies the cause or reason for something.
   Kaze de gakkoo o yasunda. (I was absent from school because of a cold.)

4 *Ja nai* is the informal form of *ja nai desu*, which means "is not."
   Sore wa sesshi ja nai wa yo. (It's not Celsius, you know.)
   In the sample conversation, Yoshiko and Reiko use this short, plain form with each other because they are close friends.

5 As a functional marker, *bakari* follows the informal past tense form of a verb and means "just" or "just now."
   Amerika e kita bakari datta kara, shiranakatta no. (I had just come to America, so I didn't know.)
   Chichi wa ima dekaketa bakari desu. (My father has just gone out.)

6 ---*nakatta* is the informal past form of the adjectival derivative ---*nai*. *Shiranakatta* means "didn't know."

7 *Sorede*, a discourse function expression, encourages the speaker to continue speaking.

8 *Nakihajimeru* (informal past tense: *nakihajimeta*) means "to start crying." It is a compound verb formed from the pre-*masu* form of a verb plus an extender, *hajimeru* ("to start" or "to begin").

nakimasu	+	*hajimemasu*	=	*nakihajimemasu*
(to cry)		(to start)		(to start crying)
arukimasu	+	*hajimemasu*	=	*arukihajimemasu*
(to walk)		(to start)		(to start walking)
kangaemasu	+	*hajimemasu*	=	*kangaehajimemasu*
(to think about)		(to start)		(to start thinking about)
hanashimasu	+	*hajimemasu*	=	*hanashihajimemasu*
(to talk)		(to start)		(to start talking)

9 ---*soo* is a dependent adjectival noun. It means "seems like" or "looks like." While --- *rashii* indicates a guess made according to some objective information, ---*soo* is usually based on someone's or something's appearance. Note: The adjective *ii* becomes *yosasoo*.
   Shinpaisoo na kao o shite. (He has a worried look on his face.)
   Isogashisoo desu ne. (They look busy.)
   Ashita wa samuku narisoo desu. (It seems as if it will get cold tomorrow.)

10 --- *tte* may replace the quotation function marker *to* in informal speech.

11 The verb *kureru* literally means "to give;" however, it is used to imply that someone did something "for me," or someone "did/gave me the favor" of doing something.
   Tomodachi ga hon o kashite kuremashita/kureta.
   (My friend lent me her book. Literally: My friend gave me the favor of lending me her book.)

12 Following are the terms used to calculate basic mathematical functions.
   tasu   (to add)   *San tasu go wa hachi.*   (Three plus five is eight.)
   hiku   (to subtract)   *Hachi hiku san wa go.*   (Eight minus three is five.)
   kakeru (to multiply)   *Ni kakeru ni wa yon.*   (Two times two is four.)
   waru   (to divide)   *Gojuu waru ni wa nijuugo.*   (Fifty divided by two is twenty-five.)

III. PARTICIPATION

1. Vocabulary

1 **From sample conversation:**

bakari (just)
hiite (minus, subtract, from)
kakete (multiply, times)
keisan shite (calculate)
kowai (fearful, be afraid)
nakihajimeta (began to cry)
omotta (thought)
shinpaisoo na kao o shite (have a worried look on one's face)
shinu (to die)
taionkei (thermometer [body])
yaku (about)

--- *de* (by ..., due to)
hyakudo (100 degrees)
kashi (Fahrenheit)
koonetsu (high fever)
mazu (first, at first)
nando (how many degrees)
sesshi (Celsius, centigrade)

shiranakatta (didn't know)
waru (to divide)

2 **Useful for activities:**

butsukaru (to hit, to strike)
guramu (gram)
joobu na (healthy, well, strong)
kashite kureru (let one borrow)
kiroguramu (kilogram)
mairu (mile)
netsu (fever)
onsu (ounce)
sagaru (to go down)
soo suru to (then)

fiito (feet)
inchi (inch)
karada (body)
kenkoo (health)
kiromeetoru (kilometer)
meetoru (meter)
ondo (temperature)
pondo (pound)
senchimeetoru (centimeter)
taion (temperature)

2. Activity, Practice, & Exercise

1 A favor for me

In small groups: Think of an action that someone did for you that you appreciated. Tell your partner about it, using the expression *-te kureta*. Your partner responds by asking about the person who you mentioned.

Example: A: *Jimu wa boku ga gakkoo o yasunda toki, nihongo no jugyoo no nooto o <u>kashite kureta</u> n da.*
(Jim let me borrow his Japanese notebook when I was absent from school.)
B: <u>*Jimu wa*</u> *nihongo no kurasu no tomodachi da ne.*
(Jim is a friend in your Japanese class, isn't he?)
A: *Un.* (Yes.)

2 Calculating in Japanese

In pairs: In Japanese, write out the necessary words to do the following calculations and solve them.

Example:
- 3 + 5 = 8   3 *tasu* 5 *wa* 8.
- 9 − 2 = 7   9 *hiku* 2 *wa* 7.
- 4 x 3 = 12   4 *kakeru* 3 *wa* 12.
- 18 ÷ 3 = 6   18 *waru* 3 *wa* 6.

1. 21 + 5 =
2. 100 − 35 =
3. 9 x 6 =
4. 32 ÷ 8 =
5. 40 + 12 − 7 =
6. 4 x 12 ÷ 3 =

3 Fahrenheit to Celsius

In small groups: Bring Fahrenheit thermometers to class. Take the temperature of your body, the classroom, and outside. Change each of the temperatures from Fahrenheit to Celsius. Refer to the formula °C = (°F − 32) / 1.8. In Japanese, group members compare the various temperatures in Celsius.

Example: A: *Watashi no taion wa sesshi 36.5 do desu.* (My body temperature is 36.5 °C.)
B: *Kyooshitsu no ondo wa sesshi 29.4 do desu.*
(The temperature of the classroom is 29.4 °C.)
C: *Soto no ondo wa sesshi 32.4 do desu.* (The temperature outside is 32.4 °C.)

4 Serious situations

In small groups: Think of an experience in which you were in a serious situation that turned out all right. Tell your group about it using the expression --- *to omotta*.

Example: A: *Koonetsu de shinu <u>to omotta</u>. Demo, kusuri o nondara, sugu netsu ga sagatta.*
(I thought I was going to die of a high fever. But the fever went down after I took some medicine.)
B: *Kuruma ni butsukaru <u>to omotta</u> ga, daijoobu datta.*
(I thought I was going to hit a car, but it was all right.)

5 The child looks happy.

Use the following expressions to write meaningful sentences.

Example: *Ureshisoo na kao* → *Kodomo no ureshisoo na kao o miru no ga suki desu.*
(I like seeing children with happy faces.)

1. *Shinpaisoo na kao* (look worried)
2. *Kenkoosoo na senshu* (look healthy)
3. *Genkisoo na gakusei* (look cheerful)
4. *Joobusoo na karada* (look strong)
5. *Muzukashisoo na shukudai* (look difficult)

6 Making mathematical equations

① In class: Using the numbers listed below, students try to make as many mathematical equations as possible in about five minutes. The equations must include at least three numbers and two different calculation words. Then students volunteer to give the teacher one of their equations, and the teacher writes them on the board. Follow the example.

Numbers to use: 3, 5, 50, 100, 150
Calculation words: *tasu, hiku, kakeru, waru*
Example: 50 x 3 - 100 = 50
Gojuu ni san o kakete, sorekara hyaku o hikimasu. Soo suru to gojuu ni naru to omoimasu.

② In pairs: Next, students talk about what happens when certain colors are mixed. The teacher writes a list of colors on the blackboard, such as *shiro, kuro, aka, ao, midori,* and *kiiro,* and the word *mazeru* (to mix). Following the example, students make sentences explaining what will happen when two colors are mixed together.

Example: A: *Aka to ao o mazemasu.*
B: *Soo suru to murasaki ni naru.*

7 Team competition

In pairs: The teacher writes the following formulas on the blackboard. The class is divided into two teams. Students from Team A pair up with students from Team B. Each pair needs a set of ten cards with mathematical questions that involve converting from one system of measurement to the other. The student from Team A draws the first card. Team B may not see the card, and A may not give B any hints as to what type of equation it is. A then tells B what to do: add, subtract, multiply, or divide certain numbers. B writes down what A says and tries to solve the equation and come up with the correct answer. A should only say numbers, not letters such as C or F, or terms such as feet or meters, because that will give B a hint. A writes B's answer on the back of the card. Then it is B's turn to give A an equation. When all of the pairs are finished, the teacher gives everyone the correct answers. Pairs give each other one point for each correct answer and then add up all of the points for their team. The team with the most points is the winner.
Note: Calculators may be used for this activity.

Calculation words: Formulas:
tasu (add)   C = 5 ÷ 9 (F - 32)   1 mi = 1.61 km
hiku (subtract)   F = 9 ÷ 5 (C + 32)   1 lb = 0.4536 kg
kakeru (multiply)   1 ft = 0.305 m   1 qt = 0.946 l
waru (divide)   1 in = 2.54 cm

Lesson 27: Review & Application

IV. PERFORMANCE

1. Application

1 Conversation completion

In small groups: The following is a conversation between students A and B. They are talking about diseases. Guess what student B would say. Choose the most appropriate sentence from below.

A: *B san, ima made ni nyuuin shita koto ga aru?* (B, have you ever been hospitalized?)
B: ( ) (Yes, once.)
A: *Nan no byooki datta no?* (What was wrong with you?)
B: ( ) (I had appendicitis.)
A: *Shujutsu shita?* (Did you have an operation?)
B: ( ) *A san wa nyuuin shita koto aru?*
   (Yes. It was an easy one, so I came home from the hospital after four days. A, have you ever been hospitalized?)
A: *Iie, nai wa. Tokidoki kaze o hiite, netsu o dashita gurai ne.*
   (No, I haven't. Sometimes I catch a cold and get a fever.)
B: ( ) (How high are the fevers?)
A: *Chiisai koro, 40 do gurai dashita koto ga atta wa.*
   (When I was little I had a fever of about 40 degrees.)
B: ( ) (What happened then?)
A: *Oisha san ga uchi e kite chuusha shite kureta no.*
   (The doctor came to my house and gave me a shot.)
B: ( ) (Did you cry?)
A: *Ee. Kodomo wa chuusha ga daikirai da mono. Demo okage de netsu ga sugu sagatta wa.*
   (Yeah. Children don't like getting shots. But, it made the fever go down quickly.)
B: ( ) (That's good.)

1. *Ee. Kantan na mono datta kara. Yokka de taiin dekita no yo.*
2. *Naita?*
3. *Moochoo.*
4. *Yokatta wa ne.*
5. *Dono kurai no netsu ga deta?*
6. *Sore de dooshita no?*
7. *Ee, ikkai aru wa.*

2 Conversation completion

In small groups: The following is a conversation between an American student (A) and a Japanese student (J) who is studying in America. They are talking about physical examinations. Guess what the American student would say in the underlined parts in the conversation. A representative from each group presents the dialogue to the class.

J: *Nihon de wa gakkoo de kenkooshindan o suru n da.* (In Japan we get health checks at school.)
A: *E, hontoo. Koko de wa* _____. (Oh, really? Here _____.)
J: *Ja, kenkooshindan o suru hi wa kimatte inai no?*
   (But, isn't there a set day when you get your physicals?)
A: *Itsu kenkooshindan o ukete mo ii kedo,* _____ .
   (You can get a physical at any time, but _____.)
J: *Minna gakkoo ga owatte kara, byooin e itte, kenkooshindan o ukeru no?*
   (Does everybody go to the hospital after school to get physicals?)
A: _____ .
J: *Soo. Nihon to wa chigau wa ne.* (Really? That's different from the Japanese way.)
A: *Gakkoo de kenkooshindan o suru n dattara,* _____ .
   (Since you get health checks at school, _____.)
J: *Soo ne. Sono toki wa jugyoo ga nai wa.* (Right. We don't have classes during it.)
A: _____ .
J: *Demo, watashi wa jugyoo no hoo ga ii wa. Minna to issho ni kenkooshindan nante, chotto hazukashii mono.*
   (Still, I would rather have classes. I'm embarrassed to get a physical with other people.)

3 Illnesses and injuries

In pairs: First, learn the expressions listed below about illnesses and injuries. As the teacher shows the class various pictures, pairs use the expressions to write a short dialogue that describes each picture.

1. *kaze o hiku*   (catch a cold)
2. *netsu ga deru/aru*   (have a fever)
3. *seki ga deru*   (have a cough)
4. *hanamizu ga deru*   (have a runny nose)
5. *mushi ni sasareru*   (get an insect bite)
6. *yakedo suru*   (get burned)
7. *kossetsu suru* (break a bone)
8. *onaka ga itai* (have a stomachache)
9. *atama ga itai* (have a headache)
10. *nodo ga itai*   (have a sore throat)

Example: A: *Kaze o hikimashita.* (I caught a cold.)
         B: *Netsu ga arimasu ka?* (Do you have a fever?)
         A: *Iie, demo atama ga itai desu.* (No, but I have a headache.)

Lesson 27

4 Discussing disasters and accidents

In small groups: Each group talks about a disaster or an accident that actually happened in this country, Japan, or somewhere else. After the first person introduces the topic, the next person asks a question using the expression --- *wa doo natta n desu ka?* Carry on the conversation, discussing what happened.

Example: A: *1995 nen ni Koobe de ooki na jishin ga arimashita.*
   (There was a big earthquake in Kobe in 1995.)
   B: *Koobe <u>wa doo natta n desu ka</u>?* (What happened to Kobe?)
   C: *Sono jishin de takusan no ie ga kowaremashita. Soshite, takusan no hito ga nakunarimashita.*
   (Many houses collapsed from the earthquake, and many people were killed.)
   D: *Takusan no dooro ya hashi mo kowareta to iu koto desu.*
   (I heard that many roads and bridges collapsed, too.)
   B: *Sore wa hidoi jishin deshita ne.* (It was a terrible earthquake, wasn't it?)

5 When I was sick ...

In pairs: Tell your partner about an illness that you had. Include kind things that other people did for you at that time.

Example: A: *Anata wa byooki ya kega o shita koto ga arimasu ka?*
   (Have you ever had an illness or an injury?)
   B: *Hai. Sukii o shite, hone o otta koto ga arimasu.* (Yes. I broke a bone skiing.)
   A: *Sono toki, dare ka ga <u>nani ka o shite kuremashita ka</u>?*
   (Did anyone do anything for you at that time?)
   B: *Hai. Tomodachi ga hana o motte, omimai ni kite <u>kuremashita</u>.*
   (Yes. My friends came to give me flowers and express their sympathy.)

6 Causes of disasters and accidents

In pairs: In class, learn the words written below related to disasters and accidents. Then in pairs, think about the causes of those disasters and accidents. Pay attention to the marker *de,* which indicates a cause.

   kootsuujiko (traffic accident), *hikookijiko* (airplane accident), *kaji* (fire), *taifuu* (typhoon),
   jishin (earthquake), *tatsumaki* (tornado), *koozui* (flood), *ooyuki* (blizzard), *tsunami* (tidal wave)

Example: *Ie ga kowaremashita.* → *Jishin <u>de</u> ie ga kowaremashita.*
   (The house collapsed from the earthquake.)

   1. *Hashi ga ochimashita.* (The bridge collapsed.) →
   2. *Ki ga taoremashita.* (The tree fell down.) →
   3. *Gakkoo ga yasumi ni narimashita.* (School was closed.) →
   4. *Densha ga tomarimashita.* (The train stopped.) →
   5. *5 nin no hito ga kega o shimashita.* (Five people were injured.) →
   6. *Oozei no hito ga nakunarimashita.* (Many people were killed.) →

2. Actualization

1 Practice the following conversation and develop your own dialogue on a similar subject with your partners.

Suiyoobi no 4jikanme, sansuu no jugyoo desu. 4 nen 6 kumi no seito wa heikooshihenkei no benkyoo o shite imasu.
(Fourth period on Wednesday is math. The 4th grade, class 6 students are learning about parallelograms.)

Suzuki sensei:	*Heikooshihenkei no tokuchoo o itte kudasai.*
	(Please tell me the characteristics of parallelograms.)
Yamada san:	*Mukaiatta hen no nagasa ga hitoshikute, heikoo desu.*
	(The sides facing each other are parallel and equal in length.)
Suzuki sensei:	*Hai, sono toori desu. Hoka ni wa?* (Yes. That's right. What else?)
Yoshida kun:	*Mukaiatta kaku ga onaji ookisa desu.* (Opposite angles are equal.)
Suzuki sensei:	*Hai, soo desu ne. Dewa, hitotsu no kaku ga 60 do da to shitara, mukaigawa no kaku wa?*
	(Yes. That's right. Then, if one corner is 60 degrees, how many degrees is the opposite angle?)
Tanaka kun:	*Mukaigawa no kaku mo 60 do desu.* (It's also 60 degrees.)
Suzuki sensei:	*Hai, dewa nokori no futatsu no kaku wa?*
	(OK. What about the two remaining corners.)
Kobayashi kun:	*Nokori no futatsu wa 360 do hiku 120 do de, 240 do desu. Nokori no futatsu wa hitoshii node, sorezore 120 do desu.*
	(Subtract 120 degrees from 360, and you get 240 degrees. They are opposite angles, so each is 120 degrees.)
Suzuki sensei:	*Hai, totemo yoku dekimashita.* (Yes. Very good.)

2 Practice the following conversation and develop your own dialogue on a similar subject with your partners.

Sansuu no jugyoo de, bunsuu no keisan o benkyoo shite imasu.
(In math class, the students are learning how to calculate fractions.)

Suzuki sensei:	*8 bun no 3 tasu 8 bun no 7 wa ikutsu desu ka?*
	(What is three-eighths plus seven-eighths?)
Yamada san:	*Eeto.* (Well.)
Suzuki sensei:	*Bunbo ga onaji dakara.* (The denominators are the same, so ...)
Yamada san:	*Bunshi dake taseba ii n desu ne. 8 bun no 10 desu.*
	(I add just the numerators, right? It's ten-eighths.)
Suzuki sensei:	*Soo desu. Dewa, Tanaka kun, 8 bun no 10 o taibunsuu ni naoshite kudasai.*
	(That's right. Then, make it into a mixed fraction.)
Tanaka kun:	*1 to 8 bun no 2 ... 1 to 4 bun no 1 desu.*
	(One and two-eighths ... it's one and a quarter.)
Suzuki sensei:	*Hai, yoku dekimashita.* (Yes. Well done.)

3 Write out the following numbers in Japanese and practice reading them.
  a) 125,737,821   b) 75,621,968,245
  c) 3,457,887,956,723   d) 72,375,806,173,438
  e) 23,456,789   f) 987,654,321,045,240

4 Team competition

In pairs: The teacher divides the class into two teams, A and B. Students then pair up with someone on the opposing team. The teacher makes 10 questions about estimating time, distance, length, price, and so on. and writes them on cards. Each pair gets one set of numbered cards in order. The Team A student draws the first card and asks the question to his/her Team B partner. The partner makes a guess, and the Team A student records the answer on a separate piece of paper. Then student B asks student A the next question. Continue to alternate asking and answering questions until all 10 have been answered. Be sure to use --- *gurai ja nakatta kana?* when answering the questions. Follow the pattern in the example. After everyone has finished, the teacher gives the correct answers so that students may check their opponent's answers. Exact answers receive 2 points and approximate answers 1 point. For example, if the correct answer is 1000 miles, 900 miles or 1100 miles may be accepted as 1-point answers. The students add up their opponents' points and then calculate the team total. The team with the most points wins.

Example of game:
  A: *Nyuu Yooku kara San Furanshisuko made wa dore gurai desu ka?*
     (About how far is it from New York to San Francisco?)
  B: *3 zen mairu gurai ja nakatta kana?* (About 3000 miles, isn't it?)

Examples of questions:
  1. *Hikooki de Nyuu Yooku kara Tookyoo made wa dore gurai kakarimasu ka?*
  2. *Jiyuu no megami no takasa wa dore gurai desu ka?*
  3. *Atarashii terebi wa ikura gurai desu ka?*
  4. *Kono gakkoo no seito wa dore gurai imasu ka?*
  5. *Fujisan no takasa wa dore gurai desu ka?*
  6. *Fune de Washinton DC kara Rondon made wa dore gurai kakarimasu ka?*
  7. *Amerika no jinkoo wa dore gurai desu ka?*
  8. *Booru pen wa ikura gurai desu ka?*
  9. *Mishishippii Gawa no nagasa wa dore gurai desu ka?*
  10. *Sapporo kara Fukuoka made wa dore gurai desu ka?*

5 Answering questions

In pairs: Answer the following questions.
  (1) *Rosu Anjerusu kara Nyuu Yooku made wa nanjikan gurai hikooki ni noru no?*
  (2) *Enpaiyaa suteeto biru wa nan meetoru/fiito aru no?*
  (3) *Famikon no sofuto wa ikura gurai na no?*

6 Mathematical equations

Individually: Calculate the following mathematical equations.
1. *Hyaku kara mazu yonjuugo o hiite, sorekara ni o kakete juuichi de waru. Soo suru to ikura ni narimasu ka?*
2. *Nijuu ni roku o kakete, sorekara sanjuu o hiite san de waru. Soshite, juu o tasu to ikura ni narimasu ka?*

3. Enrichment

1 *Kanji* for Lesson 25

| 一度 | 締切り | 来週 | 出す | 少ない |
| 健康診断 | 勉強 | 減る | 損 | |

2 *Kanji* for Lesson 26

体温計	読む	度	高熱	死ぬ
摂氏	怖い	始める	計算	華氏
引く	掛ける	割る	約	

3 Other useful *kanji*

倒、払、答、計、屈、定、受、止、比
宿題、机、苦、退院、円、店、道

4 Strategies

Since there are several ways in formulating *kanji* under type 4 (Lesson 6, 3. Enrichment, 4 Strategies), we have to establish different strategies for each sub type.

For 品、林、森、炎 duplication of same *kanji*. Usually they mean "many" or "much" of the original *kanji*.

For 明、料 individual *kanji* compound, the combined meanings create a third meaning. 明 means "bright" and 料 means "measurement." The original meaning of the component *kanji* is lost.

For 安, a compound of classifier and a *kanji* with meaning, the original meanings of both are lost and a third meaning is created. 安 means "peace" and "ease."

5 Exercise

Create some *kanji* with this approach and see whether you were able to create a few that have been recognized as *kanji*.

Lesson 28: Social studies class

I. PERSPECTIVE

1. Objectives

1 Function:

(1) Randomly expressing reasons or facts: *(Kuni) ga (attari) shite.*
(2) Guessing what might happen in the future: *Kongo wa (...) suru daroo.*
(3) Expressing disappointment, dislike, or refusal: *Yada ne.*
(4) Asking someone to do something: *(Hanashi) o shite kurenai?*

2 Language:

(1) *Moo (reisenjidai) mo (owat)ta kara, kongo wa (--- sanka sur)u daroo.*
(2) *Demo, (chikyuu) wa hitotsu shika nai (deshoo).*

3 Culture:

(1) Famous athletes

II. PREPARATION

1. Context

社会科の授業

チャイムが鳴った。社会科の授業は終りだ。しかし、授業が終わってからも、思い思いにピーター達は授業の内容について話をする。授業の中で、先生は多様性ある世界について色々な話をしてくれた。それらは、地域や民族の問題、地球全体の問題などであった。それを聞いて、クラスのみんなは考え込んでしまった。

The bell rang, and social studies class ended. Even after class was over, Peter and his friends continued to discuss what they had learned in social studies. In class, the teacher had talked about the various people of the world and their lifestyles. The teacher talked about regional, racial, and other problems that affect the entire globe. The students listened to their teacher with great interest and thought about the issues.

2. Sample Conversation

P: 国際問題は色々な所にあるんだね。
Y: スポーツの世界にもあるわよ。
J: オリンピックのことだろう。
N: 残念な話だったね。参加しない国があったりして。
P: もう冷戦時代も終わったから、今後は全部参加するだろう。
Y: でも、地域紛争はいつもどこかであるんでしょう。
N: やだね。
P: 国が違う。人が違う。考え方も違う。
J: でも、地球は一つしかないでしょう。
P: だからみんな協力するんだよ。
N: ピーターさん、今度の日本旅行の話をしてくれない。
P: オーケー。

P: *Kokusaimondai wa iroiro na tokoro ni aru n da[1] ne.*
Y: *Supootsu[2] no sekai ni mo aru wa yo.*
J: *Orinpikku no koto daroo.*
N: *Zannen na hanashi datta ne. Sanka shinai kuni ga attari shite.*
P: *Moo reisenjidai mo owatta kara, kongo wa zenbu sanka suru daroo[3].*
Y: *Demo, chiikifunsoo wa itsumo doko ka de aru n deshoo.*
N: *Yada ne.*
P: *Kuni ga chigau. Hito ga chigau. Kangaekata mo chigau.*
J: *Demo, chikyuu wa hitotsu shika nai deshoo.*
P: *Dakara minna kyooryoku suru n da yo.*
N: *Piitaa san, kondo no nihonryokoo no hanashi o shite kurenai[4]?*
P: *Ookee.*

P: There are international problems in many places, aren't there?
Y: There are problems in the sports world, too.
J: Like in the Olympics, right?
N: It's a shame. There were countries that didn't participate.
P: The Cold War is over, so from now on all countries will probably participate.
Y: But there's always a regional dispute somewhere.
N: It's terrible.
P: Countries are different, people are different, and their ways of thinking are different, too.
J: But there is only one world.
P: So everyone will cooperate.
N: Peter, could you tell us about your trip to Japan?
P: OK.

P:	ピーター スミス	*Piitaa Sumisu*	Peter Smith
Y:	やまだ よしこ	*Yamada Yoshiko*	Yoshiko Yamada
J:	ジェシー ジョーンズ	*Jeshii Joonzu*	Jessie Jones
N:	きのした のぶお	*Kinoshita Nobuo*	Nobuo Kinoshita

3. Language & Culture Notes

1 Peter uses *n da* in addition to *aru* because he is not just making a statement but stating the case with a more definite air as well.

2 Like any country, Japan takes pride in its sports and honoring the most achieved athletes. The most famous athletes of the 1990s would be baseball players Matsui, Ichiro, and Hideo Nomo, tennis player Kimiko Date, soccer player Kazuyoshi Miura, sumo wrestler Takanohana, and figure skater Midori Ito. Matsui, Ichiro, and Miura are famous for excellence in their sport and dedication to their team. Kimiko Date is Japan's top-seeded tennis player, and Midori Ito won the silver medal at the 1992 Albertville Olympics figure-skating competition. Hideo Nomo is probably the most renowned athlete of the decade. He made the headlines when, at 26 years old, he left the Kintetsu Buffalos in the spring of 1995 to sign with the Los Angeles Dodgers and became only the second Japanese to play in the Major Leagues. In his first year, Nomo had more strikeouts than any other pitcher in the league. In the spring of 1996, the L.A. Dodgers awarded him a three-year contract. Sumo wrestler Takanohana was awarded the title of *yokozuna*, Grand Sumo Champion, in the first tournament of 1995. He is a strong, dedicated wrestler and most deserving of this prestigious title.

3 *Daroo* may follow the dictionary form of a verb. It is the informal style of *deshoo*. Compared with --- *rashii* (based on the subjective judgment of the speaker), ---*soo da* (based on rumor), and --- *yoo da* (based on appearance), *daroo* is used to indicate the speaker's simple assumption.

4 *-te kurenai?* means "Won't you do --- for me?" or "Could you do --- for me?"

III. PARTICIPATION

1. Vocabulary

1 **From sample conversation:**

chigau (different)
chikyuu (a globe, earth)
kangaekata (way of thinking)
kyooryoku (cooperation)
orinpikku (Olympics)
reisenjidai (Cold War Period)
sanka suru (to participate)

chiikifunsoo (regional conflict/dispute)
iroiro na (various)
kokusaimondai (international problems/issues)
nihonryokoo (travel in/to Japan)
owatta (ended, was over)
sanka (participation)
zenbu (entire, all, whole)

2 **Useful for activities:**

Arabu (Arabian countries)
Betonamu (Vietnam)
Busshu (George Bush)

Berugii (Belgium)
Burugaria (Bulgaria)
Chekosurobakia (Czechoslovakia)

Choosen (Korea, Korean)
doopingu (drugs, doping)
Furushichofu (Khrushchev)
Gorubachofu (Mikhail Gorbachov)
Hangarii (Hungary)
Higashi Doitsu (East Germany)
Ho Chi-min (Ho Chi Minh)
hookai suru (to collapse)
Itaria (Italy)
Jonson (Lyndon B. Johnson)
Kanbojia (Cambodia)
Kankoku (Republic of Korea)
Kasutoro (Fidel Castro)
Kenedii (John F. Kennedy)
Kita Amerika (North America)
Kyuuba kiki (Cuba crisis)
kyuu Yuugo (former Yugoslavia)
Maikeru Joodan (Michael Jordan)
Minami Amerika (South America)
nakayoku suru (to get along with)
nanbaa wan (number one)
Nishi Doitsu (West Germany)
no yoo na (such as, like)
okoru (to happen)
Oranda (Holland, the Netherlands)
Oseania (Oceania)
otagai (one another)
Poorando (Poland)
Ruumania (Romania)
Sadamu Fusein (Saddam Hussein)
sanshin (strikeout)
seiji (politics)
sensoo (war)
Soren (former Soviet Union)
Wangan (the Persian Gulf)

2. Activity, Practice, & Exercise

1 Serious problems

In small groups: Discuss what kind of problems exist in a certain area, such as sports, schools, and so on. Make a few sentences about the problems using the expression *-tari, -tari, taihen desu*.

Example: *Supootsu no sekai wa doopingu ga <u>attari</u>, seiji no mondai ga <u>attari, taihen desu</u>*.

(The sports world is filled with serious problems such as drugs and political influence.)

2 Describing people and things

In small groups: One person gives a brief explanation about someone or something without identifying the name of the person or thing. Other group members try to guess the name using the expression --- *no koto daroo/deshoo*.

Example: 1) A: *Kare wa nihonjin no pitchaa de, sanshin o takusan toru n da.*

(He is a Japanese pitcher and strikes out many batters.)

B: *Sore, Nomo <u>no koto daro</u>*. (It's Nomo, right?)

2) A: *Natsu ni yukata o kite, minna de odoru no. Nihon no natsumatsuri no dansu yo.*

(Everyone wears *yukata* and dances together. It's a Japanese summer festival dance.)

B: *Sore, bon'odori <u>no koto deshoo</u>*. (It's *bon'odori*, right?)

3 World issues

In pairs: One partner gives an example of a world issue or problem. The other partner responds by saying *Iya da ne/desu ne*, and adding a comment.

Example: A: *Chiikifunsoo wa itsumo doko ka de okotte iru. Kyuu Yuugo, Arabu, Afurika ...*
(Regional conflicts are always happening somewhere. The former Yugoslavia, the Arab States, Africa ...)

B: *Hontoo ni <u>iya da ne</u>. Dooshite otagai ni nakayoku dekinai n daroo?*
(I'm sick of it. Why can't they get along with each other?)

4 World events

There have been many important world events since the end of the World War II. Following are some examples. Match each event with the names of the people who were involved with it. More than one name can be matched to one incident.

Events: *Kyuuba kiki, Betonamu sensoo, Choosen sensoo, Wangan sensoo, Soren no hookai*

People: *Busshu, Kenedii, Ho Chi-min, Sadamu Fusein, Gorubachofu, Kasutoro, Jonson, Furushichofu*

5 Could you tell me ... ?

In class: Students sit around in a circle alternating boys and girls. The teacher chooses a boy to start the activity. The boy asks the girl to his left a question, something about her that he would like to know. He asks using the target sentence --- *ni tsuite hanashi o shite kurenai?* The girl may give him an answer. If she doesn't want to answer him or doesn't like the question, she will say *yada* or *yada ne*. The girl then asks the boy to her left a question. The activity continues around the circle until everyone has had a turn at asking and answering a question. Use the following example as a guide.

Example: Boy: *Anata no suki na otoko no ko <u>ni tsuite hanashi o shite kurenai</u>?*
(Could you tell me about what type of boy you like?)

Girl: *Watashi wa supootsu man de otoko rashii otoko no ko ga suki desu. Maiku san no yoo na taipu kashira. Itsumo akarukute yasashii desu.* OR *Yada/Yada ne.*
Anata no suki na supootsu <u>ni tsuite hanashi o shite kurenai</u>?
(I like athletic, masculine guys. Maybe someone like Mike. Could you tell me about your favorite sport?)

Boy: *Boku wa basuketto ga suki desu. Ichiban suki na senshu wa Maikeru Joodan desu. Kare wa sekai de nanbaa wan no senshu da to omoimasu.*
(I like basketball. My favorite player is Michael Jordan. I think he is the greatest player in the world.)

6 Favorite sports and athletes

In pairs: The teacher makes a copy of the chart below for each student. In the column marked "Sport," students fill in any five sports of their choice. The object of this activity is for students to find one classmate who likes or is interested in each sport and has a favorite athlete for that sport. Students make as many pairs as necessary until they complete the chart or until time is up (about 15 to 20 minutes). The students may use any form of grammar that they wish, but they should try to use it correctly. Afterward, the teacher asks a few students to tell the class who likes what sport and player.

	Sport	Student	Favorite athlete
1.			
2.			
3.			
4.			
5.			

7 International problems

In pairs: There have always been many *kokusaimondai* and *chiikifunsoo* around the world. How many of them do you know? Name some world or regional issues and state where in the world the problem is/was taking place. Below is a list of geographic areas. Follow the example.

Geographic areas: *Afurika, Ajia, Yooroppa, Kita Amerika, Minami Amerika, Oseania*

Example: *Kanbojia no mondai o shitte imasu/kikimashita. Ajia ni aru mondai desu.*

8 Cold war

In pairs: During the *reisenjidai* (Cold War Period), many countries belonged to the *jiyuushugi jin'ei* (democratic or liberal group) or the *shakaishugi jin'ei* (socialist group). Categorize the following countries by the group to which they used to belong.

Amerika, Nihon, Soren, Furansu, Poorando, Chekosurobakia, Igirisu, Ruumania, Berugii, Oranda, Nishi Doitsu, Higashi Doitsu, Itaria, Kyuuba, Hangarii, Burugaria

Lesson 29: The day before the exam

I. PERSPECTIVE

1. Objectives

1 Function:

(1) Asking if someone is in (at home, office, etc.): *(Nobuo kun) imasu ka?*
(2) Asking someone to wait: *Chotto (mat)te ne.*
(3) Offering to do something for someone: *(Oshie)te ageru yo.*
(4) "By the way,": *Tokorode*

2 Language:

(1) *Chotto (mat)te ne.* (2) *Choodo ii.*
(3) *Jaa, issho ni (benkyoo) shiyoo.* (4) *(Kimi no ie) ni (it)te mo ii?*

3 Culture:

(1) Examination system

II. PREPARATION

1. Context

試験の前日

今日は試験の前日。ピーターはちょっと心配になってきた。今回の日本語の授業はよく理解できなかったのだ。のぶおの家に電話して、様子を聞いてみようと思った。ついでに、数学の試験勉強を手伝ってもらいたいと思った。

Today is the day before exams. Peter is a little worried because he didn't really understand the Japanese lesson. He called Nobuo to tell him about his situation. He hopes that Nobuo will also be able to help him study for the math test.

2. Sample Conversation

T: もしもし。木下でございます。
P: 僕はピータースミスです。のぶお君いますか。
T: はい、いますよ。ちょっと待ってね。
N: もしもし、のぶおです。
P: 僕ピーター。ちょっと日本語で分からない所があるんだけど。
N: 何。教えてあげるよ。
P: ありがとう。ところで、試験勉強は終わった。
N: あと、数学の勉強が残っているよ。
P: 数学か。丁度いい。
N: どうして。
P: 僕もこれから勉強するんだ。
N: じゃあ、一緒に勉強しよう。
P: これから、君の家に行ってもいい。
N: いいよ。

T: *Moshi moshi. Kinoshita de gozaimasu[1].*
P: *Boku wa Piitaa Sumisu desu. Nobuo kun[2] imasu ka?*
T: *Hai, imasu yo. Chotto matte[3] ne.*
N: *Moshi moshi, Nobuo desu.*
P: *Boku Piitaa. Chotto nihongo de wakaranai tokoro ga aru n dakedo.*
N: *Nani? Oshiete[4] ageru yo.*
P: *Arigatoo. Tokorode[5], shikenbenkyoo[6] wa owatta?*
N: *Ato, suugaku no benkyoo ga nokotte iru yo.*
P: *Suugaku ka. Choodo ii.*
N: *Dooshite?*
P: *Boku mo korekara benkyoo suru n da.*
N: *Jaa, issho ni benkyoo shiyoo[7].*
P: *Korekara, kimi[8] no ie ni itte mo ii?*
N: *Ii yo.*

T: Hello? This is the Kinoshita residence.
P: This is Peter Smith. Is Nobuo there?
T: Yes, he is. Just a minute.
N: Hello. This is Nobuo.
P: It's Peter. There are some things in Japanese that I don't understand, but...
N: What are they? I'll help you.
P: Thanks. By the way, did you finish studying for the tests?
N: I still have to study math. (Literally: The study of math is remaining.)
P: Math? Perfect.
N: How come?
P: Because I'm going to study after this, too.
N: Well, let's study together.
P: May I come over your house?
N: OK.

P: ピーター　スミス　　　*Piitaa Sumisu*　　　Peter Smith
T: きのした　たえこ（お母さん）　*Kinoshita Taeko (okaasan)*　　　Taeko Kinoshita (mother)
N: きのした　のぶお　　　*Kinoshita Nobuo*　　　Nobuo Kinoshita

3. Language & Culture Notes

1 *--- de gozaimasu* is a very polite expression meaning *desu*. Young students usually do not use this style.

2 As previously discussed, *--- kun* is used an alternative to *--- san*. It is only attached to male names, but it may be used by either males or females when addressing peers or people younger than oneself.

3 Notice that Mrs. Kinoshita simply says *matte* without *kudasai* to ask Peter to wait. When said in a light tone, and especially when used with *ne*, a verb in the *-te* form without *kudasai* is a friendly, informal way to request something.
   Chotto matte ne. (Wait a minute, okay?)
   Denwa shite ne. (Call me, will you?)

4 A verb in the *-te* form plus the extender *ageru* or *agemasu* is a common way to say that one will do something for someone. This form carries a connotation of favor or service.
   Oshiete agemasu yo. (I will teach/tell you.)
   Okane o kashite agemashoo ka? (Shall I lend you some money?)
   Kanojo ni shookai shite ageru yo. (I'll introduce you to her.)
   Tetsudatte agemashoo. (I'll help you/give you a hand.)

5 *Tokorode* is a discourse function word indicating the speaker's wish to change topics. It means "By the way."

6 Studying for examinations is extremely important in Japan. As in America, quizzes are given periodically in class to check students' familiarity with the course material, and tests are given at the middle and end of each term. Furthermore, tests in high school help prepare students for the most important exam they will probably ever take: the university entrance examination. College and university entrance exams are based mainly on factual knowledge and memorization. Succeeding on this test and achieving high scores is a required skill. However, this system tends to ignore other important academic skills.

7 *Shiyoo* in *benkyoo shiyoo* is the *oo* form of *suru* (to do.) The Japanese created hundreds of new vocabulary words by attaching *suru* to a noun.
   benkyoo suru (to study) → *Benkyoo shiyoo.* (Let's study.)
   ryokoo suru (to travel) → *Ryokoo shiyoo.* (Let's travel.)
   kekkon suru (to marry) → *Kekkon shiyoo.* (Let's get married.)

8 *Kimi* is the informal word for *anata*, or "you." It is used between friends and peers or by a speaker whose status (age, relationship, position) is higher than that of the listener.

III. PARTICIPATION

1. Vocabulary

1 **From sample conversation:**

choodo (just, perfect)
kimi (you)
nokotte (remain)
suugaku (mathematics)
uchi (house)

issho ni (together)
matte (wait, just a moment)
shikenbenkyoo (study for an exam)
tokorode (by the way)
wakaranai (do not understand)

2 **Useful for activities:**

chuu (be in the middle of)
ichinichi ni (a day)
kibun ga warui (feel sick)
mata kondo (some other time)
Odaiji ni. (Take care of yourself.)
-te mo ii? (May I ...?)
yoo (errand)

hokenshitsu (health room)
--- irasshaimasu ka? (Is ... there?)
kyuujitsu (holiday)
moo chotto (a little longer/more)
shiraberu (to check, look into)
Warui kedo ... (I'm sorry, but ...)

2. Activity, Practice, & Exercise

1 **Writing a telephone conversation**

In groups of three: Each group writes a telephone conversation in which (1) a person calls a friend's house, (2) a family member answers the telephone and then gives the phone to the friend, and (3) the friends talk. Group members practice the dialogue together. Change roles so that everyone gets a chance to do all three parts. Follow the example.

Example: A: *Moshi moshi, Yamada desu.* (Hello. This is Yamada.)
B: *Tanaka desu ga.* (This is Tanaka.)
A: *Ano, Hanako san, irasshaimasu ka?* (Um, is Hanako there?)
B: *Chotto matte kudasai ne.* (Just a moment.)
C: *Moshi moshi, Hanako desu.* (Hello. This is Hanako.)
A: *Aa, Hanako san. Yamada desu. Konban wa.*
   (Oh, Hanako. This is Yamada. Good evening.)

2 **Let's ... this weekend.**

In pairs: Partners are talking on the telephone. One partner asks the other to do something together over the weekend. Use the expression *Issho ni -mashoo/-oo*.

Example: 1) A: *Kondo no doyoobi, <u>issho ni</u> tsuri ni <u>ikoo</u>.* (Let's go fishing together this Saturday.)
B: *Ii ne/wa ne. Doko e iku no?* (Sounds good. Where are you going?)
A: *---gawa. Asa rokuji ni shuppatsu suru yo. Ii?*
   (The --- River. I'm leaving at six in the morning, OK?)
B: *Un/Ee. Tanoshimi da ne/wa ne.* (OK. I'm looking forward to it.)
A: *Jaa, mata.* (See you then.)
B: *Oyasuminasai.* (Good night.)

Lesson 29

2) A: *Kondo no doyoobi, issho ni eiga o mi ni ikimashoo.*
   (Let's go to the movies this Saturday.)

   B: *Warui kedo, kondo no doyoobi wa yoo ga aru n da/no.*
   (I'm sorry, but I have some errands to do on Saturday.)

   A: *Soo. Zannen ne. Jaa, mata kondo.* (I see. Oh, well. See you later.)

   B: *Ee/Un. Mata kondo issho ni ikimashoo.*
   (Yeah. Let's go somewhere together some other time.)

3 Listening comprehension and/or oral production

Individually: Listen to the following conversations. Mark (O) if the person is allowed to do the specified action, and (X) if the person is not.

Example: Gakusei: *Sensei, nooto o mite mo ii desu ka?* (May I look at my notebook?)
Sensei: *Ima wa tesuto chuu dakara dame desu.* (No. We're in the middle of a test now.)
Answer:
Nooto o miru. (Looking at the notebook.) [X]

1. Gakusei: *Sensei, hokenshitsu e itte mo ii desu ka?* (May I go to the health room?)
   Sensei: *Doo shimashita ka?* (What's the matter?)
   Gakusei: *Chotto kibun ga warui n desu.* (I feel a little sick.)
   Sensei: *Soo. Hitori de daijoobu desu ka?* (Do you? Can you go alone?)
   Gakusei: *Hai.* (Yes.)
   Sensei: *Ki o tsukete.* (Well, take care of yourself.)

2. Chichi: *Moo osoi zo. Itsu made geemu yatteru n da?*
   (It's already late. When are you finishing your game?)
   Takashi: *Ato sukoshi dakara, moo chotto yatte mo ii deshoo?*
   (I'll be done soon. Can I play a little longer?)
   Chichi: *Geemu wa ichinichi ni nijikan made no yakusoku dakara dame da yo.*
   (We made a promise that you could play up to two hours a day, didn't we?)
   Takashi: *Hai, gomennasai.* (OK. I'm sorry.)

3. A: *Anoo, koko de shashin o totte mo ii desu ka?* (Excuse me, may I take pictures here?)
   B: *Shashin wa chotto komaru n desu yo.* (It wouldn't be good.)
   A: *Dooshite desu ka?* (How come?)
   B: *Koko ni yuumei na e ga takusan arimasu kara ne.*
   (Well, because there are many famous paintings here.)
   A: *Soo desu ka. Sumimasen.* (Is that so? I'm sorry to have bothered you.)

4. Naoko: *Kon'ya, bon'odori ni itte mo ii?* (Can I join *bon'odori* tonight?)
   Haha: *Ee, demo yoru dakara, hitori wa dame yo.* (Yes, but it's at night, so don't go alone.)
   Naoko: *Taroo kun mo issho dakara daijoobu yo.* (I'll be with Taro, so don't worry.)

   Answers:
   1. *Hokenshitsu e iku.* (Going to the health room.) [   ]
   2. *Geemu o tsuzukeru.* (Continuing the game.) [   ]
   3. *Shashin o toru.* (Taking pictures.) [   ]
   4. *Bon'odori ni iku.* (Joining *bon'odori*.) [   ]

4 Guessing game

In four teams: Each group chooses a place, such as the library, gym, museum, zoo, amusement park, classroom, park, or supermarket. Think about the rules at those places and what one may and may not do there. Teams try to guess the place that other teams have chosen. Teams ask each other if one may do a specific thing at that place. Use the expression *Koko de -te mo ii desu ka*? If the place is guessed after the first question, the team gets 10 points. The second one – 8, the third one – 6, the fourth – 4, and after the fifth question – 2 points. Teams will get 1 point for six or more questions. Set the time limit for asking questions at 5 to 6 minutes. After time is up, change roles between the two teams, and then meet with the other teams.

Example: A1: *Koko de ongaku o kiite mo ii desu ka?* (May I listen to music here?)
B1: *Iie, dame desu.* (No, you may not.)
A2: *Koko de tabetari nondari shite mo ii desu ka?* (May I eat or drink here?)
B2: *Iie, dame desu.* (No, you may not.)
A3: *Koko de benkyoo shite mo ii desu ka?* (May I study here?)
B3: *Hai, ii desu.* (Yes, you may.)
A4: *Kyooshitsu desu ka?* (Is it a classroom?)
B4: *Iie, chigaimasu.* (No, it isn't.)
A1: *Toshokan desu ka?* (Is it a library?)
B1: *Hai, soo desu.* (That's right.)

The place was guessed after the fifth question, so the score is 2 points.

5 Helping a friend

In pairs: A friend has some problems with his/her Japanese homework. Offer him/her some assistance by using the verb in parentheses in each situation.

Example: A: *Chotto nihongo de wakaranai tokoro ga aru n da kedo.* (*oshieru*)
B: *Oshiete ageru yo.*

(1) *Jisho o motte kuru no o wasureta n dakedo.* (*kasu*)
(2) *Katakana no kakikata ga wakaranai n desu kedo.* (*kaku*)
(3) *Nihon no shuukyoo no kyuujitsu ni tsuite shiritai n desu kedo.* (*shiraberu*)
(4) *Nihongo no nooto o kaitai n dakedo, okane o wasureta n da.* (*kasu*)

6 What would you say?

In pairs: What would you say to your friend when
(1) you would like to visit his/her house?
(2) you would like to suggest studying together?
(3) you would like him/her to wait?

7 What would you say?

In pairs: What would you say to your teacher when
(1) you would like to visit his/her house?
(2) you would like to suggest having lunch together?
(3) you would like him/her to wait?

Lesson 30: Review & Application

IV. PERFORMANCE

1. Application

1 Conversation completion

In small groups: The following is a telephone conversation between students A and B. Student B's mother (M) first picks up the phone. Guess what each person would say in the underlined parts in the conversation. Each group presents its conversation to the class.

A: _____ .

M: *Hai, Nakai desu.* (This is the Nakai residence.)

A: *Boku wa Yamakawa Hiroshi desu. Yoshio kun imasu ka?*
   (This is Hiroshi Yamakawa. Is Yoshio there?)

M: *Hai, imasu yo.* _____ . (Yes, he is. _____ .)

B: _____ , *Yoshio desu.* (_____ , this is Yoshio.)

A: *Aa, Yoshio kun. Boku Hiroshi. Shikenbenkyoo yatteru?*
   (Hi, Yoshio. This is Hiroshi. Are you studying for the exam?)

B: _____ .

A: *Suugaku? Ja, choodo ii.* (Mathematics? Good timing.)

B: *Dooshita no?* (What's the matter?)

A: *Chotto wakaranai tokoro ga aru n da. Oshiete kurenai kana?*
   (I have some questions. Could you help me?)

B: _____ .

A: *Ja, ima kara kimi no uchi e itte mo ii?* (Well, may I come to your house now?)

B: _____ .

A: *Ja, sugu iku yo.* (OK, I'll come soon.)

2 Then and now

In groups of four or five: Talk about things that you had to do when you were a child but don't have to do now. State which you think is better, now or the past. Use the expressions *-nakya naranai* and *-nakute yoi*.

Example: A: *Mukashi (Chiisai koro) wa hayaku <u>nenakya naranakatta</u> kedo, ima wa hayaku <u>nenakute</u> mo <u>yoi</u>.*

(I had to go to bed early when I was younger, but now I don't have to.)

B: *Dochira ga ii?* (Which do you like better?)

A: *Takusan no koto ga dekiru kara, ima no hoo ga ii.*

(I prefer now because I can do many things.)

3 Making questions

In groups: Roll a die. The number that one gets corresponds to the question words written below. Make a question with the word and ask it to a group member.

1. *itsu* 2. *doko* 3. *dare* 4. *nani* 5. *dooshite* 6. *doo yatte*

Example: number → 3   A: *B san, anata no suki na kashu wa <u>dare</u> desu ka?*
  (B, who is your favorite singer?)
  B: *Madonna desu.* (Madonna.)

number → 5 B: *C san, <u>dooshite</u> itsumo jiinzu o haite imasu ka?*
  (C, why do you always wear jeans?)
  C: *Jiinzu ga suki dakara desu.* (Because I like them.)

4 Guessing countries

In pairs: On the blackboard, the teacher makes a numbered list of countries equal to the number of students in the class. Then the teacher randomly gives each student a number. The numbers correspond to the countries on the blackboard. Partners try to guess each other's country by asking questions. Each student starts with 10 points and loses one point for each question after the first that they ask. Change partners several times. The student with the most points is the winner.

Example: A: *B san no kuni wa Ajia ni arimasu ka?* (B, is your country in Asia?)
  B: *Hai.* (Yes.)
  A: *Chuugoku desu ka?* (Is it China?)
  B: *Iie, chigaimasu.* (No, it isn't.)
  A: *Nihon yori ookii desu ka?* (Is it larger than Japan?)
  B: *Iie, chiisai to omoimasu.* (I think it's smaller.)
  A: *Kankoku ka naa?* (I wonder if it's Korea.)
  B: *Hai. Atari desu.* (Yes. You got it right.) [B now has 7 points.]

5 The teacher looks busy ...

In small groups: Complete the following sentences by writing what the people are doing. Use your imagination. Use the expression *-tari, -tari*. Follow the example.

Example: *Sensei wa jugyoo no junbi o <u>shitari</u>, tesuto no ten o <u>tsuketari</u>, isogashisoo desu.*
  (The teacher looks busy preparing for class and adding up the test points.)

1. *Otoosan wa _____ , isogashisoo desu.*
   (Dad looks busy _____ .)
2. *Okaasan wa _____ , isogashisoo desu.*
   (Mom looks busy _____ .)
3. *Nihon no kookoosei wa _____ , taihensoo desu.*
   (High school students in Japan look like they're having a hard time _____ .)
4. *Chiisai kodomo wa _____ , tanoshisoo desu.*
   (The small children look happy _____ .)

6 Last week's weather

In pairs: Talk about last week's weather with one of your classmates, and write the information on a piece of paper. Be sure to include the weather and the temperature of each day. The following words may be helpful. *tenki, hare, ame, kumori, yuki*

Example: A: *Nichiyoobi no tenki wa doo datta?*
B: *Ame datta yo.*
A: *Ondo wa nando datta?*
B: *45 do gurai datta yo.*

7 Informal to formal speech

In pairs: The following expressions appeared in the Sample Conversation of Lesson 26. They are all written in the informal style. When speaking to a teacher, boss, or a stranger, one should use the formal style. Change each of the following expressions into the formal style.

1. *Taionkei o yonda.*
2. *Nando datta?*
3. *Sesshi ja nai wa yo.*
4. *Watashi wa nakihajimeta.*
5. *Daijoobu tte itte kureta.*
6. *Sesshi ni keisan shite kureta.*

8 Verb conjugation: *-nai* form

In pairs: Make verb cards and place them face down. Students take turns drawing cards and changing the verbs into the *-nai* form.

9 Review of expressions

In three groups: Following is a list of nine expressions that were learned in Lessons 16 through 29. Each group writes two sentences for each expression. This may take about 15 to 20 minutes. Groups will present their sentences to the class. Group A will present one sentence for each of the first three expressions; Group B, expressions 4-6; and Group C, expressions 7-9. Afterward, the teacher will collect all of the sentences and make a compiled list of the two or three best sentences for each expression. The list will be given to the students to be used as a study guide.

Expressions:

1. *Oya*   2. *Saa*   3. *Eeto*   4. *Masaka*   5. *Sorede*
6. *Ee?*   7. *Ja*   8. *Hontoo* 9. *Tokorode*

10 Telephone conversations

Groups of three: The teacher gives each group of students two situations in which someone is making a telephone call. The students must write a telephone conversation for each situation. The students will decide the exact details of the phone call and should try to be creative. The students may use any form of grammar that they wish, but they should try to use it correctly. Afterward, the teacher asks each group to present one of its conversations.

Examples of situations:
1. Calling a friend to get together over the weekend.
2. A student at school calling his/her parents at home.
3. A Japanese exchange student calling his/her parents in Japan.
4. Receiving an overseas phone call from one's Japanese homestay family.
5. Calling a friend to study.
6. Calling a friend to invite him/her to go somewhere together.
7. Calling a friend for advice.
8. Parent calling a teacher about his/her child's performance in class.

2. Actualization

1 Practice the following conversation and develop your own dialogue on a similar subject with your partners.

Jagaimo o hi no yoku ataru basho to hikage ni uete sodachikata no chigai o kansatsu shite imasu.
(The students are observing differences between potatoes grown in a sunny place and those grown in the shade.)

Tanaka kun:	*Hikage no jagaimo wa sodachi ga warui ne.*
	(The ones in the shade didn't grow very well.)
Yamada san:	*Soo ne. Ha mo chiisai shi, kuki mo hosoi wa ne.*
	(No, they didn't. The leaves are small and the stems are thin.)
Suzuki kun:	*Hiatari no ii jagaimo wa yoku sodatte iru yo.* (The ones in the sun grew well.)
Kobayashi kun:	*Ha mo ookii shi, kuki mo ookii wa.* (The leaves are big and the stems are thick.)
Yoshida sensei:	*Hai, dewa hotte mite kudasai.* (OK. Well, dig them out.)
Hirota san:	*Waa, sugoi. Konna ni ookii imo ga takusan tsuite iru wa.*
	(Oh, wow! So many big potatoes grew in the sun.)
Nakamura kun:	*Hikage no wa, chiisai imo ga sukoshi shika tsuite nai yo.*
	(Only a few small ones grew in the shade.)
Yoshida sensei:	*Nikkoo ga shokubutsu no seichoo ni taisetsu nanoga yoku wakarimashita ne.*
	(You can see that sunlight is important in the growth of plants.)
Zen'in:	*Hai.* (Yes.)

2 Practice the following conversation and develop your own dialogue on a similar subject with your partners.

Kotoshi wa natsuyasumi ga owatte, saisho no rika no jugyoo desu. Shukudai no monshirochoo no kansatsunikki o kurabete imasu.
(This is the first science class after the long summer vacation. The students are checking their homework: their diaries of how they raised cabbage butterflies.)

Suzuki sensei:	*Tamago kara nan nichime kurai de yoochuu ni narimashita ka.*
	(How long did it take for the eggs to become larvae?)

Hirota san:	*Mikkame desu.* (Three days.)
Kobayashi kun:	*Boku no wa, yokkame desu.* (Mine took four days.)
Suzuki sensei:	*Sorekara doo narimashita ka?* (Then what happened?)
Yoshida san:	*Nankai mo dappi shite ookiku narimashita.* (They molted many times and became big.)
Suzuki sensei:	*Yoochuu kara nani ni narimashita ka?* (What did the larvae change into?)
Nakamura kun:	*Tookame gurai de sanagi ni narimashita.* (They changed into pupa in about ten days.)
Suzuki sensei:	*Soo desu ne. Nan nichi gurai de choo ni narimashita ka?* (OK. About how many days did it take them to become butterflies?)
Yamada san:	*Isshuukan gurai desu. Totemo kirei de, soto ni hanasu no ga, chotto zannen datta desu.* (About a week. They were so beautiful that it was a shame to let them go.)

3 Practice the following conversation and develop your own dialogue on a similar subject with your partners.

Rika no jugyoo desu. Kandenchi no tsunagikata to mamedenkyuu no akarusa no chigai o kurabete imasu.
(In science class, the students are comparing the difference in brightness depending on how batteries are connected.)

Nakamura sensei:	*Kandenchi no tsunagikata wa 2 toori arimasu ne.* (There are two ways of connecting batteries, right?)
Suzuki kun:	*Chokuretsu to heiretsu desu ka?* (Connecting in series and in rows, right?)
Nakamura sensei:	*Soo desu ne. Dewa, chokuretsu to heiretsu ni denchi o tsunaide mamedenkyuu o tsukete mite kudasai.* (That's right. Then, connect batteries both ways and light up miniature bulbs.)
Hirota san:	*Are, kotchi no hoo ga akarui wa.* (Oh, this one is brighter.)
Nakamura sensei:	*Akarui hoo wa nani tsunagi desu ka?* (Which one is brighter?)
Hirota san:	*Chokuretsu desu.* (The one in a series.)
Nakamura sensei:	*Heiretsu no hoo wa doo desu ka?* (How about the one in a row?)
Tanaka kun:	*Chokuretsu yori kurai desu.* (It's darker than the one in a series.)
Nakamura sensei:	*Chokuretsu wa akarui desu ga, heiretsu no hoo ga denchi ga nagaku mochimasu.* (The one in a series is brighter, but batteries last longer in a row.)

3. Enrichment

1 *Kanji* for Lesson 28

国際問題	色々	参加	冷戦	時代
全部	地域	紛争	違う	考え方
地球	協力	今度		

2 *Kanji* for Lesson 29

君　　　　　待つ　　　　　試験　　　　　数学　　　　　残る
丁度　　　　一緒

3 Other useful *kanji*

開、閉、利、考、直、進、用、者、研究、連絡、合意

4 Strategies

This volume has introduced various strategies for recognizing and producing *kanji* with accuracy and speed. In obtaining knowledge of *kanji* as well as understanding the wisdom and culture of those who created the writing system, it is important to know that *kanji* were originally created by the Chinese. However, one should also realize that Japanese people, too, created *kanji* by changing some of the original characters and by forming *kanji* compounds. The following is a summary of the eight types of *kanji* component arrangements that are based on the six types of *kanji* formation rules that appeared in lessons 3 and 6.

Formation of *kanji* based on the eight types of component arrangements:

1. *Kanji*/Pictorial → *Kanji*/Meaning*1　　日、月
2. *Kanji* Symbol*1 + *Kanji* Symbol*2 → *Kanji*/Meaning*1　　上、下、中
3. *Kanji*/Meaning*1 + *Kanji* Symbol*1 → *Kanji*/Meaning*2　　本、末
4. *Kanji*/Meaning*1 + *Kanji* Symbol*1 → *Kanji*/Meaning*1+　　刃
5. *Kanji*/Meaning*1 + *Kanji*/Meaning*1 → *Kanji*/Meaning*1+　　林、炎、品、森
6. *Kanji*/Meaning*1 + *Kanji*/Meaning*2 → *Kanji*/Meaning*3　　明、料、安
7. *Kanji*/Meaning*1 + *Kanji*/Pronunciation*1 → *Kanji*/Meaning*1+　　語
8. *Kanji*/Meaning*1 → Transformation/borrowing → *Kanji*/Meaning*2　　楽

*1 means that it is the first symbol/meaning/pronunciation. *2 means that it is the second symbol/meaning. *3 means that it is the third meaning. *1+ means that either the original meaning is expanded (such as tree → wood), or the original meaning was modified. It is obvious that symbol alone does not have meaning by itself. It could only carry meaning when followed by a second symbol such as 上 and 下, or attached to a *kanji* with a meaning, such as 刃 or 本.

5 Exercise

Try to group the *kanji* learned in this text into the eight types of component arrangements listed in 4. Try to categorize as many *kanji* as possible.